LINE OF FIRE

LINE OF FIRE

The Autobiography of Britain's
Most Controversial Policeman

BRIAN PADDICK

with KRIS HOLLINGTON

SIMON &
SCHUSTER

London · New York · Sydney · Toronto

A CBS COMPANY

First published in Great Britain by Simon & Schuster UK Ltd, 2008
A CBS COMPANY

1 3 5 7 9 10 8 6 4 2

Simon & Schuster UK Ltd
Africa House
64–78 Kingsway
London WC2B 6AH

www.simonsays.co.uk

Simon & Schuster Australia
Sydney

PICTURE CREDITS
All photos courtesy of author, excluding:
10, 15, © TopFoto
11, © Corbis
12, 16, © PaPhotos

A CIP catalogue record for this book
is available from the British Library.

ISBN: 978-1-84737-174-4

Typeset by M Rules
Printed and bound in Great Britain by
Mackays of Chatham plc

Always tell the truth, that way you don't have to remember what you said.

MARK TWAIN

INTRODUCTION

I have recently completed thirty years in the Metropolitan Police Service and the feeling of liberation is both exciting and frightening. I have commented recently on my former boss, Sir Ian Blair, the Commissioner of Police of the Metropolis, criticising his leadership and the decisions he has made. I consider Ian not only to be a like-minded human being but, at the lowest point in my career, he was the only person I felt I could turn to. After a lifetime in a disciplined organisation where the commissioner is next to God, to criticise Sir Ian Blair is akin to a recently retired cardinal criticising a pope he worked closely alongside.

The police service has changed in some ways over the years but, as we will see in the following pages, it still remains a straight-white-male-dominated, macho organisation. Whilst in many ways it has become more liberal, in others it is slipping back into its conservative and controlling past. The restrictions placed on the freedom of even the most senior officers to comment openly and publicly about the Metropolitan Police have become more draconian. Gone are the days when there was open debate and senior officers were able to offer their own views and potential solutions. Nowadays, a senior officer can only comment on his or her own sphere of responsibility, and anything which is seen to question or criticise government is swiftly and unequivocally corrected.

This book is the product of over thirty years of pent-up frustration at not being able to talk about my experiences in the police service or to comment on social issues, particularly the most controversial areas such as sexuality and drug-taking. Finally, I am able to lay open what it has been really like to serve in the Metropolitan Police during this time: to offer an insight into police culture and practice from the era of *Life on Mars* to the era of the suicide bomber. I still find it difficult to believe that I am not about to be summoned to the commissioner's office for another dressing-down about something I have said.

It was when I decided to be open about my sexuality that my private life became a matter of public record. Certain right-wing tabloids decided that it was dangerous to have openly gay people in the senior echelons of the police service. For these, the police are the embodiment of everything conservative, and their role is to maintain the status quo and be the guardians of order; to the tabloid mind, they are the protectors and preservers of the constants that they believe people need to cling to in order to cope with the rapidly changing world in which they live. If all else fails, they argue, you can rely on the police – but not if their senior ranks are infiltrated by people so radical that they even give expression to their homosexual feelings!

Thus began a campaign of 'monstering' or 'othering', where I was portrayed not only as some kind of dangerous destabilising demon, but also as the sole cause of increases in crime across London. As far as the papers were concerned, I was part of a group who, while thankfully rare and probably mentally ill, are a dangerous breed so entirely different from 'normal people' that they must be isolated, attacked and, if possible, eliminated.

This book is also about setting the record straight about who I am and what I am. Both in my professional career and in my private life, I started out seemingly no different from everyone else, but I struggled to fit in. I struggled with who I was and I tried everything I could to conform and to comply but there are some things that I just cannot do. I cannot be anyone other than myself and I have to tell the truth as I see it. I hope you will see how I came to be the person that I am and I hope you will see why I have done things I have done. You may not agree with the lifestyle I have come to believe is right for me, and you may not agree with the decisions I have made over the past fifty years of my life, but I hope, by the end of this book, you will at least understand why.

Brian Paddick
London 2008

PART ONE

CHAPTER ONE

The doctor peered over his steel-rimmed glasses at my mother. 'My dear,' he said with a half-smile and a hint of sympathy, 'he's got you with both barrels this time.' My parents were not expecting to have any more children eleven years after Graham, their first child, was born, so this double whammy came as a bit of a shock.

John and I arrived together but the similarities ended there. I appeared an hour-and-a-quarter after my non-identical twin, and we started fighting each other as soon as we were able. We're a curious mix; I write left-handed but hold a tennis racquet in my right hand, whereas John holds a pen in his right hand and everything else in his left. And John's straight whereas I'm gay.

We competed for attention and affection from my parents; I tried so furiously that I had the opposite effect to the one I desired and became the least liked, most annoying twin. It was only when I did something wrong that I got everybody's full attention.

Since I was the difficult brother, Graham and John invariably joined forces against me in family rows and this left me feeling very lonely throughout much of my childhood. It took me more than twenty years to break out of the cycle of wanting to be liked and to just be myself.

My parents married during World War Two while my father, Anthony, was on leave; they managed to get a special licence from The Sanctuary near Westminster Abbey and he married Evelyn in the parish church in Tooting. They were a pair of keen sporting types; Dad was a cricketer and Mum was into hockey, tennis and athletics.

After they were married they didn't see each other for four years while Dad battled his way across Africa and up Italy with the Eighth Army. A major in the Royal Tank Regiment and mentioned in dispatches for gallant and distinguished service in Italy, Dad also taught fellow South Londoner General Montgomery to drive a tank.

Dad had a will of iron and rarely swore; only when he hit his thumb with a hammer when having a go at DIY, something he never quite got to grips with. Mum was once entertaining a friend in the sitting room when she looked up from her coffee to see a Rawlplug make an unexpected appearance. Dad, who was installing a new kitchen, had pushed it through the wall.

My father kept his emotions in check. While there may have been some deep, unspoken understanding between us, he never told me he loved me and I never said I loved him. He avoided physical contact with me until the last five years of his life, when we started shaking hands.

He was a very private man. Politically, along with my mother, he was a staunch Conservative, although he rarely talked about such 'private' matters. The *Daily Telegraph* dropped through the letter box each morning and they were both keen readers.

Mum had achieved exceptional success for a woman in those days. As well as being a mother of three, she had a full-time career. She had worked her way up to the number two position in a provincial building society, the South Western, and the *Daily Telegraph* wrote a feature about her in a series on women professionals. Mum was like Dad in that not much emotion showed, but this was more to do with her stoicism – 'no good being miserable, you've just got to get on with it'. When she walked in the door from work, she would plunge straight into the cooking, ironing, mending with barely a respite, scold John and me for fighting, and tell me 'not now' when I grabbed her for a hug. We were at our worst-behaved whenever my parents were entertaining. It was bad enough that attention was in short supply, but to see them spending what little available leisure time there was on others was too much to bear.

I don't remember much of my early childhood, except that I was unhappy for a lot of it. We received many wonderful Christmas and birthday presents and my parents did the very best they could for us. I craved affection desperately, a factor which has undoubtedly influenced my adult relationships. I once told Mary, my wife, that what I really wanted was just her, just to hold, be with and love. Equally, I want to give people all the attention they deserve to ensure that they are not ignored or neglected. This trait has been a driving force in both my policing and political careers.

A key emotional figure in my early life, who provided me with some precious affection, was Stella Jacquinandi, a woman Mum employed to help her with the house. Jacqui, as we called her, was a lot less forceful than my mother at telling me to let go and I latched on to her.

After the war, Dad became a technical representative for British Celanese, where he remained for the rest of his working life until he was forced to retire on age grounds. His work involved a great deal of travelling and his company car was his pride and joy. When we were living in Seeley Road in Mitcham, a short distance from Pascal's sweet factory, he was given a Morris Oxford which was too long for our garage. He spent that summer battling with bricks and mortar, reconstructing the garage so that the lengthy car would fit. The following year they gave him a Mini.

My father took this sort of thing in his stride; nothing fazed him much after the war. The only thing that filled him with dread was the threat of unemployment − a result of having been raised during the economic depression of the 1930s. It was a fear that was passed on to me.

Neither of my parents smoked cigarettes, although my dad frequently enjoyed a pipe up until his sixties, when he had a heart attack. In those days people kept cigarettes to offer guests. Mum and Dad kept them in a porcelain box with a black base and white top. One day when they were out, I nervously took one of the cigarettes from the box and lit it. When I drew in the smoke I suddenly felt burning in my throat and exploded into a coughing fit. I never smoked a cigarette again.

By then my eldest brother, Graham, had already left school and was studying at Westminster Technical College to become a chef. He got a job at Madame Prunier's, a famous fish restaurant in St James. Graham, who is six foot, four inches tall, went through a chef's hat a day as it scraped across the ceiling of the restaurant's kitchens.

My first sight of a naked female – well, of the bit that was different from a boy – came when I was six. It was on the day I stumbled across a girl offering to show hers to a group of excited boys in the playground, if they showed her theirs. I must confess I also found this quite exciting.

When did I know I was gay? As ten-year-old Wolf Cubs we were not allowed to camp overnight but we were taken on a day trip to a scout camp somewhere near Ongar in Essex. Caught in the open in torrential rain, several of us got soaked to the skin and, to my alarm, the scoutmaster ordered us to strip off our wet clothes and hang them up to dry on some bottled gas-fired ovens.

We were inside a marquee, one side of which was completely open, leaving all of us exposed. I stripped reluctantly and handed over my clothes. There were about half-a-dozen of us, all shivering, trying to hide our embarrassment. It was then that I saw a scout of about fifteen, naked and confident, striding across the grass past the open side of the marquee. He had apparently been de-bagged by his fellow scouts in some kind of horseplay. Unlike us, he appeared completely at ease without a stitch on. This was the first time I had seen a post-pubescent boy naked. I thought to myself 'That's gorgeous!'

I knew straightaway that what I felt was not 'normal', even though I didn't really understand what sex was all about yet. Despite trying to keep my secret hidden, in a school of six hundred boys, it would not be long before my peers noticed and I would suffer the consequences.

John and I both passed the eleven-plus and were sent to Bec Grammar, a real South London institution, complete with school song in Latin. The school had a tarmac playground, then an adjacent rugby field, then a high wire-mesh fence. On the other side of this was the playground of Hillcroft, the comprehensive school. As first-year pupils at Bec, we had to wear dark blue caps with white rings. They looked stupid and we knew it, as did the Hillcroft boys who took the mickey mercilessly.

We were forbidden to go on the rugby pitch during playtime, but sometimes in winter when it had snowed the headmaster would announce in morning assembly that the snow was deep enough for us to throw snowballs over the fence at the comprehensive school pupils. Our PE teacher Mr Scrouston, aka 'Screw', would warn us that if we misbehaved, 'you'll end up on the other side of the fence'.

We had been at Bec only a year when it was merged with Hillcroft, creating Ernest Bevin Comprehensive. My mother, who had campaigned to keep the grammar school, immediately moved us to Sutton Manor High School in Surrey. This had staunchly remained a grammar school in everything but name (the Tory council simply changed the names of all the schools in the borough to 'High' schools to avoid the Labour government's attempts to outlaw grammar schools).

Not long after we moved from Tooting Bec to Sutton, Mum gave me some bad news: Jacqui had died of cancer. I cannot recall exactly how I felt about this at the time but the arrival of autumn, which marked the end of the long summer holiday, combined with the fear of starting at Sutton Manor made me quite unhappy about going back to school that year. I found it difficult to make friends, and Jacqui's death probably made me even more withdrawn.

Academically, I was unremarkable. Maximum effort for unremarkable results was the story of my academic life. I had to lock myself in my room for hours, concentrating on my homework while John did his on his lap in front of the television. My plodding efforts even applied to sports. I loved swimming and won the Sutton and Cheam Swimming Club's Endeavour Cup – the prize for the one who had put most effort in without getting anywhere. I did eventually become the school swimming captain and won most of the individual events in my final year, but this achievement was mainly thanks to a lack of good competition.

As far as I was concerned, I was the only gay boy in the school and possibly the only one in all of Sutton. There were no positive gay role models to look up to at that time – entertainers like Larry 'shut that door' Grayson simply reinforced negative stereotypes – and my feeling of isolation was difficult to cope with. I certainly didn't feel able to be open with my family or friends. Every few years the subject of homosexuality would come up at home, and it was made clear that my family did not approve.

Around this time, Mum worked for the chief executive of a company whose son was gay. In conversation with her boss, unbeknown to me then, she had said to him, 'I could forgive my son for getting a girl pregnant, but I would never forgive him if he were homosexual.' She has since explained that sheer ignorance led her to think that way.

The combination of wanting to please my parents, my mother in particular, and their unambiguously negative feelings towards homosexuality, kept me firmly in the closet. It was only when I believed they might find out from someone else that I finally told them.

As far as school went, I thought I kept it well-hidden, that other people would have no idea, but it must have been fairly obvious to the other boys. After all, when I look back on those days now, I realise that some aspects of my behaviour must have seemed pretty strange.

I was bullied at school, but not until the sixth form, and even then I initially assumed that this was because I was well-behaved and always neatly turned out. My eagerness to comply was rewarded by being made deputy head prefect, while John was head prefect. Rumours – untrue, of course – circulated that the headmaster was our uncle.

It was not until we were doing revision for chemistry A-level and going through past papers that I realised the real reason for the bullying. The teacher asked: 'What's the name of a solution where the particles are evenly distributed through the liquid?'

I answered: 'Homogenous.'

A voice came from the back of the class: 'You should know all about that – *homo*.'

Then, a few days later I was in the common room when half-a-dozen upper-sixth boys piled in and grabbed me, lifted me off my feet and carried me out into the playground. It was midwinter and the open-air pool, although not operating, was two-thirds full of ice-cold water. I was saved at the last moment by a teacher on playground duty. Although traumatised by the incident, I managed to stick out the rest of the school day.

Not long after that I was dragged into the common room, where they tried to strip me naked. John heard the scuffle, wrenched open the door and rescued me. This time I immediately fled from school, only phoning Mum when I was safely home and breaking down in tears. Neither Dr Walsh, the headmaster, nor my mum, or I myself wanted to acknowledge what this was really all about. 'Just a bit of horseplay,' Dr Walsh explained to my mother.

Like so many victims of 'hate crime', where people from minorities are victimised, I was terrified and isolated with no one to turn to. John had rescued me out of loyalty but, at that time, he shared the family's attitude towards homosexuality. Despite all the advances in thinking between then and now, many school pupils still find themselves in a similar position today. Some, unable to cope, take their own lives, and I can understand why.

I decided I wanted to study medicine, so chose biology, chemistry and physics as my A-level subjects. To get accepted at Charing Cross I needed three C's at A-level. Biology and chemistry were no problem, but I wound up with an E in physics, and missed medical school by one grade.

The headmaster suggested I come back and do another year in order to retake my A-level physics but I had already filled in my application to join the police. When my grades came through, it was all the excuse I needed to post off the application. My parents were not pleased. Sutton Manor boys were expected to go to university. My twin brother was going and it was assumed that I would do the same.

Why the police? Partly because my father's fear of unemployment had rubbed off on me. I thought that as a doctor employment would be all but guaranteed, and being a policeman was certainly 'a job for life', with a good pension at the end of it. Best of all, once I'd given up my first choice, policing only required fifteen weeks of training as opposed to seven years of study for medicine.

Of course I knew that the police force would be homophobic, but I had absolutely no intention of revealing the fact that I was gay. The police force provided both the perfect cover and the necessary encouragement for me to keep my sexuality under wraps.

Dad was a high-ranking Freemason (I was to join soon enough), and my experience of the police had been limited to meeting Doug Baxter, one of his Masonic 'brothers', a very tall and broad sergeant with the force who occasionally stopped by at our home for a cup of tea.

Although my grandfather had been a policeman in the mounted branch, Mum and Dad were not keen on me joining. Nonetheless, I signed up in 1976, the year of some of the worst disturbances at the Notting Hill Carnival. In those days, police protective equipment was non-existent, and when officers were pelted with bricks they simply grabbed whatever they could to protect themselves, including dustbin lids and bits of fence. Over one hundred of them were seriously injured during that year's carnival.

CHAPTER TWO

I was ill-prepared for my interview at Paddington Green Police Station Recruitment and Selection Centre, which took place in front of two senior officers. First, they asked me what my parents thought about me joining the Metropolitan Police, a question I struggled to answer positively. Next, they asked me which newspaper I read. I didn't actually read newspapers, but I said the *Daily Telegraph*, which had dropped through the family letter box since before I was born.

Finally, the big question: 'Why do you want to join the police?'

Although I can give the reasons now, at that time, and at that moment, I didn't really know why – and said so. Fortunately, this didn't matter. This was the mid-seventies, thirty years after the end of the Second World War when thousands of ex-servicemen had joined the police, making an easy transition from one uniformed existence to another.

Now, with a full police pension available after thirty years' service, nearly all of these soldiers-turned-policemen retired in 1976. Few people were signing up to take their place because of the poor pay, tough working conditions and low morale in the force. When I joined, the police were desperate for recruits to fill the void and took anyone, including me – a naive eighteen-year-old who couldn't even explain why he wanted to join.

To this day, I have no idea what the scientific basis was for what passed for the 'medical examination'. The drill was to remove your clothes in a small cubicle and put on a white towelling dressing gown (no doubt used by fifty other potential recruits before you). You then went into a room and stood in front of three doctors. On the floor was a black rubber mat with a pair of feet outlined in white on it. You put your feet on the mat facing the panel and when told, you removed your robe. After they had had a good look at you, you were asked to turn around and touch your toes.

This desperate rush to recruit anybody with two arms, two legs and a pulse meant that, while there was a core of highly motivated, decent people who wanted to serve the public, significant numbers signed up for less noble reasons. These might have been rejected as unsuitable in more abundant times, but they now slipped in because necessity dictated that the selection process had to be rushed.

There is a real danger of history repeating itself now: sixty years after the war, my generation has hit the thirty-year barrier while, at the same time, the size of the Met has increased and is currently undergoing another spate of frantic recruitment.

When you look back at what happened thirty years ago – minor misdemeanours such as trying to get into nightclubs for free by showing a police warrant card were followed ten to fifteen years later by some of those same officers dealing drugs, taking bribes and fabricating evidence. In recent years there has been a sharp rise in officers in the nought to two year service band who are involved in misconduct, and Hendon Training School has become a hotspot for unacceptable behaviour. Unless positive action is taken now, the Metropolitan Police could end up with the same corruption problems once again.

The training course lasted fifteen weeks. We had to wait five weeks for our uniforms, providing a window during which time unsuitable officers could be rooted out. The uniform had gone through some interesting changes. Police shirts had been made from nylon but this was abandoned after a number of officers who had gone into burning buildings to rescue people emerged to find that the shirts had melted onto their skin. The police tie was changed to a clip-on after officers wearing traditionally knotted ties were nearly strangled in pub fights.

We had two pockets on the right-hand side of our trousers, plenty of room to hold one's salary of £33, paid each week in cash in a brown envelope. The larger and deeper of the two pockets held the truncheon, a fairly useless device made from very light wood, but nevertheless considered too aggressive or provocative if able to be seen by the public.

Our famous helmets, being made of pressed cork, provided hardly any protection at all. After the riots at the 1976 Notting Hill Carnival, they were reinforced, but even this was not enough. During riot-training a group of us were pelted with bricks, wooden blocks and pieces of concrete by a bunch of police constables playing the role of rioters. One of my colleagues, PC Chris Patmore, contributed to the introduction of the traditional NATO-style riot helmet (a motorcycle-style crash helmet complete with visor) after a brick struck his metal badge, driving the pin that held the helmet plate in place into his forehead. This type of training, using real rather than wooden bricks was soon abandoned because of the high number of injuries.

The accommodation at Hendon was depressing: one rectangular room with a stainless-steel sink, thin carpet tiles, thin curtains, a bed and a chair. That first night I shut the door to my room and asked myself, 'What have I done? What am *I* doing *here*?'

That initial feeling of total isolation was steadily dispelled as my group united in adversity against the early morning inspections and the relentless study and examinations. Real and lasting friendships developed in a way I had never experienced before. Such was the positive contrast with my life up until then, that I was soon reluctant to return home at the weekends and instead stayed behind with colleagues who lived too far away from London to make the journey home.

Our drill sergeant was a former army man. During foot drill we were not allowed to wear coat and gloves no matter what the temperature was. On one particularly icy morning, when one of the men arrived wearing gloves, the outraged drill sergeant growled, 'What do you think you're doing? Only girls and poofs wear gloves!'

I worked hard throughout my training and, as usual, managed to pass without distinguishing myself. Most of the time was spent learning the *Instruction Book for Constables and Sergeants* by rote. Its black cardboard cover was embossed with gold writing and its loose-leaf filing system meant that new pages could be slotted in as the law and procedures changed. Essentially, it was a catalogue of corrected mistakes.

In the exam you were given the title heading (e.g. Breathalyser Procedure) and then the paragraph headings in the margin (e.g. Inflation of the Bag) and you wrote out word for word from memory what it said in the book. The examination system was part of the whole philosophy of the police, which was to learn the job parrot fashion, to stamp on any individuality or independent thought, and instil blind obedience to those above you.

I was told that I was being posted to Holloway in North London, and that I was to live in Olive House, a section house (single officer accommodation) in Canonbury Park South in Islington. They had wanted as many London-based recruits as possible to live with their families in order to ease the pressure on police accommodation, but I couldn't wait to move out as soon as I could.

The admin sergeant at Hornsey Road police station told me I was on night duty and to report back at the station in uniform at nine-thirty p.m. When I returned I found the station in darkness, except for the basement where the lights were on as normal. The front office was lit by a couple of oil lamps.

I had heard stories of practical jokes being played on new recruits and, feeling very anxious about my first ever night on operational duty, I didn't ask whether it was normal practice to use oil lamps for lighting. Instead, I went straight down the stairs to the Parade Room, which was brilliantly lit with fluorescent tubes. The sergeant who was taking the parade introduced himself as 'Sergeant Major', which also aroused my suspicions. When he went on to explain that Inspector 'Tookey Dickson' would arrive shortly to inspect the parade, I was convinced some elaborate prank was being played but I dared not say anything.

It was lucky I kept quiet. The sergeant's name was indeed Derek Major, the inspector – who you would never call anything but 'Sir' – was John Tookey-Dickson, and the main fuse had gone on the ground floor, hence the oil lamps.

The most common phrase newly graduated recruits heard as they began their working life was 'Forget Hendon, now we'll show you what policing is *really* like.' Unfortunately, I soon learned that real policing meant doing whatever more senior constables told you to do, even if what they were telling you was clearly wrong.

You spent most of your time with the senior constables, patrolling and eating in the canteen, so they had more influence over you than the inspector or the sergeants. If those senior constables had questionable working practices, or worse, then their work ethics were passed on to new recruits who had been told at Hendon to 'Keep your eyes and ears open and your mouths shut.'

That first night I was posted to patrol in a panda car with Sean. You could either be assigned to the foot patrol, the van – NH2 – the panda or, the most glamorous of all, the area car, N4, which was crewed by the most experienced officers and would be the first to get the call to respond to a serious incident.

I was absolutely terrified. One of the first calls we took was to a sudden death. These were unpleasant to deal with and were given to the youngest officer on the team, which happened to be me . . . for eighteen months!

It was the first time I had seen a dead body. An elderly lady had deliberately taken an overdose. Her husband was there and was deeply upset, even more so when we told him that there would have to be a post mortem to rule out foul play.

One of my responsibilities was to do 'the continuity', which meant identifying the body to the pathologist as the one that I had found in the home with the empty medicine bottles. The pathologist could then confirm to the coroner at the inquest that he had conducted a post mortem on the same person the police had found.

I turned up at St Pancras Coroner's Court at eight a.m. the following morning, having worked from nine forty-five p.m. the previous night until six a.m. that morning. I walked into the mortuary exhausted, and somewhat apprehensive about what horrors I might see. I was not disappointed. There were six cadavers laid out, opened with Y-incisions; the flesh peeled back, the internal organs exposed, ready for examination. The distinctive and then unfamiliar stench of death invaded my nose and seeped into my hair and clothes.

I identified the body to the pathologist and went back to the section house for a shower and some sleep. It was difficult sleeping during the day, especially in summer – not just because of the heat, but because they always seemed to be cutting the grass with large petrol-driven lawnmowers right outside my room.

Some months later, after I had just left to go out on patrol, I received a call that a woman had come into the station to say that she had found her boyfriend dead in his bed. I went to meet her in Tollington Road, a major thoroughfare that connects Finsbury Park to Holloway, but there was no trace of her, just a large dustcart. The door of the dustcart opened and down she stepped – apparently her 'other' boyfriend was a dustman.

'Which flat is it?' I asked.

She pointed to the basement. 'Do you want to come in?' I asked.

'No thanks, I'll wait here, it's not very nice.'

I walked into what was a bedsit, very neat and well-presented but freezing cold. It consisted of one room with a bed and a sofa, a basic table and chairs, and a tiny separate kitchen which contained a gas cooker with four hobs and an oven.

On the bed, covered by a divan, was the outline of a body.

I slowly pulled back the bedclothes to reveal the dead man's face. His cheeks were full of colour, so much so that I had to touch him to make sure he was indeed dead. His skin was as cold as the air in the room. Something did not look quite right; his hair had been permed and . . . was that make-up? I pulled back the blanket a bit further. He was wearing a lacy bra, knickers, a suspender belt and stockings. Balloons half-filled with water were in the bra.

I was completely dumbstruck. Why would he be wearing women's underwear? It made no sense to a young school-leaver who had led a very sheltered life. Walking back out to the dustcart, I found the girl-friend and asked, 'Did you notice anything unusual?'

She nodded sheepishly. 'He'd promised me he was going to give that up.'

As the inspector had to attend all suspicious deaths, I asked for him to come to the scene along with detectives from the CID. I was told to stand by. After a minute or so of silence my radio crackled. 'Five-four-three? The inspector is asking why you think it's suspicious.'

I hesitated. 'Er . . . he's wearing women's underwear.'

A short while later the CID and Inspector Tookey-Dickson rolled up, along with the coroner's officer and a police photographer.

On the wall was a picture of someone I assumed to be the dead man's daughter. Seeing the photo, the coroner's officer said, 'That must have been him when he was younger.'

I had to identify the body to the pathologist – the continuity again – and give evidence in court. Tookey-Dickson told me that because the family were very upset about the circumstances in which the body was found, he had agreed with the coroner not to mention the fact that the deceased had been caught, as he put it, 'with his trousers down'.

In my testimony, I reported that I had found the man dead in bed but deliberately omitted the description of what he was wearing. The family were in the front row sobbing, but were grateful that they had at least been spared the humiliation, as they saw it, of the circumstances of his death.

Unfortunately, however, nobody thought to explain the situation to the pathologist. He took the witness box and said loudly that the body was of 'a well-nourished male dressed in women's underclothing'. Howls and sobs broke out from the family.

In the end, it turned out to be a straightforward case of carbon monoxide poisoning. The young man, desperately cold, had apparently switched on all four gas rings of the cooker to warm the room which, without sufficient ventilation, had steadily filled the room with the deadly gas.

I soon got used to the ugly sights and smells that often accompanied my job, although some were really nauseating. I arrived one afternoon at a ground-floor flat where an elderly woman had not been seen for some time. There had been complaints of a bad smell, never a good sign. As soon as I approached the house I knew that she had been dead for a while, and I forced the door. The smell was overpowering. As I searched the flat I heard a buzzing sound – bluebottle flies. Choking, I went into the bedroom at the front of the flat where the body of the woman lay in her bed. The summer sun had been blazing for days and the room was very hot. A loud humming sound came from the body. I drew back the curtains to let in some light and saw she was enveloped in a cloud of flies.

From what I could see there was nothing suspicious about this death. Undertakers were called to remove the remains. When they lifted her off the bed, the flesh that was in contact with the bed stayed right where it was, wriggling with maggots. Once the remains had finally been removed, a colleague and I searched the flat and found several thousand pounds under the mattress and stuffed into pillows.

It took less than a week for me to observe my first example of what I considered to be dubious practice. It was Friday night and I had been posted to the panda (an Austin Allegro) with Sean and we headed up to the Irish dancehall called the Gresham Ballroom on Holloway Road. This establishment was infamous for its punch-ups at closing time. Once the unsteady punters hit the street and were beyond the grasp of the thick-necked bouncers who patrolled the inside, they started on each other.

I had never seen a street fight before, let alone tried to stop one, so I was sat in the car at the Gresham, staring wide-eyed and very nervous, wondering what on earth was going to happen. As I sat transfixed, Sean suddenly shouted 'Cheeky bastard!' and screeched off in hot pursuit of a night bus.

The frantic flashing of our headlights and the sounding of our puny horn soon got the driver's attention and he pulled over. Sean got out and started talking to the driver, but I still had no idea what had happened or what to do. Should I get out of the police car and join him on the bus, or should I stay put? I remembered my old geography teacher Ivor Blake's advice, 'if in doubt, don't', and stayed in the car even though, as each minute passed, I felt increasingly strongly that I should be with my colleague. After ten minutes Sean returned.

'Did you see that?'

'No, what?'

'Cheeky sod went through a red light.'

He looked at me and said, 'When we get back to the station you can do a witness book.' It was usual practice to have another police officer as a witness so that, when the case went to court, it would be two of you against one member of the public in case they had the audacity to plead 'not guilty'.

'But I didn't see it.'

He looked at me in disbelief, as if I had just confessed to the Moors murders. The message 'Nine-nine at Holloway' came over the radio. It was code for 'tea's ready' (the code came from the Co-Op's 99 brand of tea – we never used codes for calls over the radio in the Met, except for teatime). A WPC, on this occasion it was Shirley Danes, was in charge of making tea every two hours.

I began to be aware that I was in trouble when I half overheard a conversation between Sean and some other PCs. I did not hear what Sean said exactly, but I realised it was about me when a number of the other officers started saying, in unnecessarily raised tones for my benefit, '*I'll* go witness.' Unbeknown to me, the culture was, if a more experienced officer said that he saw something, whether you actually saw it or not was beside the point – you *said* you had seen it too.

I had instantly earned a reputation as someone to be wary of, who could not be trusted to fall in with the others; someone who would not leap in as a witness as and when a more experienced officer decided that he needed one. This, together with the fact that I was always immaculately turned out, later earned me the nickname 'Peter Perfect', a character from the cartoon *Wacky Races*, the smooth posh guy with the sports car who was squeaky clean and never cheated – unlike most of the other characters.

At that time, I wasn't at all sure how to take this. Clearly, I was being perceived as different from the normal police stereotype, but I worked very hard, was good at what I did and as a result I earned colleagues' respect. Gradually, I came to realise that people were prepared to overlook the fact that you were different provided you were personable and did your job well. It would have been more comfortable for me if I had been 'one of the lads' but there were some things I was not prepared to do, and saying I saw something that I hadn't was one of them.

I was further ostracised when I became embroiled in a domestic violence case. The policy then was for the police not to get involved in domestic violence. Invariably, once the fight was over and the victim, usually the woman, had been treated in hospital for her injuries, she would have forgiven her boyfriend or her husband and would refuse to press charges. It seems incredible now, but that was the policy.

I was riding shotgun on the van when we got called by the area car to a domestic that turned out to be between a couple who were both in their seventies. Despite their age, the husband had managed to hit his wife over the head with a chair and her head was split open. She needed to go to hospital.

Unusually, that night the area car was crewed by two advanced drivers, usually the most senior officers on the relief. One of them said, 'This one's yours,' and handed the old man over to me. This was another common practice. Where more experienced officers with nothing to prove had a not very exciting or appetising arrest, they would call for the van, which invariably had a probationer on it, and hand over the arrest to the junior officer. You then had to make out that you were the one who had come across the incident and taken the decision to make the arrest. It was usually drunks and it was not a big deal; they were still drunk when the van arrived and you could see the evidence with your own eyes. But a 'griefy' domestic was another story.

Despite the fact that I knew full well what official policy was, I felt compelled, particularly after the incident with the bus, to show that I was toeing the line, although my concerns clearly showed on my face. 'Don't worry, we'll help you with your notes,' said one of the area car crew. The station sergeant was extremely unhappy when I arrived back at the station with my arrest. Sure enough, by the time the wife had had stitches in the gash in her head, she didn't want to know, and we were left with a dreaded 23/25, a refused charge.

General Order, Section 23 paragraph 25, was entitled 'Steps to allay a sense of grievance.' It went on about how, when someone is arrested 'by mistake' they are likely to be upset and everything – such as the offer of a lift home – should be done to make sure they did not make a complaint. Order 23/25 always meant a lot of work for the station sergeant, who had to write a long and detailed explanation rather than a short and simple charge sheet. A chief inspector would later have to check the entry to make sure the case was handled properly.

On that occasion, the very unimpressed sergeant told me to go and write up the arrest notes. The two area car drivers came with me to the canteen, the usual place for writing arrest notes, and one of them said, 'Okay, you just write what we tell you.'

I was angry at having been stitched up with an arrest which, according to the rules then in force, should never have been made. Now they were going to add insult to injury by telling me what to write. Completely ignoring convention and without a thought for their senior status on the relief I said, 'Haven't you got me into enough trouble as it is?'

They had never heard such insolence. They simply could not believe that a probationer barely out of training school had dared to speak like this to *them*, the elite of the team, both of them advanced drivers. Neither of them talked to me again for *two years*.

Whenever I went out on night duty patrol with one particular panda car driver, the first stop was the 'tube station' – our term for the off-licence. We would buy a couple of 'tubes' of Foster's lager which we stowed under the front passenger seat of the police car. We would wait for a lull, go to the Kentucky Fried Chicken (Kentucky Fried Pigeon, we called it) and then sit in the car eating chicken and drinking Fosters. It may sound shocking now but we never had more than one and it was accepted practice in what was one of the hardest-working divisions in the Met.

Kevin and I were in the panda and had just come from the 'tube station' when we came across a drunk. We radioed for the van but it was busy, so after waiting for a few minutes we decided to take him in ourselves. We put him in the back of the car, (always a struggle with drunks). Prisoners always sit behind the front passenger seat in a police car so they cannot attack the driver from behind. The arresting officer sits next to him behind the driver.

Kevin never hung about. As we roared off at speed back to the police station, the 'tubes' of Fosters slid out from under the seat landing at the feet of the drunk. He looked down and could not believe his luck!

In those days, the unofficial police policy across the Met was to try to avoid arresting people for drink-driving – because the police were drink-driving themselves. After we had breathalysed a suspected drunk-driver we would tell them to lock the car and get a taxi home. We told them that if we came back that night and found the car had gone, we would come straight round to their home and arrest them. This was complete rubbish since we had no power to do this; in fact in those days it was only if you caught a person actually driving that you could breathalyse them. Generally, the warning system worked, although some people refused to blow up the bag or tried to get away when we asked them to stop, in which case we arrested them.

There was other dubious behaviour at Holloway. One night officers brought in a suspected child molester and the night duty detective sergeant and one of the area car drivers, who knew each other well, took the suspect into the divisional surgeon's room where the police doctor examined ill or injured prisoners. You could hear the slaps coming from the room for several minutes.

One night Kevin and I brought in a squaddie for drink driving. He had crashed into a lamp-post.

One of the sergeants at Holloway did not like to be disturbed with prisoners when he was on night duty. That night his patience was already wearing very thin; as he tried in vain to get a name and address the squaddie told the sergeant where to go and what to do while he was there. The sergeant purposefully placed his pen down on the desk next to the charge sheet, stood up, leaned across the desk and gave the prisoner one almighty backhand, breaking his nose and sending blood spraying across the table.

The on-call divisional surgeon was called to take a blood sample to analyse the amount of alcohol in the squaddie's bloodstream and he asked what had happened. We sheepishly explained, out of the sergeant's hearing, and the surgeon simply said, 'Well, that's nothing compared to what the Red Caps will do to him. They'll give him a good kicking before he goes back to the barracks.' And that was that. The soldier never complained.

A controversial law from that time was the 'sus' law – sus being a suspected person loitering with intent to commit an indictable offence, contrary to S.4 Vagrancy Act 1824. This law allowed the police to arrest someone on grounds of suspicion alone. There was no need for a victim or a witness, and so this was open to abuse. The usual evidence given in court was 'the usual three car-door handles, your worship'. Police officers would keep a suspected criminal under observation. If they saw the suspect try three separate car-door handles or put their shoulder to three front doors, this was considered to be good evidence of 'sus'. The Caribbean community in particular complained that the police were abusing this law in order persecute young black men unfairly.

I was in court one day with an unrelated matter when I spotted an officer I knew who had arrested a young black man on sus. The man had pleaded guilty, and I told the officer I was pleased to see the sus law being used properly: after all, the accused had pleaded guilty so presumably the PC's reason for arresting him had been justified. 'Well,' said the officer with a conspiratorial air, 'if you want to know the truth, he saw us and just started running away. We chased him and when we caught him I said he could either be nicked for attempted burglary or sus and he chose sus.'

Attempted burglary in those days was likely to result in imprisonment whereas, with magistrates already becoming disenchanted with the numbers being brought before them for sus, pleading guilty to the lesser offence was likely to result in a fine. The young man had taken the soft option.

There was very little in the way of helping people cope with the effects of traumatic experiences. During one night duty, three young people had been driving in an MGB roadster with the roof down in St Paul's Road in Islington when the driver tried to take a bend in the road too fast. The sports car struck the kerb, flipped over and skidded upside down for at least fifty yards. The passenger in the rear, who had not been wearing a seatbelt, was thrown clear and had only minor injuries. The heads of the two in the front, who were strapped in, had been grated along the road, killing them instantly.

A very young and inexperienced WPC was asked to do the continuity, having seen the bodies at the scene. She travelled with them in the ambulance to the mortuary and identified them to the pathologist the following morning.

She had not dealt with a fatal accident before, and arrived back from the mortuary very upset. A fellow constable alerted a sergeant, who came out into the yard where the young lady and I happened to be. He stood over the WPC and said, 'For God's sake pull yourself together and grow up.'

This was typical of the compassion and understanding of post-traumatic stress in those days.

We spent a lot of time in hospital casualty departments and had an excellent relationship with the nurses who, like us, were relatively poorly paid, did shift work and often had to put up with difficult members of the public. Even today I cannot watch *Casualty* or *Holby City* (I am told that this is no great loss) because it reminds me all too vividly of some of the more gruesome cases we ended up bringing into casualty.

I was once called to 'suspects on premises' (burglary in progress) to find a drunken Irishman attempting to break into a flat in a six-storey block in Archway which was surrounded by iron railings, the kind with the spear-shaped tips.

Kevin chased him up the stairs until he got to the roof while I waited on the ground in case he got away from him. Our suspect ran to the edge and yelled, 'Don't come any closer or I'll jump!'

The officer approached, and the suspect jumped, landing on the spiked railings. Incredibly, he was still conscious, moaning and bleeding with the railing having pierced his thigh, groin and hip.

The fire brigade were unable to use the oxyacetylene cutters as the metal would heat up and burn him. In the end, he was cut free with a powerful pneumatic saw while we struggled to hold him steady. We then helped the ambulance men wheel him into the ambulance, balanced between two trolley-stretchers with the railings hanging in between. He was still moaning when we wheeled him into casualty.

Another gruesome case involved me being called to the Nag's Head pub in Holloway to find that somebody had been glassed. His cheek had been sliced open like the lid of a tomato soup can, and the wound was so deep that it was possible to see his teeth and gums glistening in the street light through the huge gash; flesh from his cheek flapped open as he shook uncontrollably from shock. It was a busy Friday night and no ambulances were available so we took him to casualty in the van.

There were lighter moments. Once I was on foot patrol with Shirley Danes when we stumbled across a man propped up against a wall. He was completely drunk and it took us about five minutes to realise he was trying to tell us that he was outside his own front door. There was no point in arresting him if we could get him safely inside his own home, so I searched his pockets while Shirley held him upright. We could not find a key and no one answered the door. Spotting that the top part of the front sash window was open, I decided to see whether I could squeeze my way in and then open the front door.

There was a low wall about eighteen inches high between the front garden and the pavement, so we sat him there facing the house, Shirley gripping his shoulder trying to keep him balanced. The window was a bit too high for me to climb in so I got Shirley to give me a leg-up. There we were, both in full police uniform, Shirley bending down grabbing hold of my shin and me with my bum in the air with one arm and shoulder inside the front room and the rest of me hanging out of the window.

As we both wobbled, with me struggling to push myself through the gap, we both had an onset of the giggles. Shirley, hardly able to talk through her laughter, suddenly exclaimed, 'Where's he gone?' I twisted around and looked over my shoulder to see the man had fallen backwards over the wall with his back on the pavement. All I could see were his boots and his legs up to his knees still firmly planted in the front garden whilst the rest of him had disappeared.

'You know what?' I said, 'I think I'm stuck.' We both burst into the kind of mad hysterical laughter of the 'you had to be there' variety, with tears running down our faces. Shirley didn't know whether to rescue me or the drunk. We got him in eventually, and he would have awoken the next morning with absolutely no idea what great lengths had been gone to to get him into his bed. At least I hoped it was *his* bed.

There was going to be a pageant at Olympia to mark the Met's 150th anniversary. Serving officers and cadets would dress up in old police uniforms and re-enact scenes from days gone by. To publicise this, there was going to be an item on the London edition of the BBC *Nationwide* programme, where they were planning to interview three officers – a sergeant with twenty-five years service who would talk about how things had changed, a WPC who had joined when the Women's Police was a separate department with a limited role, and a young officer who had recently joined who would talk about the future.

I had previously been selected by the superintendent to audition for a pilot of *Junior Police 5*, a spin-off of an early version of *Crimewatch* presented by Shaw keep 'em peeled' Taylor. For the pilot show I was interviewed by a panel of teenagers who concluded that I was the sort of cop who went round beating them up, so in the end my appearance was not to be.

I was on night duty and asleep by eight a.m. when the section house warden let himself into my room and left a note above my sink. He woke me up, so I read the note which said, 'Phone the superintendent at 2pm'. Thinking I had done something seriously wrong, I could not get back to sleep. When I rang him, I was amazed to hear he wanted me to represent the Met on *Nationwide* – that very evening. It was my twentieth birthday, my first away from home. I called Mum from the call box in the section house to tell her that although I would not be at home for the first time ever on my birthday, she would at least be able to see me on television.

That night there happened to be a strike by workers at ITV so the fact that there was nothing else on the box only added to my nerves as I travelled down to the BBC TV Centre in Wood Lane. Millions would be watching me; the image of the Met was in my hands. This was going to be a live broadcast, and thanks to a mixture of nervousness and the heat from the studio lights, I began to feel faint.

The cameras rolled and the presenter, Bob Wellings, gave a brief introduction before 'rolling VT', the pre-recorded video of the scenes from the Olympia show. While the microphones were off, he explained to the sergeant what he was going to ask him and then did the same with the WPC. Before he had a chance to tell me anything the director shouted 'End VT, five seconds Bob!' and we were on air, live on BBC1.

Having interviewed the other two, Bob turned to me and said, 'Last but not least, Brian Paddick. You're pretty new to the force and I understand you've got some pretty good O-levels and even some good A-levels. Why did you join the police?'

'I thought it was a job where you could get on by your own efforts,' I offered nervously, which I thought sounded better than 'I couldn't stand the idea of any more academic work.'

'So you see yourself as another Sir Robert Mark, do you?' said Bob laughing.

'I'm not sure if anybody could be as good as he was, but I'd like to get to the top where he was.' (I often repeat myself when I'm very nervous.)

Laughing again, Bob said, 'So you see yourself as a future commissioner?'

'Yes, I do.'

Not for the last time in my career, I thought I had said nothing controversial but I had put my foot right in it. I had insulted the new commissioner, Sir David McNee, by saying that nobody could be as good as Sir Robert Mark. When I arrived in the canteen back at the section house later that evening the women behind the counter shouted 'Commissioner!' From that day forth the title stuck.

CHAPTER THREE

At the end of my probationary period I had to sit the final Probationers' Examination and I got eighty-nine per cent. After the results came in I had a confirmation interview with Chief Superintendent Polkinghorne, who encouraged me to keep studying for sergeant. 'Where do you see yourself in thirty years' time?' he asked me.

'Commander,' I replied with some confidence.

He wasn't impressed. 'Hmmm . . .' he said with a frown, 'when I was in your position I wanted to be a sergeant.'

Around this time our outdated section house began an eighteen-month renovation and so we were sent to Harold Scott House in Limehouse near the Thames.

These section houses were all-male affairs, and the only time we encountered women socially was at the Empire Leicester Square nightclub and at the monthly section house disco in the police gym (I once won the prize for the 'Best Twister'). There was one attractive male PC whom I had been admiring, but he lived in the other wing of Olive House and so it was a case of admiring him from a distance. To my great surprise he wound up in the room next to mine when we transferred to Limehouse.

Late one night, there was a knock on my door and I was shocked to see him standing there in his underpants. 'I've noticed something about you, Brian,' he said. 'The way you look at me and some of the other guys.' My heart raced. He knew – but how? I remembered my first day at the section house when the sergeant had told me that it was okay to have a girl in your room overnight, but 'no blokes'.

My first thought was that I had been 'outed' and my career was over. I thought I would be ostracised by my colleagues to the extent that they might in future ignore my calls for 'urgent assistance' – the policeman's emergency cry for help. When you were part of the relief, it was not simply a case of wanting to be liked by the team you worked with or wanting to get on well with your colleagues, it was a case of safety.

'Can I come in?'

Terrified that someone would see him there I said yes. He told me not to worry, that he wasn't going to tell anyone. He had realised that I was gay and he wanted to sleep with me. How many more people knew? I was petrified; I was twenty-one years old and I had not had sex with anybody, male or female, and here was this guy suddenly out of the blue, in my bedroom and wearing only a pair of Y-fronts.

He could see how distressed I was. 'All I want to do is sleep with you,' he said, 'we don't even have to touch.' I was in turmoil. For ten years, since that sight of the naked scout, I had fantasised about having sex with another man – and I did not even know what to do. To suddenly be propositioned by this attractive man brought a mixture of desire and absolute terror. It was astonishing that the only PC in the whole section house who I really fancied happened to be the one who was now within touching distance. Trembling, I nodded and we went to bed. After a while we fell asleep. Several hours later I woke up to find that I wasn't shaking any more; my desire overcame my fear and I started stroking him.

I had very mixed feelings about this first sexual encounter. Everything I had learnt screamed out at me that this was wrong – it went against what I had been taught, my experiences at school, and the life my parents expected me to lead. It was contrary to the whole culture of the police – the bullying at school would be nothing compared to the horrors I would now face if anyone found out.

At the same time there was something about this that felt instinctively right.

My initial confusion was only made worse by Barry's behaviour. We continued to meet in my room whenever our shifts coincided, which was about once every four weeks. I once persuaded him to go for a drink with me, so he took me miles away out into the suburbs where no one would recognise us. I told him I wanted a relationship, but all he wanted was sex; gay relationships never lasted, he said, and were too dangerous for policemen, so I stopped seeing him any more. I decided that if I couldn't have a gay relationship, then I would simply have to try and go straight.

Although my sexual desires were focused on men, I resisted the temptation to put these feelings into practice. I convinced myself that what I really wanted was a best friend whose company would be constant, with whom I would go out and socialise, and with whom I would share intimate moments. Given the homophobic culture of the police, and of society generally at that time, I believed it would be impossible for that person to be a man. There was no choice for me but to find a woman to be my lifelong companion.

During a week of night duty while we were still at Harold Scott House, I was posted for one night to Bethnal Green Police Station because of a demonstration in the area. In all, there were nine male officers and one female. I was paired with the female officer and we really hit it off; in fact I had never had such a good time on patrol before.

We started seeing each other outside of work and after many happy months together I thought Jenny was the one – so I got down on one knee and to my delight she accepted. Jenny's parents were living in Cyprus and invited us to spend two weeks with them. Although we were engaged, Jenny's parents didn't believe in sex before marriage and her mother hung a sheet from a washing line stretched across the room with a bed either side – a method which proved to be entirely ineffective.

This was the first time we had spent more than a night or a weekend together and, to my horror, I found out that we did not get on at all. By the time the two weeks were up it was clear it was never going to work and I told Jenny once we arrived back in the UK. She threw the ring back at me and I left.

Besides the inevitable emotional upset, I was also distraught because this had been a genuine, determined effort on my part to play it straight and I thought I had succeeded. Although we had done everything but full sex, all the indications were that it was possible. It had felt strange to begin with (Barry was a very different shape to Jenny!), but it was wonderful to share such intimacy with someone without the guilt that had been associated with sex with Barry.

After the break-up I went home to see Mother. The moment she answered the door she realised I was very upset. Whatever's the matter?' she asked. I walked into the lounge, sat in one of the armchairs next to a nest of glass-topped tables and took the engagement ring out of my pocket. I placed it on the glass.

'Oh, thank God for that,' she said. 'I thought you were going to tell me you were queer.'

Needless to say this set things back in terms of coming out to her.

I was still a PC at Holloway when we were joined on our relief by WPC Fiona Pilborough, a beautiful, blonde and voluptuous woman with a fresh china-doll face. She became Holloway's 'most wanted' among the male officers even though she made it clear from the start that she would never date somebody on the same team. In a moment of fate I was transferred to the crime squad and seized my opportunity.

A short time after we started going out I called round to her section house to find her in her nightdress. I was quite embarrassed. 'Do you want me to come back later?' I asked.

With a very firm 'No!' she grabbed my arm and pulled me inside, slammed the door and locked it behind me. She then began removing my clothes. I was suddenly petrified and it was some encounters later before I finally overcame my fear and achieved my long-awaited goal.

Despite this slow start, Fiona proudly boasted to her friend (while I was still in the room), that I was 'like a kid with a new toy'. I blushed, albeit proudly, but I soon began to feel that the sex I was having with

Fiona had little to do with love and intimacy. While I initially thought she might be 'the one', she turned out to be anything but.

Until then, Fiona and I continued our relationship and actually became engaged.

Encouraged by my chief superintendent, I had continued with my studies for the sergeant's exam immediately after finishing my probation and could not believe it when the results came in: I had come sixth out of the one thousand people who took the exam that year.

The top one hundred had an automatic right to apply for accelerated promotion. The first part of the process involved appearing before a selection panel which was chaired by a deputy assistant commissioner from New Scotland Yard. He asked me the dreaded question: 'If we put you forward for accelerated promotion and you were offered the chance to study for a university degree, would you take it?'

I had hardly stopped studying since the day I joined the police and, knowing that there was only one acceptable answer (it had been decided that all senior police officers should have a degree), I said yes straight away. The rest of the interview was a formality.

Next, I was sent to Preston for three days of tests and interviews based on the Civil Service Selection Board process. After my usual nervous start, I really began to enjoy the process and did well enough to qualify for a year at the Police Staff College at Bramshill as a sergeant and, subject to one year's satisfactory performance back in the Met, promotion to inspector.

Back at Holloway it was decided that I needed some CID experience before I was promoted. Normally you could only be promoted sergeant after you had completed five years' service, but those on accelerated promotion were promoted after four. This was still six months away.

The CID was a very popular career option. You did not have to wear uniform, you rarely did night duty, and you never had to walk the beat in the cold and rain. It was a much sought-after role – but not by me. I didn't want to go into it at all.

In the 1970s the CID had a reputation for being corrupt, an

extraordinary drinking culture, and was even more homophobic than officers on the relief. Every Friday afternoon when I was on duty I could smell the booze from the CID office as the detectives began yet another drinking session. The superintendent, and the chief superintendent, sometimes dropped in.

I much preferred the discipline of the uniformed branch of the police as opposed to the unstructured culture of the CID. I decided that I was going to have to fail the selection interview, which would be chaired by the local detective chief inspector.

The DCI asked me questions such as, 'Who is the current target criminal?' This was the easiest question of all as the answer was prominently displayed on a big poster in the station but I replied 'I don't know' to most of the questions.

After what was the worst performance I thought I could possibly produce, I was told I had been successful and was to start the following week. Although the DCI was probably under strict instructions from the superintendent to pass me, and despite the fact that I did not want the job, I was still expected to comply with the tradition of buying the DCI a bottle of scotch for selecting me. I didn't, and that did not go down very well.

As the CID involved working in plain clothes, sometimes undercover, officers had to lose the neat policeman's haircut because it was a clear giveaway. All of the CID officers grew their hair long in keeping with the fashion of the day. I couldn't bear to have long hair so I had the idea of becoming a skinhead.

I went and bought myself a black Harrington jacket with tartan lining, white Fred Perry polo shirts, heavy black brogues, white socks and drainpipe jeans held up with red braces. As I walked down the Hornsey Road, people crossed the street to avoid me. This was an interesting lesson in how people are judged by appearance; a simple costume change had completely altered people's perception of me.

After three months I was allowed to leave the Crime Squad and become Holloway's first ever acting sergeant (officers usually went straight from PC to sergeant but I did not have enough service). As this was a first, we had to improvise. We got a set of sergeant's metal epaulette badges and cut one of the stripes off. I ran Holloway's front office until I reached four years of service and was given a sergeant's position in Brixton in November 1980.

The sergeants' stripes sat heavily on my shoulders. I was acutely aware of my youth, especially as I had to give orders to older and more experienced constables. I sometimes over-compensated for this by throwing my weight around, which brought me into conflict with some of the senior PCs, particularly the lazy ones.

One cold, damp night duty I was driving my Hillman Hunter supervision car when I passed a couple of women officers and as there was little going on, I offered them a lift. As we were driving along, I could hear them talking in the back.

'What are you two talking about?' I asked.

One of the women, Sue Luke, replied: 'Sarge – why don't you just be yourself?'

Sue Thomas (as she is now), you changed my life.

From then on I tried my best to be the same person, no matter what the circumstances were, whether I was at home, at a social occasion or at work. Clearly you have to modify your behaviour depending on the circumstances, but I wanted to be genuine; what you see is what you get, whether you like it or not. People respect you for being who you are, although what I did in the bedroom was my affair.

CHAPTER FOUR

After a few months at Brixton, I was sent on the Special Course, an accelerated promotion course, at Bramshill, the Police Staff College in Hampshire.

'Accelerated' was a bit of a misleading term as the course lasted for a year. It involved a mixture of practical exercises, along with academic work which included essays in sociology, politics and social policy, during which you took and were expected to pass the national inspector's exam.

The chief superintendent in charge of the course was also an officer in the Territorial Army and he thought it a good test of character for us to be taken on a week of extreme cross-country exercises across Dartmoor. We found ourselves wading chest-deep through ice-cold rivers and trying to navigate the moors in thick fog before spending a night under canvas. To my surprise, I thoroughly enjoyed the experience, and my esteem amongst the instructors rose considerably through this difficult week.

We also engaged in practical exercises during another week when we took over a village near Grantham and acted out scenarios like trying to capture a blackmailer and searching for an armed suspect in the woods.

By strange coincidence, when it was my turn to play the role of the inspector, I was given an exercise which involved the case of a gay man who was being blackmailed. By dealing with the victim sensitively I managed to persuade him to cooperate with us. I set up an operation with undercover officers and police dog units to capture the blackmailer when he came to pick up the payment from the victim.

As soon as we had arrested him red-handed with the money tucked inside his jacket, a halt was called to the exercise.

At Bramshill I met a handsome sergeant from Kent called Malcolm Sparrow who seemed to have it all. He played tennis and hockey for his county, had a double-first from Cambridge in mathematics and was married to a charming woman. He was developing mathematical formulae for the automatic recognition of fingerprints by computers. He left a few years later to join the academic staff at Harvard.

Much to my surprise, I learned that Malcolm was a committed born-again Christian. He completely shattered the negative stereotype I had of a Christian as a weak, weedy, feeble person in need of an emotional crutch. He was the complete opposite, someone who greatly impressed me.

As we talked about religion and my negative preconceptions, he suggested I read John's Gospel in a modern translation of the Bible. My parents were not at all religious; the only time I had been to church was for church parades about once every six weeks when I was in The Cub Scouts and I doubted that Christianity could have any meaning for me.

Following the encounter with Malcolm, I read John's Gospel with an open mind and I was convinced. A short time later I found myself at Cheam Baptist Church being baptised by total immersion by Pastor David Abernethy.

My finding God had a traumatic effect on Fiona. The Christian way is to abstain from sex before marriage and she did not take this news very well. She tried her hardest to talk me out of my new-found religion but I remained adamant. Faced with the prospect of no sex for a while, Fiona told me she could no longer remain engaged to me. She called my mother to tell her that I was going mad, adding 'If Brian isn't careful, he'll end up in a bare room with just a Bible!'

It was not long before I found my future wife, however. I had met Norman and Hilary Stone at Cheam Baptist Church and they had bemoaned the fact that their daughter Mary was totally uninterested in religion and refused to come to any services. When they started talking to her about this upwardly mobile young policeman they managed to tempt her along and we started going out.

Mary was beautiful, always immaculately dressed, and our senses of humour dovetailed perfectly. We were both very affectionate and, knowing my religious beliefs, there was no pressure from Mary to have sex. We often talked about it and we were intimate together, but we were both happy to wait until we were married. Mary was kind, and very supportive of my demanding job. Her renewed interest in going to church pleased her parents and we genuinely fell in love with each other. Everything seemed to be going well and after a year or so she was also baptised. We were engaged soon afterwards.

CHAPTER FIVE

The Bramshill course finished on Fridays and at the weekend I typically returned to London and, once a month, to Brixton police station to collect my payslip. One weekend in April 1981 I saw plain clothes officers on virtually every street corner. I did not know it, but this was part of Operation Swamp, a clampdown on street robbery in Brixton's town centre. About a thousand black men (including three members of the Lambeth Community Relations Council) were stopped and searched in the 'Triangle', the three most deprived streets in the area. It was as if an army of occupation had descended.

Relations between the police and locals were already strained and, while there was no evidence I was aware of, rumours were rife that any black person who was unlucky enough to be arrested was beaten up. Add to this the police's aggressive tactics in Operation Swamp and the fuse was lit. It was just a matter of time.

When Brixton exploded I was pressing my police uniform in my parents' house. I was watching the television news when I thought, 'Hang on, that street looks familiar.' I watched in shock as I saw police officers I knew coming under a barrage of missiles. Many of my colleagues had been injured by bricks and bottles.

I jumped into my brand-new £5,000 pageant-blue MGB GT in my freshly pressed uniform and headed for the heart of Brixton.

In retrospect, this was not a very bright thing for a young sergeant to do.

Twenty minutes later I was stuck in traffic in Acre Lane when a group of about fifty young men appeared. 'If they see me I'm dead,' I said to myself, and desperately tried to hide behind the steering wheel. I frantically wriggled my way out of my jacket while the youths smashed a shop window. As I sat low in the car the traffic began to move. I had escaped, but worse was to come.

Policemen were arriving from all over London. Unlike today, there was no 'Service Mobilisation Plan', a well-choreographed and practised system of getting large numbers of officers to the point of serious disorder within hours. Calls were being made to section houses across the capital asking off-duty officers to turn out. Nobody had a clue as to how many reinforcements might show up.

At the station I was given ten officers and six plastic shields and was told to clear Mayall Road in the heart of the riot so the fire brigade could get in and put out fires started by petrol bombs. Rioters armed with bricks, broken paving slabs and lumps of concrete were waiting for us. A burning pub was in the process of collapsing as we arrived in the street.

I split my ten men into two groups of five in a scrum formation, shields to the front, and pressed forwards. Concrete missiles pounded off us but somehow we managed to get close enough to the rioters to get them nervous enough to start fleeing. One of my men broke away and started chasing them. I screamed at him to come back, which he thankfully did. It was only four years later, in 1985, that we learned what could happen if an officer became isolated in a riot situation when PC Keith Blakelock was hacked to death during the riots at the Broadwater Farm Estate in North London while he tried to clear a path for the fire brigade.

It was not until I saw the TV coverage of the Brixton riots that I realised what a dangerous situation we had been in. There were almost three hundred police injuries and sixty-five serious civilian

injuries. Fifty-six police vehicles were destroyed and thirty buildings had to be demolished.

It felt surreal to be back at Bramshill after such a weekend. The
chief inspector was angry when I told him that I had been on
Brixton's frontline. 'What would have happened if you were
injured, you would have missed the rest of the course!' I told
him I simply could not stand there and watch while my colleagues
were attacked and injured. I had to do something. The chief superintendent, the course director, agreed I had done the right thing.

Part of the Special Course involved spending two weeks in another
police force of our choice. There had been copycat riots in St
Paul's in Bristol, so I asked to go there. Even though this was a
much smaller area than Brixton, the policing was just as confrontational. Six officers in the back of an armed Land Rover
would pile out, grab a black suspect, and drive off again because it
was unsafe for them to stop. They were policing without the support of the community, by force rather than by consent. Although
this type of policing was confined to a very small area it was a
glimpse into the abyss; this is what policing would be like if we lost
the consent of the people.

We were out one night when some officers called up on the
radio; they were chasing a drug dealer. I was in a car with an
inspector and we joined in the chase. We saw the suspect sprinting
along the pavement. The inspector yelled at me, 'Get out and
run!' I jumped out, effectively taking over the chase from the two
PCs who were some way behind. I steadily gained on the suspect
and got my hands on his shoulders, but then he twisted around and
pushed me off balance, sending me sprawling onto the ground,
tearing a deep jagged gash in my knee.

Scrambling up, I carried on and was gaining on the suspect
again when he turned in to the front garden of a terraced house.
Thinking he was safe, he slowed down, ambled up the path to the
front door and opened it with a key as I arrived at the front garden
gate. Turning to grin at me as I sprinted up the path, he slammed

the door as hard as he could in my face. To his horror, he slammed it so hard that it simply bounced open again. I stepped over the threshold and arrested him.

I got my knee seen to at the Bristol Royal Infirmary at five a.m. It was the end of my night shift and I was shattered. The young casualty doctor decided to get the gravel out with a nail brush dipped in disinfectant and then stitched it up – all without anaesthetic.

At the end of the course, I was awarded an A grade and my leadership ability was described as 'outstanding'. Although my academic work was not very good, it was good enough to earn me a scholarship to the university of my choice – or at least any university prepared to have me. For the moment though, it was time to get back to Brixton.

Brixton became the most valuable education of my police life. My attempts to change things in the Met were fuelled by my experiences in April 1981. My empathy with minority communities, my hostility to the discriminatory use of 'stop and search', my commitment to policing with the consent of the community – all had their origins in the riot and shaped my policing of the community when I went back at the end of the course.

Lord Scarman was asked to investigate what had gone wrong. He argued that there needed to be a balance between law enforcement and preservation of the peace. It was the very heavy-handed approach of the police in Brixton that had kicked off the riot. Ultimately, it was an anti-police riot. Various politicians appeared in front of the TV cameras to condemn the people involved in the rioting; the 'Uprising' as it became known in Brixtonian folklore.

While there clearly could be no excuse for such criminal behaviour, these people really felt that they had no choice because nobody was listening to them or their concerns about their situation generally, and the police in particular. They felt they had no option but to rise up against the police after Operation Swamp; many saw it as a battle for their human rights.

*

In January 1982, I returned to Brixton to work with exactly the same people on the same shift, who seemed to have become racist while I was away.

Of course it was not that my colleagues had changed at all; it was, as Lord Scarman had said, the 'liberalising effects of education'. Spending a year away from the canteen culture of the police force in an academic environment had changed me. I had been so successfully inculcated into the police canteen culture that I had become blind to my own racism.

For three months I was one of the sergeants in charge of the Railton Road patrol, known locally as 'the frontline' and at the core of the riots. I was given six constables to carry out foot patrols and ordered to improve our relations with the community. Not an easy task. The tension remained so high that we had a bus full of constables waiting on standby just on the edge of the area we were patrolling, ready to pile in at a moment's notice.

It was during this time that I first began to understand Brixton's relationship with cannabis. Once, when we tried to stop and search a young black man for possession of cannabis he ran off. We chased him as far as a house in Railton Road, which we knew was used as an illegal gambling den by some middle-aged Caribbean men. Sure enough, a forty-something black guy answered the door.

Catching my breath, I said, 'We're chasing a young suspect and he ran into this house.'

The man asked me, 'Wha' ya wan'im for?'

'Cannabis.'

The door slammed in my face.

A few weeks later we were chasing a youth who was suspected of having stolen a handbag and he ran into the same gambling den. Not holding out much hope, I knocked on the door and it was opened by the same man.

'Wha' ya wan'im for?'

'Stealing a handbag.'

He looked at me, shook his head and disappeared inside, leaving the door ajar. A few moments later he pushed the young guy out and into my arms. These incidents did not seem too significant to me at the time. It was only when I later returned as the borough commander to face the problems peculiar to Brixton that I realised their true importance in terms of tackling crime.

Railton Road remained a drug hotspot. Number one was a troublesome address and, after a number of complaints, the police raided it. The raid was carried out so violently that the contents of the property were all but destroyed, which led to all future potentially controversial police raids being videotaped.

Despite this, drug dealing continued from this local authority house and with the council's agreement it was decided to take the extreme step of demolishing it.

In this post-riot time the Labour MP Clive Soley had the bright idea of taking ten young police officers and ten young black people from deprived inner city areas to a foreign country where they would have no choice but to talk to each other as the inhabitants did not speak English.

Because I had been in charge of community policing in Brixton I was asked if I wanted to go. I was warned I would have to take annual leave; the police were not prepared for us to go 'on duty', although the trip would be paid for by Soley's backers. The youths and youth workers came from Brixton, Lewisham and Toxteth in Liverpool, and we met at six-thirty a.m. at Euston station to catch the coach that would take us across on the ferry to the Netherlands.

We were based in a hotel in Amsterdam from where we would go on coach trips to other parts of Holland. To our surprise, there were some genuinely good discussions – despite the Toxteth lads making full use of the liberal cannabis laws; they took delight in blowing smoke in our direction while reminding us that we could not arrest them.

For me it was very interesting to be able to spend that amount of time with these young men and I managed to get on very well with all of them. This experience helped to demolish some of the stereotypes of black people, and some of their stereotyped opinions of the police.

The period I spent as a sergeant at Brixton and on the Special Course changed my views on many things but I was still struggling with my youth, especially when I was promoted to inspector at Fulham in 1983, at the age of twenty-four.

PART TWO

CHAPTER SIX

My first tour of duty as an inspector was a night shift and waiting in my 'corres. tray', a small metal locker with a lockable door and an opening at the top where correspondence could be posted, was a file marked 'STAFF – IN CONFIDENCE'. It contained a report about a young WPC who was off sick every two or three days each month. A minute had been written in biro on the bottom of the report by the chief superintendent: 'Inspector Paddick to deal'. My initial thought was embarrassment – how was I, a very young man, going to talk to a woman I had never met before about her period pains? Then I remembered a girlfriend who had suffered from a similar affliction and I decided to consult her.

The following night I called the WPC in, and in as fatherly a tone as I could manage, I recommended a particular painkiller that appeared to be most effective, especially when taken with iron tablets, but if she had any doubts she really ought to see her doctor. The periodic sick leave had to stop, however (I cannot begin to imagine the trouble such an order would cause today).

The WPC seemed genuinely pleased that I might have found a potential solution to her ills and that I had been concerned enough to give her healthcare advice rather than just tell her off for being sick too often. It certainly helped – her sickness record was no longer an issue in the months that followed.

One of the 'perks' of being at Fulham was the football. With first division clubs Chelsea and Fulham on our patch, I spent a great deal of time policing the stadiums as whenever one team was playing away, the other was at home.

During one of the first matches I attended, I made another error of judgement. A very long-in-service chief inspector felt that officers under my command were not doing their jobs adequately. He told me, 'If I find they're not where they should be, I'm going to kick their arses all around the ground.'

I liked the sound of this phrase and decided to make it my own; I repeated it when I spoke to my sergeants. While they may have taken such a harsh telling-off from an older, more experienced officer, they could hardly believe what this twenty-four-year-old (who looked about fifteen) was saying. The sergeants passed on what I had said to all of the constables. It became obvious that the hostility aimed in my direction was more than the usual 'Bramshill w★★★★★'.

'Okay, what have I done wrong?' I asked the chief sergeant.

'Sir, you can't tell us you're going to kick our arses around the ground.'

I reflected for a moment.

'Sergeant, once the match has finished I want to see you and your officers in the back yard at Fulham police station,' I said firmly.

He was not pleased to hear this and neither were his officers. Quite what they thought I was going to do to them when they got there I do not know, but the last thing they were expecting when they dutifully arrived back at the police station was an apology.

I stood on the external metal staircase of one of the small buildings in the back yard and looked down at the twenty officers, feeling a little like Julius Caesar addressing an army. 'I realise now that I shouldn't have said what I did this afternoon. I'm sorry, it was inappropriate. Thank you for doing a good job despite that.'

Twenty open mouths looked back at me. It was unheard of for an inspector to apologise to junior officers. At training school, officers are taught that the senior officer is always right. By admitting I had made a mistake I won their respect, and this was made clear to me when the sergeant came up to me in full view of the others and shook my hand.

At the end of each football match, it was traditional for the senior officers to meet with the commander (who came along each Saturday just to watch the game from one of the best seats in the stand), the superintendent and the chief superintendent for a 'debrief' – which meant sharing the contents of a bottle of scotch. On this particular day it had been my turn to supply the scotch.

The superintendent at Fulham at that time was not well liked. After we had all had our fill and the others had left, he handed me the remnants of the bottle and told me to place it in a 'safe repository'. This strange turn of phrase I immediately recognised as a quote from Masonic ritual.

My father was quite senior in the lodge and my brother and uncle were also members. I was curious about it but all they would tell me was that they thought I would enjoy it if I joined, so I did. There were lodges with many police members and there were many allegations that they 'looked after each other', so I wanted to make sure there were no accusations against me of using the Masons to make my way up through the ranks. I was glad to discover that there was only one other officer in my father's lodge, the sergeant from Sutton, Doug Baxter. You have to be twenty-one to join the Freemasons and it was not long after my birthday, while I was still a constable, that I accepted my father's invitation to join.

I asked the superintendent if he was 'on the square' and his attitude changed completely; suddenly he became my best friend and showed me his Masonic regalia, the decorated apron worn in Masonic meetings depicting the role and rank of the wearer. I found his complete volte-face quite disappointing, but it was not the last time someone's attitude towards me was to change instantly when he discovered my Masonic links.

In 1985, under the new Metropolitan Commissioner Sir Kenneth Newman, a book – known as 'The Blue Book' – was published on policing principles in which Newman wrote that being a Freemason was inconsistent with being a police officer. With increasing mistrust of the police generally and amongst minority groups in particular, Newman felt that membership of a 'secret society' (or a 'society of secrets' as Freemasons would argue) would only add to public suspicion that the police could not be trusted.

The commissioner's views resulted in the rebellious formation of a lodge exclusively for police officers, 'The Knights of St James', so-called for the area of London where New Scotland Yard is based. It was a typical response of junior officers to their bosses' attempts to change them.

When I talked to my father about 'The Blue Book' he said he had expected me to call him; he had read about it in the *Daily Telegraph*. He agreed that I had no choice but to no longer attend meetings.

One night duty, a local well-known criminal attempted a smash-and-grab at a shop on a main road just as the area car was driving past. The driver, who appeared to model himself on the TV show *The Sweeney*, grabbed the unlucky thief while his hands were still on the inside of the window and punched him in the face. They put him in handcuffs, even though he promised to 'come quietly', and dragged him down to the station.

The arrest, and most importantly the punch, was witnessed by two ambulance men who happened to be driving past at the time and they decided to make a complaint. In those days all complaints against the police had to be dealt with by an inspector. Their outrage was plain to see when I met them; they told me that there was no need for the officer to have struck the prisoner.

I went to the custody suite and asked the burglar what happened (burglary is stealing when you are trespassing, even if it's only your hands that are doing the trespassing inside a broken shop window). He told me, 'I was caught bang to rights. I deserved everything I got.' This was tricky. I didn't want to suggest to the guy that he ought to make a complaint since I had some loyalty to my staff but, on the other hand, I wanted to ensure that he had every opportunity to express a grievance.

'You're okay about the way you've been treated?'

'I've no complaints.'

I went back to the ambulance crew. 'Look, the prisoner doesn't want to know.'

'We don't care; *we* want to make a complaint.'

Until very recently, the police were not legally obliged to record 'third party' complaints unless the prisoner himself complained, so I did not have to make an official report. But this was still an awkward situation: I was torn between wanting to see justice done and my loyalty to the team. Encouraging the prisoner to make a complaint when he was not interested could have potentially damaged my ability to lead the team, but I didn't want to send the ambulance crew away feeling they had been short-changed.

I decided to take the unprecedented step of taking the ambulance crew into the charge room to meet the criminal. It was a high-risk strategy. I told the prisoner about the ambulance crew and that they were not taking no for an answer; they needed to hear it from him. He agreed to meet them. He told them, 'Look, I appreciate what you're trying to do but I've got no complaints, I was out of order. Thanks again but I really don't want to know.'

'Well, if you're sure . . .' This was followed by thanks and handshakes all round and the ambulance crew left happy. I was feeling pretty pleased with myself that my gamble had paid off and all parties were happy when a friendly sergeant came up to me and asked 'Can I have a word, guv?'

He told me that one of the other sergeants had it in for me, and had told the arresting officers and the rest of the team that I had brought the prisoner and the ambulance crew together so that they could collude in building a cast-iron case against the arresting officers.

This should have taught me a number of valuable lessons. Unorthodox solutions sometimes pay off, but there will always be people who deliberately misinterpret your actions in order to damage your reputation. I could also have learnt that those closest to you would sometimes turn out to be your worst enemies. Looking back on what was to come, I clearly did not learn those lessons here.

Kenneth Newman became commissioner in 1982 and brought in the new and what was then radical idea of 'policing by objectives'. This involved setting targets and formulating action plans to achieve them. Previously we just tackled crime as it happened and hoped it would go down as a result. Newman envisioned a far more proactive approach that involved analysing where and when crime was being committed and targeting problem areas at peak times in an effort to cut down on crime.

Every division had to produce its first ever divisional plan, including analysis, objectives and action plans. Lucky me – as the only inspector with O-Level mathematics, I was selected as the planning inspector. It was with great reluctance that I gave up my operational role to take charge of planning, a nightmare that only came to an end when I left Fulham to go to university.

CHAPTER SEVEN

I had been given an application form where you state which courses
you want to apply for, and choose five universities. Assistant
Commissioner Geoffrey Dear (who later became the chief constable
of the West Midlands and resigned in 1989 when he uncovered extensive corruption in the Crime Squad) suggested that I started at the top
and worked my way down.

Very late in the application process, I was extremely surprised to
learn I had been granted an interview at The Queen's College, Oxford.
I went up to see the admissions tutor, Peter Neumann, a very pleasant
well-spoken chap with a large, balding head. We had coffee and chatted about life in general and after a while he suggested I should move
on to see the politics don, Geoffrey Marshall.

Marshall was a diminutive figure, a frail-looking man in his late
fifties who was far more serious and businesslike than Neumann. I
took a seat in his expansive rooms, which were exactly how you
would expect an Oxford professor's room to look; shelves and shelves
of books, portraits, papers, journals, and old furniture. Then began
a fairly serious discussion where he asked me what I expected to get
from Oxford, and how I expected to cope with economics and
philosophy when I had only studied politics at Bramshill.

After about ten minutes of talking, Marshall, deadpan and without
pausing, suddenly changed the subject: 'Do you drink light ale?'

I never had, but thought it best to nod fervently. He walked over
to the corner of the room where there was a plastic crate full of
bottles.

'Well,' he said, 'we had better have a drink then to celebrate your success.'

I later learnt that he had been impressed by a previous policeman who had studied at Queen's. He had not only proved himself a good student but had also become a positive influence on his fellow students who, while academically brilliant, lacked 'real-world' experience and the dedication that comes when your employer is paying for both your tuition and your salary while you study.

I found my success incredibly bizarre. Peter Burt, a friend from church, who was to be best man at my wedding, was in his final year at Queen's studying mathematics. I had visited him there and was overawed by the history and grandeur of the place, particularly the dining hall with its wood-panelling, high ceiling, and large portraits on the walls. I never dreamt I would one day be there on my own account.

I was due to start at Queen's in October 1983. On 17 September, Mary and I were married at Cheam Baptist Church. Baptist churches are deliberately stark in appearance, with little in the way of decoration and no central aisle along which the bride might otherwise make a grand entrance. Mary, who appeared immaculate even after she had just got out of bed, stunned everyone in the church with her beauty; in her flowing white bridal gown, she seemed to float as she approached me from the side aisle at the front of the church. In keeping with the setting, I did not repeat my twin brother's top-hat-and-tails wedding but opted for a lounge suit. We exchanged our vows surrounded by flowers.

The ageing organist, who sometimes struggled with the more difficult pieces, had been set a very tough assignment but rose to the occasion magnificently. Mendelssohn's Wedding March opened the proceedings and Widor's Toccata played us out. This was, as far as I was concerned, a one-off; I wanted it to be unforgettable and it truly was. Mary was the only woman I ever really wanted to marry. We were soulmates and I was truly the happiest I'd ever been on that day.

We had a grand reception at Bourne Hall in Ewell paid for by Mary's parents, an incredibly generous gesture as they could ill-afford such extravagance. After our honeymoon in Madeira we returned to the UK and to Oxford. Our new home was a Thames Valley Police house just inside the Oxford ring road.

That summer I had attended a conference at Windsor Great Lodge hosted by Lord Vaizey and his family. He found out I was going to Oxford, so he invited me to supper to meet his daughter Polly who was already there. He also invited the Right Honourable Michael Sieff, then chairman of Marks & Spencer.

When he learned that my wife was looking for a job and had considerable experience in retail (Mary worked as a beauty consultant for Estée Lauder), Sieff said that he would find her employment at M&S in Oxford. On her first day Mary arrived at work to be told to fill a freezer with frozen turkeys. She stuck the day out, but this was not the kind of retail Mary was used to or expecting, and she did not go back.

We found life in Oxford quite difficult to begin with. It was the first time Mary had ever been away from her family home and I was having enough trouble getting adjusted to university life so our time together as newly-weds was limited.

Mary soon found work as a receptionist for a solicitor's firm opposite the Oxford Union, work she was intellectually overqualified for, and within a few weeks she was promoted to the cashier's department.

Still a keen Christian, I attended St Aldate's Anglican Church in the heart of Oxford. Michael Green, the canon, was a famous Anglican evangelist, and about a thousand people attended each service. For Mary, who was a reluctant Christian, it was far too much, and while I was drawn more and more into my religion Mary became repelled by it. It upset me deeply to think that we were heading in different directions so soon in our marriage.

Despite this, I still played a very active role at St Aldate's. Once a year, Michael Green, along with other clergy and students from the university, would go to another part of the country to convert the locals. I went on one of these missions and I loved every minute of it, trying to engage with people; the spirit of camaraderie amongst us was wonderful.

Oxford terms were eight weeks long and each week was given a number. 'Noughth' week of the first term involved preliminary meetings with the two tutors for that term, together with between two (philosophy) and five (politics) other students. We were given the topic for the week and allocated an essay title and a list of reading. The following week students were picked out at random to read out their essay to the class who would, along with the tutor, criticise as you went along.

Some of the essay titles were scarier than others; our first philosophy essay title was in Latin so the first thing I had to do was find someone who could translate it for me. I was petrified of being asked to read out my essay. One of my tutors said he had not met a nervous policeman before. Directing six lanes of traffic at the Nag's Head when the traffic lights were out was no problem, but reading out an essay in front of half a dozen people was terrifying.

I felt completely out of my depth. All my fellow students were at least seven years younger than me, had at least three A grades at A-level (some had five) and had passed the entrance examinations. Police officers who had gone to other universities told me they had to complete two essays a term; I was doing two essays a week. We had very limited help with our studies; after one hour you left the tutor with your reading list and the essay title and that was it until the next week. I do not know how I survived that first term, and only just managed to scrape through the exams at the end of the first year, which I had to pass in order to continue.

The only saving grace was economics, for which the tutor and renowned economist Dieter Helm suggested buying *Modern Micro-Economics* by A. Koutsoyiannis. Dieter set the questions for each of the essays based on the chapters of the book, so it was simply a case of copying out the relevant parts and disguising the fact that, most of the time, I didn't understand what I was writing.

On the sporting front I managed to secure a place in the college rugby team and also joined the university's swimming team, eventually becoming captain. The standard of rugby was not particularly high and I was able to play in the forwards in my favourite position of flanker. I had been selected to be vice captain of the college team when I was kicked in the side of the head in a grudge match against 'former members' of college. This left me with double vision for three weeks and so I decided to end my rugby-playing career.

A Queen's tradition that gave me some cause for concern followed the annual rugby club dinner when 'freshers' were expected to strip naked and 'streak' around the college's back quad. Even in those days I was sufficiently aware to realise that if it leaked out that a police inspector was about to streak in a public place, the opportunities for a good headline and a series of colourful pictures in a tabloid newspaper would be too good to miss.

I debated with the captain whether or not a dispensation was available, and weighed this possibility against the loss of credibility I would suffer by not taking part. I also consulted my parents and we came up with the idea of me wearing my mother's swimming cap as a disguise. It was decorated with tufts of light-brown nylon 'hair', so it might be possible to deny it was me in any photos.

On the fateful evening, after downing several glasses of wine during dinner, I whipped out the bathing cap and donned it before my team-mates, who thought a police inspector streaking in a woman's wig was an even greater spectacle than doing it without. We launched into our streak at top speed around the back quad but, unfortunately, our little fun-run coincided with the end of an organ (no pun intended) recital in the college chapel. I watched in horror as the doors opened and out came Oxford's most esteemed members of the blue-rinse brigade. Their faces were a picture of delight and disgust as we stampeded past. To my relief, no one photographed the occasion.

The terms only made up twenty-four weeks of the year and for the remaining twenty-eight weeks my time was my own. I was under no obligation to return to the Met. One of the aims of a scholarship was to immerse oneself in a different culture, so I stayed in Oxford and tried to make up some time with Mary and catch up with my studies.

I also helped to run a youth club in the centre of Oxford which was owned by the church. It was open to any young people who wanted to play pool or table tennis, listen to music, chat, and so on. Coffee was fivepence a cup but it was on the house to anyone prepared to sit down and listen to me talk about Christianity for five minutes during the 'God slot' halfway through the evening.

Kids from poor housing estates as well as punk rockers and glue sniffers made good use of the club. It was a good place to escape from the cold and, occasionally, a young person would come looking for help. One particular evening a very handsome young guy of about eighteen, with a huge spider's web tattoo on his neck, told me he had been arrested the day before for glue sniffing. Apparently, the police surgeon told him he would die if he did not give up. With tears in his eyes, he told me he didn't want to die but found it hard to give up when everyone around him was doing it. I never saw him again. This incident touched me deeply.

Another rather scary-looking, tall, thin punk-rocker with a huge Mohican and dressed in black had been thrown out of the local home- less persons' refuge and found his way to us. He was desperate and really had nowhere to live, so I phoned Mary and she agreed he could come home and sleep on our sofa in the lounge.

I explained to him he could only be in the house when either Mary or I were there, and only as long as he stayed off the glue. He accepted our offer. Unlike some of the students we invited back for dinner, this young man was extremely well-mannered and leapt up to clear the plates and wash up each evening as soon as we had finished dinner. He provided yet another very strong example about the dangers of judg- ing people by how they look.

A few nights after he had come to stay with us, I was at home when I received a reverse-charge call from a telephone box in the city centre. It was our punk, in tears and practically incoherent although I could just about make out that he had gone back on the glue and as a result he would not be coming 'home'. We never saw him again.

When it came to the end of term report, students had to appear wearing the college gown in front of the head of the college, the provost, then Lord Blake.

Sitting either side of him were two tutors who read out what they thought of your performance. At the end of the second year I was astonished when my philosophy tutor said that teaching me philosophy of mind was like 'a discussion between equals'.

As a consequence, the governing body had decided to award me an academic prize which amounted to £15 a year, just enough for a textbook.

As finals loomed, Mary and I agreed that it would not be a good idea for us to move back to London during my final examinations, so we moved during the Easter break and Mary lived in our new home in North Sutton while I settled into a room in college.

Oxford had not been kind to our marriage. While Mary felt isolated from friends and family, I immersed myself, perhaps too enthusiastically, in university life. Besides this, our religious convictions had diverged. We were still unmistakably in love, as visitors to our home often pointed out. Oxford was such a great place to live, with countryside an easy walk from our front door and we had some very good times together, despite the underlying tensions.

Incredibly hard academic work, sport, religious activity and life with Mary had pushed the issues I had with my sexuality into the background. In my experience, when things are going well, unresolved issues – even fundamental ones – are manageable. It is only when unexpected events beyond one's own control cause things to go very seriously wrong that something has to give.

The final examinations were a really dreadful challenge. The whole degree was based on the marks you achieved in these examinations. There were twelve three-hour papers over a period of three weeks.

The intense pressure was made all the worse because we had to wear the traditional dark suit, white shirt, white bow-tie and gown, and carry our mortar boards into the exam room – at the height of summer.

I cannot remember anything of the exams themselves, but I came away with a very good 2:1 and graduated in 1987. The ceremony involved dressing up once more and walking in a crocodile line to the Radcliffe Camera, an old, circular theatre building. Students went in wearing their undergraduate gowns before somebody uttered some Latin phrase and we all filed out, put on our graduate gowns and then filed back in as graduates.

My parents were there and were delighted to see me receive my degree. It was a truly remarkable moment. It seemed unbelievable that I had a degree from Oxford, a place I would never have had a chance of entering if I had tried to apply straight from school.

CHAPTER EIGHT

When I returned to the force from university, I was sent to Deptford, a testing posting for any inspector.

There were, as ever, some 'interesting' characters. Inspector Alan Reed was an old, and old-fashioned, cop whose favourite saying was, 'Police officers are never happy unless they're moaning, and it's my job to make them happy.'

Being a duty officer in a busy borough, death was something I encountered on a regular basis.

One of the most profoundly upsetting suicides I was called to took place the day after Boxing Day. A woman with a history of depression had gone to keep her weekly appointment with her psychiatrist at Lewisham Hospital, but because it was between Christmas and New Year, the clinic was closed and there was no one available to see her.

She crossed the road and walked up the stairs of an old-fashioned tower block until she reached the ninth floor. There were windows on each landing that could easily be opened. On her way down she struck the concrete canopy that came out from the tower block over the entrance before hitting the street.

Her handbag lay a few feet away and from this we got her address. I went round straight away and knocked on the door. A timid-looking man wearing glasses and a sleeveless cardigan opened the door. 'Oh hello, officer, how can I help you?'

'Do you know Jane Smith?

'Oh yes, that's my wife. Is everything Okay?'

'Do you mind if I come in, sir?' I stepped in and was shown into the living room to find a Christmas tree and two very happy kids aged about five and seven playing on the floor with their presents. I stared at them for a few moments, swallowed hard and suggested we went into different room.

'I've got some very bad news, I'm afraid. Your wife appears to have taken her own life.'

His reaction was deadpan. 'Oh dear, she has been depressed a lot recently.'

I had been pretty upset at seeing the kids but his ability to take it in his stride made it a lot easier for me – until he said, 'Inspector, how did she do it?'

I wondered how on earth I could possibly answer this delicately. I can't remember what I said except that I explained in as gentle a tone as I could manage.

The death that affected me the most, however, was the one that involved one of my own officers. Steve was a good-humoured, tall, slim, red-headed twenty-four-year-old PC on my team at Lewisham. He had been raised alone by his father since he was two years old. His father went back to college to study to become a teacher so he could earn a good income and do the very best for his son. Steve, his father, and their Dobermann dog lived together in a maisonette in South Norwood.

Steve was a keen marksman and belonged to a police shooting club. On this particular evening, he left before work for the basement of Croydon police station to practise. 'You go ahead,' his father had said. 'I'll take the dog for a walk.' His father took their Dobermann for a stroll on Blackheath Common, where they were both run over by someone who was apparently driving far too fast, instantly killing both man and dog.

I always arrived early for my shift so I knew everything that had been going on before I took over responsibility. I was informed the moment I arrived and it was down to me to tell Steve what had happened. The inspector's office was in a single-storey building on the other side of the yard from the main police station. I watched as

Steve, who was always very professional and immaculately turned out, strode confidently towards my office. He bounded into the room with a cheeky grin on his face. 'You asked to see me, sir?'

I can't remember much about the conversation that followed, except that it was one of the most emotional in my professional life and ended with Steve sobbing on my shoulder and me crying along with him.

His girlfriend, a WPC called Karen, joined us and helped to console him. We travelled together to Greenwich Hospital to formally identify the body. Unfortunately, because it was now very late, Steve's father's possessions had been locked away in the safe overnight which meant he would have to return in the morning.

We would normally have arranged for somebody from the early turn to pick him up, but I could not bear the thought of him having to go through this with a stranger as he was so deeply upset. I went home at the end of my shift at six a.m., showered and changed and went to pick Steve up myself.

I became Steve's unofficial driver and counsellor, driving him and Karen to the court hearings and the inquest. I also went to his father's funeral. It was a privilege to have shared that time with Steve when he was at his most vulnerable and at his most upset. I get a good feeling from helping other people, particularly when it means putting myself out; helping Steve was something I willingly did.

Steve did not take his father's death very well and I could well understand his bitterness, especially as the driver all but got away with it. The skid-marks stretched over three different types of road surface and therefore the accident reconstruction officers were unable to give an accurate estimate of the speed of the car. In those days, a conviction for death by dangerous driving could only be achieved if you were able to prove excessive speed, and the young driver received no more than a fine for driving without due care and attention – hardly justice.

A few weeks later I was moved on to become the acting chief inspector at Lewisham and was no longer in charge of Steve's team. I was, however, responsible for controlling the overtime on his and every other team, which was at that time completely out of control and way beyond our budget. I was forced to use some pretty draconian measures to reduce the hours being claimed. Steve came to see me, and after a fairly heated discussion about whether this was fair on the officers he said, 'You're just like the rest of them, you don't care about us.'

The pain that those words caused me was intense. After all we had been through together, after what I had done for him, it was difficult to take. The hurt stayed with me for twenty years until it was wiped away in the aftermath of the 7 July bombings when Steve and I met each other for the first time since that encounter.

As usual, managing police officers threw up its periodic surprises, but there was one incident in particular which nearly cost me my career and it was all thanks to my officers wanting to show me their loyalty. One night duty at Lewisham I was checking the Occurrence Book, a large hardbound volume in which all the incidents in the police station area are recorded, when I heard a commotion coming from the charge room.

When I got there, I found a young black woman being held down on the floor by four officers holding a limb apiece. Sergeant Gerard was one of them. 'What's going on?' I asked him.

The woman had been arrested for a 'cab bilking' – running from a taxi without paying. Gerard had handed her over to a female officer to be searched when she suddenly kicked up a fuss. This had escalated until the officers were forced to take hold of her, put her on the floor and wait for her to calm down.

Unusually, there were three female officers at the station that evening so I told them to take her into the detention room, a short-term holding cell. 'We [male officers] will wait outside,' I said. 'Leave the door slightly ajar; shout if there are any problems and we'll come in.'

I could see that one or two of the male officers, who were very protective of their female colleagues, were not too happy about this.

The woman was searched and the WPCs emerged from the detention room. I stuck my head in the cell and asked the prisoner, 'Is everything okay now?' She nodded. I repeated the same question to Sergeant Gerard, who said, 'Yes, sir.'

I thought that was the end of it, but no. The prisoner decided to make a complaint, insisting she had been indecently assaulted by one of the female officers. Unbeknown to me, she was backed up to some extent by another prisoner in the charge room who happened to be the son of a serving police officer.

The allegations were passed on to the complaints department at Catford. They thought they had a 'runner' and decided to throw their full weight into the investigation. Their star witness turned out to be anything but. The investigating team were forced to travel to Oxford prison to interview him because he'd since been jailed for another offence.

Undeterred, they employed some heavy-handed tactics. The lead investigator was a determined individual who investigated the incident as if he were already fully convinced of the guilt of the officers involved. One morning at about seven a.m., three chief inspectors and three sergeants arrived at Lewisham to take away the three female officers for questioning, only to find, much to their annoyance, that two of them were off sick.

I later found out that when all the officers involved in the incident were interviewed they deliberately failed to mention that I had been there. Nobody had asked them to, but they made a deliberate effort not to involve me. Usually junior officers, quite rightly, complain that senior officers get away with things as blame is pushed down the ranks as far as it will go. For my team to deliberately try to leave me out of the situation was loyalty indeed.

Once I found out that one of the chief inspectors was treating my officers like criminals, even though I was no longer on their team, there was no way I could stand by and let it pass. I told my superintendent that I was there on the night in question and that I should be interviewed as well. I had by this time been selected for promotion to chief inspector and was already an acting chief inspector at Lewisham.

At about eleven-thirty the same morning, I received a phone call from the chief inspector leading the investigation who said, 'Mr

Paddick, I understand you want to come and talk to us.' I agreed to be interviewed straight away and drove over to their offices in Catford, hoping this would be over quickly as Mary and I were about to go on holiday to the Maldives. I had just had my typhoid inoculation and was beginning to feel its flu-like side-effects by the time I arrived.

The chief inspector seemed friendly enough to start with, but his sergeant wrote down everything I said. When I got to the point where I said I heard a commotion and walked down into the charge room, the chief inspector said, 'At this point, Mr Paddick, I have to warn you that you are not obliged to say anything . . .' He added that I was not under arrest, that I could leave at any time and that I was entitled to a solicitor. Somewhat taken aback, I stated that I had come as a witness and had nothing to hide.

It was a very tough interview. He even had the nerve to ask me, 'Did you indecently assault this woman?' It was a female officer who was accused of indecent assault but rather than pointing that out, I simply replied with a firm 'No.' While my interrogators had a break for lunch, I was told to sit in the corridor and not move, despite the assurances that I was not under arrest and could leave at any time.

The interview dragged on for over four hours; when it was over I had to sign forty-two pages of interview notes.

Unbeknown to me initially, the chief inspector had written a report claiming that because of the seriousness of the allegation I was facing and the possibility of disciplinary action, my promotion should be frozen. Not for the last time in my career, standing up and telling the truth was to bring serious repercussions.

While the investigation dragged on and on, work continued apace at Lewisham. A female officer came to me to tell me that Phil, a tall, pale, blond PC was being bullied by colleagues on my old team because they thought he was gay. She asked me if I would talk to him because they were giving him a very hard time.

I called Phil into my office and told him what the WPC had told me. He was adamant. 'It's not true, I'm not gay, and I can handle the situation without your help.'

I wasn't sure whether to believe him so I just made sure the offer was there: 'If you do need to talk to somebody, just bear in mind that some senior officers have very different views from others,' I said, in a ham-fisted attempt to reassure him that I would be supportive were he in fact gay.

I continued as acting chief inspector and continued dedicating myself to work. Mary found the long hours I put in hard to understand, considering the ongoing investigation might cost me my career. On top of all this, I fell ill with pleurisy and was forced to take some time off to recover.

When I was at home convalescing, I got a phone call from Phil. It was unheard of for a PC to call a chief inspector at home, especially when the chief inspector was off sick. Phil was very friendly with the girls in the administration department and had coaxed my number out of them.

His voice trembled as he asked if I would come and see him. I was feeling pretty rough but he had no way of getting to me so I asked for the address and drove over. 'I'm staying at my girlfriend's place,' he explained, throwing me temporarily off the scent. When I arrived, the door was answered by a very sweet blonde girl. Inside, Phil was sitting in an armchair while the girl perched herself on the arm.

Phil told me that he shared his flat with another man. He had come home in the early hours of the morning and his flatmate had beaten him up. 'I don't want anything done,' he said, 'but if I tell him that a senior police officer knows about it, it might stop him doing it again.'

'Why did your flatmate attack you?' I asked him. He said he didn't know. 'Is it because of your sexuality?'

Phil looked at the girl, who nodded encouragingly. Very hesitantly he said yes.

'Well, I'm not as straight as I look,' I replied, and Phil nearly fell off his chair.

I had already decided I would provide him with as much reassurance as I possibly could and that I would keep his confidence, so sharing the same secret with him seemed the best thing to do.

Phil had been out to a gay club with his boyfriend and had brought him back to the flat. His homophobic flatmate had attacked them both but Phil didn't want anything done about it.

At the time I met Phil and his boyfriend there was no support for gay male officers. While on the surface it may have seemed odd, the disparity between the way gay men and lesbian women were treated in the police was entirely explicable. This was largely thanks to stereotypes maintained by the police's macho culture.

The entirely false stereotyped image held by the majority of police officers towards lesbians was that they were tough and butch. This, coupled with the typical straight man's fantasy of two women having sex with each other, made being a lesbian woman in the police force reasonably acceptable, so most lesbians tended to be open enough to be able to form informal networks. Female officers were already in the minority and tended to stick together, so lesbian officers had less to fear in terms of being undermined by their female colleagues.

Conversely, gay men were thought to be feminine and delicate, limp-wristed and camp, which was entirely the opposite of the macho culture. Generally, if you were a gay male, it was much better for you if you stayed in the closet. Despite my having nearly fifteen years' service by this point, the only other gay officers I knew were Phil and my first lover (who later claimed he was not really gay anyway).

It was a momentous occasion when, in 1990, about ten gay police officers met in Steph's Restaurant in Soho. There were some officers, including the person who is now the chairman of the Gay Police Association (formerly the Lesbian and Gay Police Association) who were open even then, and were suffering at the hands of their straight colleagues. Apart from physical and verbal abuse, the organisation's first chairman, Paul Cahill, had his car vandalised while it was in a police car park. Incidents like this kept the rest of us well and truly in the closet with the door locked.

*

The combination of work, my ill health and my battle with my own sexuality was a constant pressure. Added to this was the investigation, which progressed steadily but interminably. I had heard that the recommendation from the area commander was that I should face a full disciplinary board. I was facing the prospect of losing my job. If everything else had been going well in my life then it would have been relatively easy for me to handle the pressure of the investigation but it simply became too great – something was going to have to give way; I was finding it increasingly hard to continue living a lie.

Mary's trust was such that she didn't question it when I told her that Phil and his boyfriend were going to take me to a nightclub, just to reassure me that there was nothing strange about gay clubs. We went to the Hippodrome in Leicester Square which had a gay night on Mondays.

I was incredibly nervous, not wanting Phil and his partner Padraic to let me out of their sight in case something happened to me. I had a lot to learn. Okay, there were men dancing with each other, and I spotted the odd couple kissing, but it all seemed, well . . . strangely normal, like a night out at the straight clubs I had been to as a PC but with hardly any women. No one tried to chat me up, touch me or do anything the uninitiated and paranoid straight man might think might happen to him if he strayed into the wrong club. On the other hand, it was a revelation. I simply had no idea that there were so many gay men in London, let alone in one club on one night.

I agonised over what to do for some time until a particular incident made up my mind for me. I was alone in the house; Mary had gone out for a run with her brother Richard. The film *My Beautiful Laundrette*, which features a gay relationship, was on TV. I had not seen it before and was watching with no little interest when Mary arrived home during the scene where Daniel Day Lewis's character makes out with Omar at the laundrette, just as Omar's uncle is arriving for the opening ceremony.

I felt very uncomfortable as Mary and I watched these two young men kissing. I was worried about her reaction. Then she said, referring to the uncle and his mistress, 'Oh no! They're going to catch them!' I took her sympathy towards the men in the film as an indication that she might be sympathetic to my situation and I determined to tell her.

Of course, there never is a right moment for these sorts of life-changing revelations. We were having dinner in a very good Chinese restaurant in Ewell and I talked to Mary about Phil and how he was getting on. Mary looked at me and said casually, 'You'll think I'm being very stupid . . . but you don't have any inclinations in that direction, do you?'

I looked at my wife – and I did not have to say anything.

As the tears welled up in her eyes, Mary brushed them aside. Without saying much more, I paid the bill and drove us home. I told her that I had always been gay but that I loved her and that I really wanted the marriage to work. I had tried so hard to overcome my sexuality, but I now realised that I just had to be myself. Mary was remarkable, as always. There was no massive row, and she even thanked me for being honest with her.

Some time later, Mary said that if I had told her I was leaving her for another woman she would never have forgiven me. Instead, she realised I needed something that she would never be able to give me.

Metaphorically, I had been standing on the top diving board for a long time, looking over the edge, too scared to jump. More than anything I wanted to be honest. I loved and respected Mary so much that I had to tell her; it was too painful for me and too unfair to her to continue living the lie. At the moment that my feet left the board, doubts assailed me as to whether this was a wise move, how painful it would be when I hit the water, depending how many people were in the landing zone – and how many others I might hurt in the process.

Incredibly, now that this fundamental secret of my sexuality had been revealed, Mary and I felt closer than ever; but at the same time the marriage was over – separation and divorce were inevitable.

Understandably, Mary did not want to be seen as responsible for the breakdown of our marriage so I had no option but to tell my parents the truth about why we were splitting up. I first spoke to my twin brother on the telephone; he asked me not to tell Mum and Dad, fearing it would upset them too much. This did nothing either to reassure or dissuade me. Naturally, I was worried about what their reaction would be. I was scared I would lose them – that they might never talk to me again.

While I suspected, and certainly hoped, that my mother would sooner or later employ her oft-used expression 'san fairy Ann' (ce ne fait rien) in relation to this as she had with so many of life's devastating blows, I had no idea what my father's response would be and was much more concerned about this. Despite believing that I was not very close to my father, the fact that I was so worried about how it would affect him, perhaps tells a different, subconscious story.

I went to see them. Dad, who was in his seventies, sat in an armchair while my mother took her seat on the sofa. 'I've got to tell you both something,' I said, 'I'm exactly same person today as I was yesterday. The only difference is that you are about to know something about me today that you didn't know about me yesterday.'

My dad turned to face me and said, 'Are you trying to tell us you're gay?'

Not bad for seventy! He was very stoical and added something like, 'Well, that's very clear then.' Mum, meanwhile, was in tears.

The next day I telephoned Mum, who was still in shock. I asked if I could talk to Dad. 'No you can't, he's taken it very badly.' Apparently, after his initially stoical response, he had become very upset. It would be quite some time before Mum considered it safe for me to talk to him again.

I next went to visit my older brother to tell him and his wife, although I cannot believe Mum had not tipped them off before I arrived. Sally's instant response was 'It doesn't matter to us,' to which Graham, who was an Anglican priest, added, 'No it doesn't, but it's quite clear what the Bible says.' Recently, though, he told me he does not agree with this and that a far more tolerant approach to homosexuality is needed.

CHAPTER NINE

After having my promotion blocked for eighteen months while the incident at Lewisham was investigated, I was very keen to move on as a full chief inspector, so I jumped at the first opportunity I saw. This happened to be the head of the planning unit in Personnel and Training at Scotland Yard. I was back doing the job I had hated at Fulham, but at least it was a promotion.

My job in the planning unit was so boring that there is hardly anything about it worth recording. Besides writing the department's annual report, I was also responsible for that part of the commissioner's annual report which referred to personnel and training. The thought of having to do this for another year was too much to bear, but I spotted a potential escape route. The problem was that it meant going back to university.

As part of an innovative strategy at the Met it had been decided that officers with 'high potential' should have a business degree. Budgets, targets, planning, management of change and the use of computers had all become part of senior officers' work. The Met, along with British Telecom, British Petroleum, Coopers and Lybrand and Natwest, formed a consortium which asked Warwick Business School to produce a tailor-made business degree.

Although my bosses did not want me to go, the fact that I was one of the few suitable candidates for the MBA who was willing to go meant that my escape request was granted.

The catch was that it would mean another fifteen months of full-time study at Warwick University. Considering I had joined the police because I didn't want to do any more academic work after school, I wasn't doing very well.

The first part of the course brought back memories of my first term at Oxford – a desperate race to try and keep up – except that this time I was grappling with accounting instead of philosophy.

Warwick managed to exceed even Oxford in terms of volume of work and deadlines. After a day of lectures and classroom work, there were more lectures after dinner. These would be followed by preparation for our own presentations to be given the following day. We could choose between a good night's sleep or getting the work done.

The MBA gave me the framework and the language to analyse and explain things that were going on in the police that I had previously dealt with instinctively. It was hugely important in terms of equipping me to deal with progressive change. It taught me an understanding of what the obstacles were and how to win over enough support from stakeholders and bosses to get ideas through – or how to get around the obstacles if one's path was blocked. Out of all the courses I had been on, the MBA was far and away the most important in terms of the practical application of ideas to real-life situations.

Sadly, only fifteen police officers ever attended the MBA course over a period of three years, so as soon as the contract was up the Met pulled out. Nothing replaced it and now, if a police officer wants to do a degree or an MBA, then it would have to be in his or her own time and largely at their own expense. I have enormous admiration for people like my niece, who successfully completed an MBA degree while carrying on with the day job.

I was somewhat disappointed when I returned to the Met from Warwick to find that there was no job waiting for me. Personnel had had fifteen months' notice to find me something while I was on the course.

I went to talk to a superintendent about what job I would do next.

He said, 'Let's go through the other people on the course and see what they're going to be doing.'

The superintendent stopped at the name Graham James. 'We've got him down for a staff officer.' He looked up, thought for a moment and said, 'No, he's too fat.'

I wasn't sure what a person's fatness had to do with becoming the staff officer to a senior officer, but I quickly pulled in my stomach and said, 'What about me?'

'Yes, we'll give that some thought. In the meantime, perhaps you can just amuse yourself.'

It took a couple of months, but finally I was interviewed by the senior officer for the position of his staff officer. He was a well-spoken, placid individual. There were other candidates but, as he explained, 'It's not so much a case of experience or ability – it's about chemistry.' Chemistry was all well and good, but I was planning to work for him, not marry him. Nevertheless, the 'chemistry' was right and I got the job.

The senior officer worked in complaints and discipline. One of the highlights of my day was receiving a call detailing the latest tales of woe in terms of police officers' misconduct. This was a real eye-opener for me, as I had not encountered any serious misconduct during my service.

One example included the tale of a probationer constable and a van driver who had to check a warehouse where the alarm had gone off. After they were satisfied that their callout had been a false alarm, the van driver gave the doors a good shake and said, 'These doors aren't very secure, why don't we come back tomorrow and screw the place?'

The young probationer, hardly able to believe what she had just heard, duly reported the driver to her inspector, who informed the Complaints Investigation Bureau (CIB). The following night, officers from CIB lay in wait and ambushed the van driver who was caught red-handed with the crowbar.

In another case, a team in the East End of London decided to play a trick on a probationer WPC. They arranged for her to be called to a suspected burglary in progress. The premises were in fact a disused warehouse in the docklands where one of the other prankster officers leapt out at her with a white sheet over his head. She ran off screaming – straight off the end of the dock, where she fell thirty feet and broke both her legs.

Whenever the senior officer came into my outer office, which he had to pass through to get to his, he would look over my shoulder to see what I was up to. Once he caught me reading the monthly Police Federation magazine, which featured a piece on homosexuality.

The previous edition had published an outrageously homophobic article, written by an inspector from a Home Counties force, claiming that there was no place for homosexuals in the police. The following month there was a double page of letters written by numerous officers, both straight and gay, criticising his views and supporting gay and lesbian officers.

Nervously, I explained to him what had happened. 'I know,' he said to me in a tone of some disgust as he looked thoughtfully off into the distance, 'they're out there you know, they're out there!' I thought to myself, 'And they're in here as well, if only you knew it!'

Having spent fifteen months at Warwick and then returned to a desk job, I was extremely keen to get out of the office and into operational policing again. With my senior officer's agreement, I commanded various events at Wembley Stadium. I also became a sub-Bronze commander in charge of officers on the street during the Carnival weekend at Notting Hill and ended up policing this event in one guise or another for nine consecutive years. Mostly, I was in the thick of things, and one incident, which occurred in 1992, made it clear to me just how dangerous Carnival can be.

On my patch there was an 'illegal' sound system. As well as the procession of floats through the streets, there are fixed sound systems throughout the Carnival area, all of which are supposed to be licensed by the Carnival organisers. Despite our attempts to seal off the area well in advance to prevent this sort of thing happening, this one had set itself up without authorisation and was playing heavy ragga-jungle, a kind of high-octane Jamaican reggae, to about three hundred revellers.

In the interests of keeping the peace we had let this illegal system carry on, but as the Carnival had to be shut down at seven p.m., I eventually had to tell them to turn off their sound system.

A sergeant accompanied me as I made my way to the front. It was summer, and we were in our shirtsleeves (no stab vests in those days), armed only with the regulation wooden truncheon. After yelling over the music, I managed to convey the message to the DJ that he had to close down.

At this point somebody in the crowd reached over the barrier, grabbed hold of the microphone and shouted, 'The police have come to close us down! We're not going to let them, are we?' This was met with a huge roar from a suddenly menacing crowd and three hundred unfriendly faces turned to glare at us. 'Time to beat a hasty retreat, I think,' I told my sergeant, and we tried to back out through the crowd.

We were pelted with half-full cans of beer and empty bottles and were kicked and punched as we tried to push our way through. All I could see was a sea of angry faces and staring eyes; I began to wonder if we were going to get out alive. Ignoring the assaults, we put our heads down and fought our way out. The crowd jeered and bayed after us as we escaped into another street.

Back at the briefing centre, nursing our injuries while still shaking and in shock, I described what happened to Chief Superintendent Daniel Grainger, who thought our 'little story' was 'quite amusing' and chuckled over it. During the following few days I was unable to sleep and became increasingly restless, a classic symptom of post-traumatic stress disorder.

Having worked in the Personnel department, I was one of the few people who knew about the Occupational Health department and I telephoned them for help. They sent me a leaflet entitled 'After a Traumatic Incident', and I was left to sort myself out. This was at least one step forward from the sergeant's reaction to the distressed officer in the back yard at Holloway when I was a PC, but occupational health obviously still had quite some way to go if it was ever going to be effective.

Despite this experience, I enjoyed policing public events enormously and I regularly practised at the Public Order Training Centre, then at Hounslow Heath, being bombarded with wooden bricks and the occasional, very real, petrol bomb. As soon as I could, I took the week-long course to qualify as an advanced trained senior officer.

We would spend two days every six months training and exercising with 'serials' (one inspector, three sergeants and eighteen constables) of officers. We had to clear the streets of 'rioters' in the mock town that had been built for the purpose. As the senior officer, you had to devise a clearance plan based on the information you were given on the day, and then put the plan into action, briefing the officers and then shouting orders out on the ground while running around the site avoiding the missiles and the petrol bombs.

At another Carnival, I was asked to be the conscience of the designated senior officer for baton guns (the official name for a 'rubber bullet' is 'baton round'). At that time there were strict regulations laid down by the Home Office on the use of baton guns. Only the commissioner could order their use and he would only do so on the basis of a personal account given to him by the designated senior officer at the scene. Baton guns could only be used when all conventional methods had failed.

As the senior officer's 'conscience', I had a pocket recorder taped to my riot glove on which I was to record the exact wording of the commander's decisions. This way, a detailed record would be available for the inevitable public inquiry that would follow any riot.

A decade later, the rule had changed from the commissioner alone being able to give the order to use plastic bullets, to a situation where a commander could give the order for someone to be shot in the back of the head without warning and without reference to anyone else. Such was the change in the levels of responsibility and the protection afforded to the man at the top of the Met.

One of the benefits of being a staff officer to a senior officer was that you could use the weight of their position to get the posting you wanted. After eighteen months in the job, I said that I wanted to go back to Brixton. Brixton Chief Superintendent Bill Wilson was very concerned about community tension and the likelihood of another riot and didn't want to lose his current very able and experienced Chief Inspector (Operations) Alan Webb, who had been selected to command the area's Territorial Support Group. Alan would have to stay at Brixton until 'the end of the summer'.

Much to my dismay, rather than going back to my old stomping ground, I was put in temporary charge of the Territorial Support Group in South East London. At first I was horrified – the TSG were the elite 'riot squad' who prided themselves on their physical fitness and exceptionally high levels of testosterone. The thought of going into an even more straight, macho branch of the police was decidedly unnerving for a gay man.

In July 1993, I took charge of 4 Area TSG, which was based in Thornton Heath.

Luckily, I was very physically fit and secured the respect of my fellow TSG officers by being able to keep up with them on gruelling runs, with press-ups, and by being enthusiastically petrol-bombed by colleagues in training sessions on Hounslow Heath.

I will never forget the agony of the 'shield run', a 500-metre sprint with boots and gloves and a very heavy three-quarter-length plastic shield. No matter how hard I trained and how fit I became, the shield run was a killer. It had to be completed within a certain time and I never managed to end up in better than the middle range of ability.

TSG officers have to be so physically fit because they are expected to be able to run some distance in full kit to the scene of trouble and, once there, expected to fight. Anyone who has been in one will tell you that fighting in a riot is truly exhausting.

CHAPTER TEN

After spending the summer with the TSG, on 13 September 1993 I finally made it back to Brixton as chief inspector in Personnel and Training. I was responsible for delivering training to officers, based on changes made to legislation and police practice, and for all personnel issues from sickness and welfare to postings and selections.

One of my responsibilities was to chair the selection processes for specialist jobs in the borough, one of which involved finding an officer to join a unit set up to deal with 'sensitive crimes' (later to be called hate crimes) where people were being targeted because of their minority status, along with domestic violence. While predominantly racial or domestic, some homophobic crimes were dealt with by this unit.

The panel consisted of a married uniformed sergeant and a female constable who were already working on the unit. In the end we selected a married woman for the job, but one of the unsuccessful candidates put in a complaint against me. In interview she had used the expression 'sexual preference' and I had pointed out in her written feedback that 'sexual orientation' was a more appropriate term, since sexuality is not a preference, but generally something you are born with.

In her complaint she said that she had heard I was homosexual, and that she believed I was homosexual, and claimed that she had been discriminated against because she was straight. When I was confronted with this allegation I was simultaneously concerned to learn that rumours were going round the Met about my sexuality, and angry that she had unjustly attacked my integrity over the selection process. Everything had been done properly, with no discussion of the merits of any candidate until we had individually recorded our own findings on everyone and her complaint was dismissed.

Through the Lesbian and Gay Police Association I had heard there was an openly gay chief superintendent in North London and I went to see him. His name was Peter Twist, one of the most extraordinary characters that has ever donned a policeman's uniform.

A real trailblazer, Peter Twist was a larger than life, extremely in-your-face and extrovert officer. When I told him about the complaint that had been made against me his eyes lit up. 'Brian,' he told me confidently, 'we've *arrived*. When the straights start complaining that *we're* discriminating against *them*, then we've arrived!' This was not exactly the reaction I either wanted or expected, but I supposed he had a point.

Before the allegations were made against me by the female candidate, I had confided that I was gay to my chief superintendent, Bill Wilson. He saw himself as a liberal and arty individual, no doubt influenced by his wife Jacqueline Wilson, the famous author of children's books. Bill, his wife, my then partner and I visited a couple of art galleries where there was an exhibition of modern American art, including many of Andy Warhol's and Jackson Pollock's paintings.

Things had certainly moved on in my private life. I had begun my first gay relationship some months after separating from Mary. Unlike most gay men, I had developed a lasting relationship with one of the first gay men I met – a relationship which, to date, remains my longest. Not long after Paul and I started going out, we went on a holiday in Ibiza, where I was stung by barbed comments made by other guests as we lazed around the pool. We had taken a 'don't know until you get there' cheap, last-minute package and ended up in a family hotel in Santa Eulàlia. Never having been on holiday with a man before, I had no idea how obvious it was to others that we were lovers and how intolerant they would be, even in Ibiza.

Eventually, Paul moved into a place in Kemptown (aka Camptown) in Brighton and I travelled down from London whenever I could, having made the difficult move back to live with my parents after the divorce. Eventually Paul and I decided to buy a small house in Horley, Surrey, which was halfway between his work and mine. These were still the days when you had to ask permission from the police to cohabit with someone in a property. They needed to know that you were not associating with the wrong sort, someone with a criminal background.

I was still at Lewisham when I put in my report and was soon summoned to the chief superintendent's office. 'Are you sure this is a good idea, living with another man? People will talk you know.' I tried to pass Paul off as a friend who, like me, had nothing left after a recent separation and the only way we could afford to buy a house was to buy one together. I am hopeless at lying and he did not believe a word of it.

When Paul moved on to a much bigger and better paid job in London, we decided to stay in Horley and bought a larger house. We both had very demanding jobs and long journeys to and from work, so the time we had together, particularly during the week, was limited. It was an unremarkable story of two guys living in suburbia with as many straight friends as gay, and outings to gay venues were few and far between.

It was almost as though I was in another marriage, where only the sex of my partner had changed. I had never had the chance to 'play the field', going as soon as I did from marriage to a long-term gay relationship. Being married, and then being in a relationship around the time of the emergence of the terrible reality of AIDS, quite possibly saved my life when so many others, unaware of the dangers, lost their own. Not everything was perfect, but I settled into my new gay lifestyle with relative ease.

On Wednesday 9 March 1994, at nine thirty-four p.m., PC Simon Carroll and PC Jim Seymour had become suspicious about two men on a motorcycle and decided to pull them over. Their suspicions were proved correct as the man riding pillion was a drug dealer and prison escapee. Unfortunately, he was also carrying a gun.

As the officers climbed out of their car, the escapee opened fire, hitting both men in the legs. He walked up to them as they lay helpless and in shock on the ground. Both men were fully convinced they were staring death in the face, that in a few moments they would be shot in cold blood. Instead, their would-be killer turned away, climbed back on the motorbike and rode off.

This episode had a devastating effect on the two officers' colleagues, who were all ordered back to the station as soon as cover had been arranged. As is common in these situations, they started feeling guilty that it was not they who had been wounded and that they had not been able to prevent it happening. The most traumatised officer was the one who had been posted to the station's front office that day. Arguably, he was in the safest place – but that also meant he felt the most helpless.

I was called in from home to take care of the welfare issues surrounding the shooting. I gathered all the officers from the team together and we were joined by counsellors from the recently formed Occupational Health department to give what they called a 'hot debrief' – to talk to the team about how they felt in order to help them get over the incident.

The two OH counsellors said it was important that they spoke to the officers alone. I agreed, but ten minutes later the doors burst open and the team stormed out of the room, obviously in a real fury. The officers complained that the counsellors had no operational experience and so were unable to empathise with them. They had no idea what life was like on the streets, or any understanding of the dangers police officers faced everyday. OH had improved since I had consulted them, but clearly still had a long way to go.

I continued to do everything I could to support the officers who had been shot, visiting them on numerous occasions in hospital and then while they recovered at home. We arranged for one of the officer's families to be met off a flight at Heathrow and taken directly to the hospital.

One thing we learnt from this experience was that the shot officers were very sensitive to any perceived falling away of interest by the senior management. Although the chief superintendent visited them in hospital, for them this was just not enough. One of them later told me, 'I hate the chief superintendent more than I hate the man who shot me.'

As a consequence of the shooting, our bosses at Scotland Yard decreed that every officer should be issued with bullet- and stab-proof vests. The irony of this, of course, was that both officers had been shot in the legs.

When the current superintendent at Brixton moved on, although I was in a support role, I argued successfully that I had the longest service and experience as a chief inspector and managed to secure the position of temporary superintendent. I took over responsibility for day-to-day operations across uniform, CID and support departments, a position I held for six months.

When the Sheehy Report into the structure of the police was finally debated in Parliament, one of the few recommendations to make its way through the Commons was to abolish the ranks of deputy chief constable (deputy assistant commissioner in the Met), chief superintendent and chief inspector. In anticipation, officers in those ranks who were close to retirement were offered a severance package and many took the chance to leave.

Then, in the House of Lords, the abolition of the rank of chief inspector was defeated. By this time dozens of chief inspectors had taken the money and run, so the Met found itself short of chief inspectors, and detective chief inspectors in particular. It was decided that high-potential uniformed chief inspectors would be deployed as detectives and so, after eighteen years in uniform (or as a 'wooden top' as CID officers liked to call us), I was suddenly and miraculously transformed into Detective Chief Inspector Paddick over a weekend and on 16 January 1995, I was put in charge of the CID office at Notting Hill.

The uniformed superintendent in charge at Notting Hill was very enthusiastic about my arrival as he hated the CID and I, as a uniformed officer with almost no CID experience, was one of his wildest dreams come true. His extreme dislike of the CID stemmed from the dark days when his father, who despised corruption, was a detective and witnessed widespread corruption, with brown envelopes stuffed with cash being passed around.

The CID was a completely different culture to the uniformed branch. Uniformed officers worked strict hours and were replaced by another team at the end of their shift. In the CID, a typical ratio was one sergeant to two detective constables, as against a ratio of one to ten in the uniformed branch. Detective sergeants and detective inspectors were practitioners as well as supervisors, and handled the more serious criminal investigations. This meant that CID teams were much more close-knit.

When I called my first office meeting I was met with a wall of silence by the detectives, despite my best efforts to engage everyone in the office in cheery conversation and popular debate. I was an unknown quantity, and they were suspicious of their 'instant detective' boss.

In an effort to show my detective inspectors that I was completely open and honest, I told them that I was relying on them to help me through and that I saw it as my job to defend the CID to the hilt, even if it meant upsetting the superintendent. Not only did the DIs (particularly Ray McCullough) become mentors and friends, they won over the rest of the office.

I was still paranoid about my sexuality and believed that CID culture was even further behind than the rest of the force when it came to homosexuals. It was still a very macho, alcohol-fuelled culture but I soon discovered that attitudes, particularly amongst the younger detectives, were changing.

A long-established CID tradition was the office luncheon, which was held about once every three months. Everyone downed tools at one p.m. and trooped off to a local pub or restaurant for a meal, washed down with large quantities of alcohol in a drinking session that could continue into the night.

Although I disapproved of the practice, I was also acutely aware that it is not possible to change a well-established culture by running headlong in the opposite direction. I therefore invented a new event: rather than office lunches, we had office 'high-teas'. Everyone had to start work at seven a.m. and no one left for the restaurant until three in the afternoon, so everyone was off duty.

Alcohol loosened my detectives' tongues, although they would never call me anything other than 'guv'nor'. Rumours had gone before me about my sexuality, but rather than say anything explicitly, a detective sidled up to me at one of the high teas and said, 'By the way, guv, I share a house with a couple of lesbians.'

Another said, 'My uncle used to run a deli in the King's Road and he had several gay customers.' It was their way of letting me know they knew but that it didn't matter to them. They did enough to reassure me that it was okay with them.

Over the next ten months I fought a constant battle against the totally unreasonable cuts in CID overtime at the same time as the superintendent attempted to increase our workload significantly. From a uniformed senior management perspective, CID was a nightmare in terms of the amount of overtime they ate up. Uniformed senior management, who didn't understand or had never experienced CID culture, saw the overtime as a combination of inefficiency and greed. This is not what I found. The officers under my command were conscientious professionals, and the high overtime was due to a combination of far too few CID officers, along with the fact that those serving retained ownership of their cases to the bitter end. While uniformed officers would pass unfinished cases on to the next shift, there was no 'next shift' in the CID, only sheer professional dedication. Of course limits had to be imposed, but the higher per-head overtime bill was justified.

Every step was dogged by argument, and even when our street robbery problem reached epidemic levels, the superintendent would not allow the formation of a specialist robbery squad to tackle the issue. So, instead, I established a Street Crime Investigation unit.

During my time at Notting Hill, I felt as though the superintendent was continually trying to undermine my authority – so much so that I believed it amounted to homophobic bullying.

These work-related pressures were only exacerbated by the fact that after seven years, I was on my own again. Paul and I, because of our exhausting work schedules and long commutes, had moved to Pimlico. The bright lights of the big city brought with it distractions and we were already drifting apart when Paul fell for a charming, intelligent and handsome young man. He has been much luckier in love than me; the two of them are still together after all this time.

Our parting was mutually agreed and civil but, unfortunately for me, it meant moving out of our luxury apartment in Pimlico (well, comfortable basement flat where you could hear the Victoria Line trains rumbling past just a few metres below), and moving to a studio flat in Petty France, just around the corner from New Scotland Yard. The block relied on communal heating and hot water, and if you weren't up and in the shower before seven in the mornings, the hot water was gone. It was freezing in winter, the metal casement windows were not double glazed, and the radiators rarely rose above lukewarm.

The property market was in recession at that time, which meant Paul and I were left with negative equity. Rather than selling up and leaving with a healthy deposit, I was left owing Paul £15,000. I had very little furniture and no bed, so for the first couple of months I slept on the floor.

I was feeling particularly low and vulnerable when things came to a head at work during one of our regular pub quizzes. One of the questions was, 'Who is the local MP?' Shouting, so that everyone in the room could hear, the superintendent said, 'Oh, he's that poof, isn't he?' He then reached across the table towards me and added loudly, 'Sorry, Brian, I didn't mean to upset you.' From my perspective, he had outed me to every other person in the room.

I approached the personnel manager who said she did not believe the superintendent was homophobic, but if that is what I believed, I should go to the Headquarters Equal Opportunities unit. I did, and spoke to Susie Bragg who advised me that although sexual orientation was included in the Met's Equal Opportunities statement, she felt that the Met was not yet ready for a DCI to take a grievance out against a superintendent on the grounds of homophobia. A detective chief superintendent who had worked on Equal Ops had already warned me that the change in policy 'was a shield and not a flag'. There was really nothing more I could do.

The following week I was away from the office on an interview techniques course when I was summoned to see a deputy assistant commissioner at Central London headquarters in Canon Row. He said, 'Your superintendent tells me that you don't agree with his policing style, and the senior management team at Notting Hill is too small to have that sort of disagreement. On Monday I'm moving you to the Central London Crime Squad.'

CHAPTER ELEVEN

It was at this point that I met James Renolleau, the man who would eventually play a major role in both my private life and my career. I had gone out with some friends to a club in the West End when a tall, dark, handsome and charming Frenchman introduced himself; one thing led to another and we started dating. James was a French former model who had worked for, among others, Yves St Laurent in Paris. He had come over to the UK for a long weekend and never gone back. He told me he had given up a job as a social worker, looking after children in care, to nurse his ill lover who had died six months previously.

James and I spent increasing amounts of time together and he became a regular visitor to my little flat in Petty France. His arrival, which coincided with this particularly low point in my life, really lifted my spirits, and it was not long before I had fallen for him.

Reinvigorated by our rapidly blossoming relationship, I arrived at the Central Area Crime Squad in Notting Dale in the Notting Hill Division on 13 November 1995. I was nominally in charge of the intelligence unit there while I waited for promotion to superintendent. Although my superintendent was able to get me moved, he couldn't block my promotion. I had got through the relevant assessment and had been placed on the 'select' list.

Then, around this time, I discovered James was on police bail. The family of his deceased ex alleged that he had stolen from him. James rented a basement room in a house in Hackney, and when I spoke to his landlady, Andria, she supported James absolutely and told me he had only taken items of sentimental value; things like a tennis racquet and a bird-bath.

Andria was also a counsellor and suggested that this reaction was to be expected of a grieving family; that they would find someone they could focus their anger on. Although initially nervous about James's brush with the law, I accepted this explanation, and when James was due to return to Stoke Newington police station I agreed to go with him, although I only went as far as the postbox on the opposite side of the road. I certainly did not want anyone suggesting I was trying to influence the investigation.

James went in with the duty solicitor, Ruth Ross, who had been allocated to him when he was first arrested. A short time later they emerged to say that the police were not going to take any further action as there was no evidence to support the allegations.

Things continued to improve as our relationship developed. James found a job working in the bookshop at Westminster Abbey, but there were some aspects of his behaviour which, although subtle, had begun to worry me. Being blinded by love, however, I did my best to ignore them.

The earliest warning sign came in the kitchenette in Petty France about six months after we first met. I received a birthday card from one of my dearest and longest-standing friends, Neil, and while there had been a sexual element to our relationship that had long since passed and we just remained (and still remain) very good friends. When James saw the card he demanded to know who Neil was. When I told him, he ripped the card up and threw it in the bin. This lack of trust and his controlling behaviour gradually came to dominate our relationship.

I felt sure that James's behaviour was the result of negative experiences when he was younger. This included a belief that people generally could not be trusted and that some misdemeanours justified physical punishment. What had happened in his own life began to affect our relationship.

At work, I again took the first available position that came up and worried about getting a good operational posting later. There was a vacancy in the Personnel department for a superintendent in charge of secondments and exchanges. In those days, many officers were seconded to other organisations as 'career development opportunities'. Some were seconded to charities like the Prince's Trust, where the work of the charity had some connection with diverting youths away from crime. Other officers were involved in an exchange with another officer of similar rank in another police force; in the case of the Sir Arthur Conan Doyle Foundation, the exchange was with the Swiss police.

It all seemed fairly straightforward but what I did not realise was that this was a 'Trojan horse' promotion. When I met my new commander, he began talking about the new 'tenure of post' policy and how he wanted me to take the lead on it.

There was a long-established tradition in the Met that once an officer had been selected for a specialist department – whether as a detective or a dog handler, an officer in the mounted branch or a traffic officer – they remained in that department until the day they left the police.

In what became perhaps one of the most despised policies ever introduced by a commissioner, Sir Paul Condon decided it would be beneficial to introduce a time limit after which specialist officers would be returned to uniformed duties. Experienced detectives would return to work shifts in uniform, sharing their investigative expertise with their uniformed colleagues. Their places would then be taken by young uniformed officers who wanted to develop their detective skills.

Sir Paul also felt there should be movement of uniformed officers between the quieter suburbs and inner city areas. Traditionally, first postings after training had been to inner city areas. As officers matured, had families and bought homes in the suburbs, they would migrate outwards, embracing the more sedate pace of policing in outer London. Throwing experienced officers back into inner London would help balance the teams policing the more difficult and testing areas and help share the extra cost of commuting more fairly between younger and older officers. The idea made absolute sense but for one fact – this plan involved dealing with human beings who had vested interests in staying exactly where they were.

Imagine my joy when I learned that I had been 'selected' to devise a workable policy for the 'tenure of post' plan, and that I would be the officer charged with marketing the policy to reluctant specialists and older uniformed officers. I went on a one-man roadshow, trying to convince officers that what was a nightmare scenario for them was for the greater good.

My unpopularity with the superintendent at Notting Hill paled into insignificance compared with the reactions I received when I stepped into the lion's den to tell roomfuls of experienced detectives that, under this programme, they would have to work shifts and patrol the streets in uniform.

None of the longer-serving officers and none of the specialist officers wanted the policy, and few of the younger officers were enthusiastic about it despite the increased opportunities it would give them; the turkeys were not voting for Christmas and the potential beneficiaries had little appetite.

Although this was a very stressful and unpleasant experience, I was able to cope, helped by the occasional stiff G&T when I returned home to James after a particularly gruelling and confrontational meeting. What didn't help, however, was that James didn't trust me. James checked the numbers on my mobile phone and when he saw a work colleague's number, he would accuse me of having an affair simply on the grounds that I had the telephone number of a man he did not know.

Meanwhile, at work I produced draft after draft of the tenure of post policy document before discussing each one, line by line, with my commander, who had overall responsibility for the project. His usual reaction was, 'I don't know what I want, but it isn't that.'

After ten months of intense work and negotiation, the commander and I ended up in front of the commissioner and his top team with what we believed to be the best possible plan. Ten-year limits were imposed for both specialist and uniformed officers, except for those with more than twenty-two years' service, the point where you get your Long Service and Good Conduct medal, who were to be exempt.

After we had given our presentation, Sir Paul told the rest of the

Met's leadership: 'As commissioner I think it is only right that I take the lead on this one. I think this is an excellent policy, clearly in the best interests of the organisation, but I am happy to hear colleagues' views.' Roughly translated, this meant 'Don't waste your breath, we're having it' and with little debate the tenure of post policy was launched.

A few years later, when Sir John Stevens became commissioner, the single objective given to him by the Home Office on his appointment was to get the Met off its knees after the devastating MacPherson Report into the tragic murder of Stephen Lawrence. Stevens, himself an experienced detective, immediately abolished tenure, a politically astute move which won him a great deal of support.

Having successfully done my master's bidding, I was given additional responsibilities and placed in charge of Leadership and Management Development in the Personnel department. Working with the Management Resource Centre, the Met's internal consultants, I set about trying to identify the principles used by the cream of the Met's leadership in an effort to provide future leaders with useful guidelines.

The result of months of interviews and research was a list of nine leadership principles, each with a two-line description, which we felt accurately described good leadership.

Good leadership is about capability – knowing what you are doing and knowing when you need to use the skills and abilities of those around you. It is about confidence – taking firm control, positively demonstrating to others that you know what you are doing. It is important to get your decision-making right by taking all relevant information into account when considering consequences, and consulting others if appropriate. Effective communication is one of the essential skills of a good leader; everyone must be kept informed and face-to-face discussions should be held wherever possible.

Enthusiasm, too, is useful, but not if it has no direction. You need to demonstrate drive and determination, especially when things get tough, but you have to make sure your own and everyone else's efforts are channelled in the right direction. If you are to keep everyone on-side, you need to demonstrate fairness by being objective, consistent and sensitive.

If you make a mistake admit it, and if others deserve credit make sure they get it rather than taking it yourself. Innovation and flexibility are necessary leadership requirements. Trying something you think is better is all very well, but you must be prepared to change if it does not work out. Be flexible to suit the circumstances – no two situations are ever exactly the same.

People always want to follow someone they can trust, so integrity, honesty, and being open and genuine in setting the standards for conduct and behaviour, are as important as tackling unacceptable decisions or actions by others. Teamwork means taking others' views and needs into account and taking a genuine interest in your own team members as individuals.

We used these principles to produce leadership guidance for each rank and grade in the Met, with practical examples of how they could better lead. To my satisfaction, these principles became embedded in recruitment and specialist training, and candidates for promotion were questioned on their knowledge of the principles.

CHAPTER TWELVE

After spending such a long time desk-bound, no matter how productive that time had been, I really needed to get back to operational policing. After having had an interview with Assistant Commissioner Denis O'Connor (who covered South West London) about leadership, and knowing there was going to be a vacancy at Brixton, I said to him, 'If you're looking for a chief superintendent for Brixton, then I'm your man.'

He looked at me with a quizzical expression as if he didn't know whether to take me seriously or not. He went off without saying a word. The following week he asked to see me. 'Why should give I you Brixton?' he asked me.

It turned out he had already earmarked someone else for that post, but he had been impressed by my forthrightness and said he was prepared to offer me divisional commander at Merton. I was disappointed not to get Brixton, but was nonetheless delighted, and gratefully accepted.

I was in Sainsbury's in Victoria Street on an August Sunday morning, buying croissants for breakfast when someone in the checkout queue mentioned that Princess Diana had died. I was, like most people, completely stunned. Having been the press spokesperson for the Notting Hill Carnival a few days previously, I was asked to repeat this role for the funeral of Diana.

Notting Hill had involved a number of press briefings, but this was my first exposure to an extremely intensive, worldwide media operation. On 4 September 1997, the day before the funeral, I was driven from Scotland Yard to Buckingham Palace to Hyde Park and back again to do countless interviews with UK TV and radio, the BBC World Service and many American TV crews. Diana's funeral broke the record for the most covered and most watched event in the USA since the moon landing. The BBC said the broadcast was the largest in its history.

Although I was quite nervous to start with, knowing that millions were watching, I soon settled into it. It was extremely busy in the run-up to the funeral, and we decided it would not be appropriate to do any broadcasts after nine a.m. on the day itself. As a result, I was able to walk through the arch at Horseguards Parade and down Whitehall towards Westminster Abbey where the streets were free of traffic; one million people were packed along the three and a half mile procession route.

I was outside Westminster Abbey just as Lord Spencer, Diana's brother, gave his famous and controversial eulogy, calling her the 'most hunted person of the modern age'. Like most people, I thought it was incredibly powerful and was moved by the crowd's spontaneous applause.

PART THREE

CHAPTER THIRTEEN

Thanks to its diversity, Merton provided a broad spectrum of crime and social issues. The local population in Mitcham were largely poorly educated white working class and the few Asian and Caribbean families that lived in the area suffered a disproportionate amount of racial abuse, thanks in part to the activities of the National Front.

By contrast, Wimbledon was affluent. The larger Asian population consisted mainly of successful business or professional people, and a smattering of millionaires and public figures, including Mike Fuller who was to become the UK's first black chief constable. The policing issues were testing but they were manageable; there was time to do things properly and, most importantly, there were enough officers in Merton who, most of the time, were able to deal comfortably with the demands placed on them. Of course, Wimbledon also hosted the most famous tennis tournament in the world, which brought its own policing challenges.

Although Wimbledon only lasted for a fortnight, the planning was an all-year-round job, since we had to consider everything from traffic flow to terrorism, from ticket touts to stalkers. We also practised for all manner of potential terrorist scenarios, and non-terrorist accidents such as a petrol tanker crashing and exploding in the midst of the tournament.

During the tournament, as the Gold commander, I was on duty in uniform from seven a.m. until ten p.m. for the entire two weeks. Although it didn't happen very often, I was sometimes able to stand behind the baseline on centre court and watch a game or two.

*

One Thursday, some officers from the Complaints Investigation Bureau (CIB) arrived in my office to tell me that on Monday they were planning to arrest one of my officers on the robbery squad who was currently working for the unit that handled police informants, one of the most sensitive jobs on the division. They told me he would almost inevitably be charged with serious corruption offences.

I asked the CIB officers how I could now leave this man in such a sensitive position for another three days. They insisted that I do nothing, that it had to happen this way, and eventually I acquiesced. They searched his home and the CID office in Wimbledon before charging him.

As the borough commander you are responsible for your officers' welfare even if they are arrested. I took this duty very seriously and kept in close contact with the accused officer until the pressure became too great for him and he refused to speak to anybody connected with the police.

I continued to leave messages for him, just to keep in touch and check that he was okay, but he never replied. At his trial at the Old Bailey he was acquitted and reinstated. I met him several years later when I was a commander. He had retired by then but was still active, working with serial offenders, trying to steer them away from a life of crime. He visited them at home or in prison with someone from the local authority to help them try to find a home and a job. Despite his background and his hard-bitten attitude, it was only when we met at this time that he was able to tell me how much he appreciated my support. Before he had been arrested I didn't know him well, but later discovered he was a really caring man who saw the best in people.

I had a particularly good relationship with Police Federation representatives from Wimbledon, whom I used to meet with regularly. On one particular occasion I was about to conclude a meeting when one of them remarked, 'That was a bit of a strange one, one of your officers making a false entry in his arrest notes.'

'What officer?'

'Perhaps I shouldn't have said anything.'

I soon found out the full story. Two uniformed officers working in plain clothes were on patrol in an unmarked car. At the end of their official tour of duty one officer went home while the other, without authority and putting himself at risk, went back on patrol to watch a disqualified driver he thought was about to drive.

A few minutes later the suspect took off in the car. The officer called for assistance and the suspect was arrested. At about five a.m. the officer sent a pager message to his colleague who had gone home saying, 'I've arrested a disqualified driver and I've written in my notes that you were there with me.' This was to cover the fact that he should not have been out in plain clothes on his own without authorisation.

As soon as the other officer came on duty that morning, he told his sergeant about the pager message and she reported it to the DCI. Rather than treating it as a disciplinary issue, the DCI removed the officer from plain-clothes duties and took no further action.

For me, the deliberate telling of lies in an official document was a serious breach of discipline. If the case had gone to trial, and the officer had either given evidence or had his statement read out in court, he would have been guilty of perjury, an offence that typically merits a custodial sentence. Dealing with this kind of breach of discipline informally was unacceptable. After discussing the matter with my superintendent, I reported the DCI for neglect of duty in failing to take appropriate action as well as calling for a formal investigation of the officer for falsification of evidence.

To report one of my own senior managers for an alleged breach of discipline was unprecedented. The normal thing to do is to push the blame down to the lowest rank possible; it was rare for a DCI to find himself disciplined but there were two important points to be made:

1. The importance of integrity.
2. To try and reassure all my officers that, no matter what level they were at, the same standards of conduct and behaviour were expected from all of them and the consequences of any breaches would be the same – no matter their rank.

Unfortunately, those charged with investigating the case did not adopt such a hard line as I did and both issues were resolved 'informally' after I had left to go on the Strategic Command Course.

Another case in point was that of PC Mark Tuffy. I received a phone call from a senior officer: 'Brian, I want you to do me a favour and take this officer on for me. He's currently employed in plain clothes but an allegation of rape has been made against him. He met this girl at a dance and took her home and they were playing strip poker, so she was asking for it really.'

The fact that he used the word 'dance' was an indication of how dated his views were before he even got to the 'she was asking for it' line. The case against Tuffy was never proved.

I reluctantly agreed to take PC Tuffy. I later discovered that he had previously been employed at Lambeth where he was involved in the death of a young black man called Brian Douglas on 7 May 1995. Brian died of head injuries inflicted by Tuffy's police baton, and the case had become a cause célèbre. Again, no prosecution was ever brought, and now this man was one of my uniformed officers based at Wimbledon. There were rumours among the officers about his conduct, including what appeared to me to be a further serious allegation which was never substantiated.

In the latter days of my career I saw some encouraging signs that police officers were not prepared to put up with colleagues' misconduct and that complaints were being dealt with more effectively. Tuffy left the police early in 2007 – he resigned after being convicted of racially aggravated assault.

Most of the time there is only one complainant and two police officers. Without an independent witness, or supporting evidence such as forensics, if the officers stick together the complainant has no chance of proving their misconduct. Although they are a tiny minority, the damage caused by 'criminals in police uniform' is incalculable.

Merton threw several challenges my way, but I coped well and enjoyed my time there immensely. Unfortunately, my relationship with James had taken a very disastrous and violent turn.

James became more and more distrustful the longer we were together. As I was the divisional commander, something would invariably come up at the last minute, sometimes delaying me just as I was about to leave the office. James, however, thought something else was going on. It was all about controlling me, making sure that I was not going to leave him; something I had no intention of doing. I loved him and could not imagine life without him.

These incidents didn't take place that often and there were many very good times in between. Even my mother found James absolutely charming and appeared to accept him wholeheartedly (although I subsequently discovered that my father was suspicious but never wanted to say anything).

James was by this time in complete and total control of me and became very aggressive in arguments. During one row he grabbed me by the lapels and slammed me against the kitchen wall.

Things came to a crisis when we were about to go on holiday with my parents to stay with James's parents in France. He had stormed out after an argument and I ran after him, calling for him to come back. When I caught up with him he wheeled round and floored me with a punch and started kicking me while I lay in the gutter. All I could do was curl up in a ball and try to protect my head with my arms while I waited for him to stop. My main thought as I lay there was how embarrassing it would be if someone called the police and I, a senior police officer, was found to be the victim of domestic violence.

I had dealt with numerous incidents of domestic violence in my time in the police and I could never understand why people put up with the levels of abuse and intimidation they experienced at the hands of the person they loved. It is impossible to know what it is like to be in such a situation unless you have experienced it yourself; and this is something I would not wish on my worst enemy.

I think most people are unaware just how widespread domestic violence is, not only among traditional couples in heterosexual relationships but in same sex couples as well. No matter how good a leader, how well-educated, intelligent, physically strong and emotionally aware you are, it is still possible to find yourself controlled in the way James controlled me during our time together.

By the time James had finished with me I was shaking and in shock. I went back into the flat and cleaned myself up. I called Andria, James's former landlady and a counsellor, who advised me I needed to make it clear that this behaviour was unacceptable and that, if it ever happened again, it would be the end of our relationship.

I found James and told him I had spoken to Andria. I secured a promise that this would never happen again, and we went off on our holiday – a holiday which my parents loved, describing it as the best they had ever had. If they had only known what had happened a few days before . . .

CHAPTER FOURTEEN

On 22 April 1993, Stephen Lawrence, a young black teenager, was out with his friend Dwayne Brooks when they were chased by a group of white youths. While Dwayne escaped, eighteen-year-old Stephen was fatally stabbed. No one to date has been convicted of his murder. The killing received little publicity at the time but it gradually became another cause-célèbre and a milestone in British policing in relation to issues of race and so-called 'hate crimes' where people are targeted for being different.

The subsequent Macpherson Inquiry into the Lawrence case concluded that, because of 'institutional racism', along with a good measure of police incompetence, mistakes had been made which prevented a successful conclusion to the murder investigation.

On 22 February 1999, the day the Macpherson Report was due to be published, all senior officers of the Metropolitan Police were called together in the briefing room at Lambeth support headquarters, just across the river from the Palace of Westminster. The meeting started with a live link-up to Parliament where the Home Secretary announced the report's conclusions.

The commissioner, Sir Paul Condon, watched in a separate room. We had to wait as he digested the speech and decided on his response. The sense of expectation was high when he finally strode purposefully into the briefing room. Many of the most senior officers expressed their support by breaking into spontaneous applause. After a few moments' silence, Condon said: 'I'm staying. We're changing.' He had refused to accept that the Met was institutionally racist, but now he said he would implement changes that would transform the way serious investigations were handled.

The author of these changes was a real maverick, Deputy Assistant Commissioner John Grieve, the former head of the Flying Squad and the Anti-Terrorist Branch. Grieve was a real character, much liked by those who worked with him; he was very intelligent and extremely well read.

Grieve transformed the police approach to hate crime – the way the police responded to and investigated crimes involving race, sexuality, religion and disability. This not only had a significant effect on police-community relations in the UK, but also influenced policing internationally as other forces around the world adopted his ideas.

He introduced the concept of an enhanced level of service for the victims of hate crime and established family liaison officers – police officers who would look after victims and their family members. This concept was extended from hate crime to fatal incidents generally, from road traffic accidents to murder. He also introduced the concept of Gold groups – multi-agency groups, including community representatives, who would work together to ensure everything was done appropriately and with the help and support of the local community.

Every senior officer at the event was charged with briefing their staff on the outcome of the Lawrence Inquiry and the Met's proposed response. I developed a presentation which I personally delivered at dozens of training days over the next few months.

Some officers had difficulty with the idea of an enhanced level of service. They suggested that if you were white you would get second-class treatment, but all Grieve was asking for was a level of service appropriate to the crime, while taking into account the distrust of the police held by some victims from minority communities.

Race is a highly emotive issue, particularly in the police service. Whether you are trying to deal with the issue of a disproportionate number of black people being stopped and searched or deliver an enhanced level of service to the victims of hate crime, it is better to take race out of the equation if you want to change police officers' attitudes.

I tried to do this by recalling the example of an old lady who had been robbed of her pension and Christmas bonus as she emerged from the post office in Wimbledon. The officer who dealt with the crime had a whip-round among his colleagues and succeeded in more than replacing the money that had been stolen. In contrast, when I had been a detective inspector at Notting Hill there had been a series of Rolex watch robberies, but at no time had any of the officers suggested a whip-round for the loss of these people's expensive jewellery.

These cases were examples of how police officers instinctively reacted differently to different victims, depending on the needs of the victim. All Grieve was saying was that people who were picked on because they were different and because they were vulnerable had had a more terrifying experience than if they were simply a victim of a random crime. The crime was likely to happen to them again, they had been hurt both physically and emotionally, and it was frightening to know that people hated you that much simply because of your skin colour or, as in my case, your sexuality. I knew only too well what it was like to be the victim of a hate crime from the bullying I had faced at school.

In addition, the history of the relationship between many minorities and the police had been one of perceived conflict and discrimination. As a result there was a level of distrust which was not present in the majority white population, and this distrust had to be overcome.

What Grieve was unable to change was how the police dealt with people from ethnic minorities who were suspects, particularly in relation to stop-and-search. A black preacher who gave evidence to the Lawrence Inquiry said that black people felt 'over-policed and under-protected', which was exactly how I felt as a gay man. As far as the black community was concerned, and as far as the gay community was concerned, the police were more interested in us as suspects than in helping us when we were victims.

One manifestation of this was the disproportionate stopping and searching of black people by the police. Even if there is discrimination in the workplace and in the labour market, even if black people are found disproportionately in areas of deprivation and as a result of these pressures are statistically more likely to be involved in crime, those who actually *commit* crime are still only a tiny proportion of the overall black population. Police officers need to understand that they need far stronger grounds than this to justify the fact that they are six to eight times more likely to stop and search a black person in the street than a white person.

I was having dinner with a black friend when an eighteen-year-old white, public-school educated acquaintance of his joined us for a drink at the end of the meal. The public schoolboy told me he got his cannabis from Brixton, and on the hundreds of occasions he had travelled there he had never been stopped and searched by the police. This demonstrated to me that the high numbers of cannabis offences recorded against black people are not necessarily because more black people than white use cannabis, but because blacks tend to get stopped and searched far more than whites.

Eventually, as the Deputy Assistant Commissioner (DAC) with responsibility for stop and search, I wrote a formal paper and gave a series of lectures on the subject. I explained how the police approach needed to change to become less discriminatory and more accurate. I gave the report to my boss but he did not take it any further. It was a constant frustration that many of my ideas were never even discussed by the top team because I never had a seat at the top table.

All that police officers want is to be professional, effective and arrest criminals. If you can show them that, by changing their approach, they can accurately target criminals and make more arrests then they will listen. By identifying known prolific criminals, by looking at those who keep getting arrested, and by getting accurate descriptions of people who have just committed an offence from the victim, it is possible to achieve these outcomes without reference to race while, at the same time, dealing with the racial profiling that currently leads to the unjust targeting of black people.

James and I tended to have a gin and tonic before dinner, which I would usually prepare. James was a heavy smoker and would generally stay in the lounge while I cooked.

One evening I emerged from a steam-filled kitchen to tell him that dinner was ready and caught him smoking a cannabis joint. Shocked and angry, I told him that not only was he breaking the law but he was also putting my job at risk. Sensing that something was boiling over on the cooker, I dived back into the kitchen and when I reappeared in the lounge James had put everything away.

There had not yet been a debate about what police officers should do if they caught loved ones or family members committing minor offences. The only reference is in the 'Blue Book' published during Sir Kenneth Newman's reign as commissioner, and describes a scenario where an off-duty officer is at a party and someone there is smoking cannabis. It suggests that the reasonable course is to alert the person whose party it is and to leave without taking any further action. Where you draw the line is a difficult judgement call; what do you do if you are a police officer and it is your son whom you suspect of having the occasional joint in his bedroom?

I was deeply in love with James – imagine catching your husband or wife smoking a joint; it makes a clear and objective decision very difficult. Short of illegally evicting him from the flat (he paid a contribution towards the bills and the mortgage) or calling my colleagues to arrest him, I don't know what else I was supposed to do.

There was no way I was condoning or allowing James to smoke cannabis; I did all I could reasonably do to stop him smoking it, and explained what the consequences would be for me if he continued the habit. His smoking of cannabis rarely ever happened; when it did, there would be a row and he would desist . . . until the next time.

CHAPTER FIFTEEN

As usual I had plenty on my plate at work and I was fighting very stiff competition to get on to the Strategic Command Course (you cannot get promoted beyond chief superintendent without completing the SCC). The course was open to superintendents and chief superintendents, and the selection process involved two and a half days of tests and interviews.

I knew from having gone through a similar process to get on to the Accelerated Promotion programme that the assessors wanted to look at you as an individual as well as a police officer. I was determined that I was going to be selected for being myself, not for pretending to be something I was not, and that included my sexuality.

On the first day, candidates fill in an interview aid questionnaire – something for the interviewers to go on. One of the questions was 'What is the most difficult decision you have had to make (a) in your professional life and (b) in your private life. I thought carefully and in answer to (b) I wrote 'Deciding to tell my wife that I was gay after we had been married for five years.'

During one of the interviews I was asked whether anyone in my own force knew about my sexuality.

I recalled talking to one of my chief inspectors when I asked him if people knew I was gay. He told me that everyone knew and it did not make any difference to them.

'And it does not make any difference to us, either,' said the interviewer.

I was then picked out for a co-director's interview. Only a handful of candidates were put through this ordeal and there was much speculation as to its relevance. Some believed it was because you were borderline, others that it was simply a random sample.

We talked about selection processes and I was asked if it was ever justified to positively discriminate. I trod carefully. I said that if there were three equally good candidates for a job, matched exactly for ability, experience and all-round suitability and one of them was black, and the force wanted to increase the number of black and minority ethnic candidates, then politically there was an argument to select the black candidate. The formal written feedback from that interview read 'Mr Paddick was completely open and honest in interview, which was a serious mistake on his part.'

Not serious enough for me not to be selected.

Finding how best to get to the course was proving tricky. It was due to start in April 2000. At the time I did not own a car and Bramshill is quite a difficult place to get to by public transport. I spoke to my finance and resources manager about the difference in cost between all the travel and incidental expenses I could claim and the cost of hiring a small car.

After exchanging a few emails, I was told that there was little difference between the two and it made more practical sense in terms of opportunity costs to hire a small car than claim all the expenses. I arranged to pick up the car every Sunday afternoon and return it on Friday afternoon when the course had finished for the week. It would be garaged at the police station until I needed it again on the Sunday.

My superintendent at Merton had applied at the same time as me, and he was very hopeful that he was going to be successful. When the results came through, he apparently expressed surprise that I had been selected while he had not.

A couple of weeks into the course, the superintendent asked to see me. He had by this time become the acting borough commander, and told me that he wanted the hire car back because it was too expensive. I told him about my discussion with the finance and resources manager who had worked out that it was cost neutral. He picked up the telephone while I sat in front of him and called the F&R manager who confirmed this. The superintendent put the phone down, looked back at me and said, 'It might well be cost neutral but there is a limit on the number of hire cars we can have and we're short of transport. I need your hire car back.'

I left him without comment and telephoned the area fleet manager who controlled the supply of cars. He said there was no limit to the number of cars the borough could hire; the only limit was the cost. I went back and told the superintendent, who replied, 'Fair enough, but I want you to pay the line rental on your official mobile for the duration of the course. I'm sure you would do the same if you were in my position. It's my duty to look after the budget for the borough.'

'If I was in your position,' I replied impetuously, 'I'd be thinking, this man could be a commander in a few months' time, I'd better look after him.'

I used the car for one more week, then hired an Easy Rentacar and bought my own mobile telephone, both out of my own pocket (although I started claiming the expenses I was entitled to as I no longer had the official hire car). With a mixture of resentment and satisfaction, I handed over the keys to the hire car and my officially provided mobile telephone to the chief superintendent's PA.

Some months later, while still on the course, I received a call from the commander for South West London. 'I've had a complaint from a superintendent that you've threatened him. He says you told him you were going to get your own back once you reached commander.'

With a sigh I explained the whole saga to the commander who said, 'To be honest, I didn't think it sounded like you. I think we can leave it there.'

Things came to a head in my relationship with James in 2000 while I was on the Strategic Command Course. Seeing him only at weekends made life very difficult and rows began not long after I arrived home each Friday.

I confided in a woman superintendent who was on the same course, telling her about what life was like with James. She was horrified, and couldn't believe I was still with him; her extreme reaction helped me to realise that James's behaviour was totally unreasonable.

I was very pleasantly surprised to find that I had been sent a pair of centre court tickets from the All-England Club as a thank you for several years I spent policing Wimbledon. While the club had always made tickets available then, I had been unable to use them because I was always on duty; this was the first opportunity I had to enjoy the tennis. The big day coincided with the marriage of one of James's cousins in France, someone I had never met. When I explained the clash during one Friday lunch break, James said he understood perfectly: 'You must go to the tennis, it's the only chance you'll get.'

On reflection, I wasn't sure it was right to accept the tickets, and knowing James would be pleased that I could go with him to the wedding, I put them back in the post with a thank-you note that afternoon.

James went back to work while I went to the dentist. When I returned, a note was waiting for me from James in which he said, as I had put tennis before his family, I wouldn't be seeing him that weekend; he had packed an overnight bag and stormed out.

I tried to call him but his mobile was switched off. This was the last straw. It was then that I resolved that it was over. Not surprisingly, James refused to accept my decision and tried to enlist our friends to help reverse it. I was by then in the middle of a course at Fitzwilliam College at Cambridge University, part of the Senor Command Course. From the conversations we were having over the telephone, it was clear that James was not taking my decision to leave him seriously.

One Tuesday I came back to London on the train, having called James to tell him that we needed to go out for dinner and talk face to face. I sat with him in the flat and said, 'James, you're not hearing what I'm saying to you. It's over. I don't want to be with you anymore.' We didn't go to dinner because James got up in a temper and walked out, slamming the door behind him.

I caught the train back to Cambridge, where I turned off my phone and went to bed. When I got up there were fourteen voicemail messages from James and, as I listened to them, it was clear that he was getting more and more drunk and more and more angry with each message. Although I deleted them and wrote them off as drunken rage, with what was to happen some fifteen months later, I wished I had kept some of them.

While I was still away, he began clearing the flat of everything he felt he had any possible claim to – some of his claims were rather dubious, making me recall the allegations made by his previous ex's family. I also returned the money he had paid towards the mortgage on the flat in compliance with the legal agreement he had insisted was put in place a year or so earlier.

It had been a very difficult relationship. James had successfully isolated me from my friends and had continually told me that I was not the sort of person anyone else would want. After his long and sustained campaign I had even begun to doubt my own abilities; I had very low self-esteem.

CHAPTER SIXTEEN

At the end of the course, I eagerly awaited advertisements for commander or assistant chief constable posts. I applied for the post of commander in both the City of London Police and in the Met. If you are ambitious, you should also apply to other forces outside London to increase your range of experience, but I was a Londoner through and through and I wanted to stay in my home city. The interview for the Met would be held on the Thursday and the interview for the City of London on the Friday of the same week.

With my promotion to commander, I thought my opportunity to be in charge at Brixton would come but I was told that the commissioner had decided to experiment with what he called 'big ships, little ships', where the importance of the captain of the ship would depend on the size of the command. After Westminster, Lambeth was the biggest, and arguably the most demanding, of all the London boroughs and he was going to put a commander in charge.

I had wanted to take charge of Brixton, which is within the borough of Lambeth, ever since I had been there as a sergeant and it was hinted that if I was promoted that was the job I would get. How exactly the Met selects its most senior officers still remains a mystery to me, but I went into the interview with confidence, believing I had been pencilled-in for a specific job at commander level.

Candidates appeared before six members of the Police Authority, a mixture of politicians, magistrates and independent members. The new commissioner, Sir John Stevens, was also present, but he did not have to ask any questions. The only question I remember from that interview came from Rachael Whittaker, head of the Human Resources Committee. She asked, 'Mr Paddick, you were the author of the tenure of post policy. Do you think it was the right policy at the right time or do you feel it was a mistake?'

Fully aware that Sir John had abolished the tenure of post policy as soon as he took over, I said, indicating the commissioner, 'I have to be careful how I answer this one otherwise something will be thrown at me by the gentleman on the left.' To my relief, there were chuckles all round.

The results were due to be announced at Friday lunchtime. I was furiously preparing for the City of London panel when, one hour before that interview was due to start, I received a call from Sir John Stevens telling me to pull out of the interview because I had been selected for the post of commander of the Metropolitan Police. He was not a man to be argued with and I immediately did as he asked.

This was what I had wanted ever since my confirmation interview at the end of my first two years; I could hardly believe I had achieved the rank of commander or that I would soon be on my way to take charge of Lambeth. I did what any gay man would do when he had achieved his life's dream.

I went shopping! I went to my then favourite clothes store, Jaeger, and bought two pairs of trousers, one leather jacket and a pair of shoes.

The pay increase from chief superintendent to commander was substantial in those days and, wanting to put memories of James well and truly behind me, the extra money gave me the opportunity to move out of the flat we had shared to a better property in a prestigious development in Marsham Street, formerly the nursing home for Westminster Hospital.

My celebrations were brought to an abrupt halt on Monday morning, when I was summoned to see the head of Internal Investigation, Andy Hayman. An anonymous letter had arrived on Deputy

Commissioner Ian Blair's desk on the morning of my appearance before the selection panel, alleging that I had taken an operational police vehicle from the Borough of Merton and used it to go to and from the Strategic Command Course for the entire six months. I had, the letter claimed, deprived operational officers of the use of the vehicle and had impaired the operational effectiveness of the borough as a result. The writer went on to say that this amounted to corruption, and that to ensure that the matter was properly dealt with, the letter had been copied to a national newspaper.

Sure enough an enquiry came in from the *Daily Mirror* asking whether there was any substance to the allegation. Andy Hayman told me that his people had interrogated the police computer system and had discovered the exchange of emails between me and the F&R manager at Merton. I was entitled to use a hire car and giving it and my mobile phone back after only three weeks on the course was more than could have been expected of me.

Andy then said, 'You probably know who's done this and we've got a pretty good idea as well, but as you've just got your promotion, I suggest we leave it there. It's not very pleasant to know we have colleagues like this, but it's best if you move on.' I wasn't sure who the author of the letter was. My superintendent at Merton knew I had returned the car after two weeks so it could not have been him.

Reluctant to let the matter go, but buoyed up by my success, I agreed not take it any further. The matter was never investigated fully so I can't be sure who sent the letter, but it was an important lesson: however popular you are or try to be, you can still become the victim of professional jealousy or homophobia.

In October 2000 I was told that I would take over at Lambeth on 1 January 2001. Knowing that the outgoing borough commander was not going to be around at Christmas because he was taking time off to be with his family, I decided that on Christmas morning I would visit each of the stations in Lambeth – Kennington, Clapham, Brixton and Streatham – before heading on to my parents' house for Christmas lunch.

*

On Christmas Eve I was at home alone, still in the flat I had shared with James, and ready for my tour of the police stations in the morning, when I picked up a magazine called *Positive Nation* which supported people with HIV and AIDS. The outgoing commander had given it to me because it featured a Lambeth officer, PC Andy Hewlett, who was on the cover as the first openly HIV-positive police officer. Andy's colleagues had been very supportive and the commander, who was proud of Andy, suggested I read it.

I opened the front cover and on the contents page there was a series of thumbnail photographs, one of which looked strangely familiar. I turned to the feature in question, which told the story of a young man who had contracted HIV and nearly died of AIDS but how, thanks to improvements in anti-retroviral drugs, had recovered and was living a normal life. From one of the other photos, none of which showed his face, I realised who it was

My heart thudded into the pit of my stomach as I realised that this was the man I had been with for the past three months.

A few months after James and I had split up, I had started seeing someone else. Although we practised safe sex to begin with, as we grew more confident with each other we began to do things that were not safe, although neither of us said anything or discussed the issue. Excellent organisations like the Terrence Higgins Trust, based on years of experience and research, suggest that many gay men engage in unsafe sex as a result of lack of self-esteem or self-loathing, or placing no value on themselves. After three and a half years of being with James, at that time I could have ticked all those boxes.

I immediately called my new man on his mobile. My first words were, 'I've seen the article.' I asked him why he had never said anything to me about his HIV status. He said the longer the relationship had gone on, the more difficult it had been for him to tell me. He was in the North of England with his parents and said it was difficult for him to talk. I said I understood and hung up.

There I was, on my own on Christmas Eve in the flat where I had lived with an abusive partner, and with no one to talk to about the honestly held belief that I must have contracted HIV, which had taken hold of me since I'd read the article. I had never felt so alone or so frightened. I frantically went through the pages of the telephone directory and eventually managed to get through to an AIDS helpline. The person I spoke to was very understanding, but confirmed that I had put myself at very high risk of contracting HIV; the more I sought reassurance, the more likely he told me I was to have the virus.

In those days it normally took forty-eight hours to get a test result, and even then one couldn't be sure that the result was accurate until three months after the last contact with the infected partner. At that time the virus could not be detected directly; it took three months for the antibodies produced in one's system to fight the virus to reach levels that could be detected. To my despair, I also discovered that I would have to wait a week for the initial test because all the clinics were closed for the Christmas holidays.

I was beside myself with worry and didn't know what to do or who to call; out of complete desperation I phoned James. I knew that his previous partner had died of AIDS and that at least he would understand the issues. I was looking for some reassurance from him that I would be okay. He was matter of fact, cold and detached. He told me that I was stupid and offered neither hope nor comfort.

The next morning, I got up after a restless, worried night, showered, and dressed in my uniform. I picked up the four king-size tins of Quality Street I had bought from the Nine Elms Sainsbury's, one for each station I was to visit, and tried my best to put on a cheerful face as I engaged in a tour of my new domain. The officers appeared surprised and genuinely pleased to see me – and the Quality Street.

I got through the rest of Christmas Day, and then Boxing Day, in the agonising position of wanting to share my concerns with my parents but not wanting to worry them. It was not the best Christmas I had ever spent.

I managed to get an HIV test after a week. The counsellor, recognising my distress, put the analysis through as urgent and I got the initial test result back the same day – negative. I would have to go through the same experience every month for the next three months before I could be sure that I was clear of the virus. Things are very different today. The last time I had an HIV test I asked the doctor when I would get the result and he said, 'By the time I've got this plaster on.' It is always nerve-racking, even when you know it's highly unlikely you could have contracted the virus, but if you are sexually active, having regular sexual health checks is a good thing to do even if you have no symptoms.

With trust having broken down, I could not continue my relationship with the guy I had been going out with. After a dignified period, I started seeing another young man named Michael and known to his friends as 'Gucci Michael' – he was then the floor manager of Gucci in Sloane Street.

We hit it off immediately, and as the relationship developed I felt this was the start of a long and permanent relationship.

Michael is a great character, bright and witty and bursting with energy, and even as we were about to embark on some of the darkest days of my life, he was able to keep smiling and to pull me through.

After we had been seeing each other for about five months, Michael's landlord decided to put the rent up, so I suggested he move in with me until he was able to find alternative accommodation. He moved in and did not move out again for many years. Unfortunately, being somewhat of a *fashionista* there was no way that his vast array of clothes – shoes, coats, suits, not to mention casual wear – was going to fit into my one-bedroom flat; even the two enormous free-standing wardrobes we bought to accommodate his collection were not able to contain all of his designer gear.

Michael went on to the Internet every day in a frantic search for suitable alternative accommodation with more storage. He discovered we could afford to buy a large two-bedroom flat in Vauxhall for the same price as the one-bedroom flat I owned in Westminster.

As well as working for Gucci, my partner Michael was a party animal. He had been going to London clubs for years and knew many people from the scene, including one of those involved in a new club, the Shadow Lounge. Because of Michael's connections we were given VIP treatment there.

Despite references in the press to Elton John being a member of the Shadow Lounge, I never saw him there, but one Friday night I was with Michael in the VIP area when he introduced me to David Furnish, Elton's partner, who was enjoying a night out with his friend Patrick Cox, the shoe designer. In his job, Michael often looked after David and Elton when they came in to Gucci to shop.

That Friday, David and Patrick sat next to each other on the bench that runs in a wide semicircle around the wall of the VIP area. Michael sat down next to Patrick and I sat next to David. Michael, a wonderful raconteur and real social animal was off into a deep conversation with Patrick leaving me to talk with David, who was absolutely charming and totally engaging. So began what turned out to be an enduring friendship between David and me.

My regular attendance at the Shadow Lounge had not gone unnoticed. I was again summoned to see Andy Hayman, the head of Internal Investigation, who told me there had been an anonymous phone call to Crime Stoppers in which someone alleged that I was associating with a drug dealer in the club. The caller also alleged that I had tipped off the manager of the club that the police were going to raid the premises, resulting in posters appearing on the walls warning drug users they would be expelled and the police called. I had noticed these posters had recently appeared in the club.

Andy Hayman had asked his staff to check out the story. They checked with the local police in Westminster, with the Clubs and Vice section, and with other departments at the Yard who might have been involved, but nobody had planned to raid the club for drugs.

Hayman said that when he found that no raid was planned, he knew that the allegation was malicious and decided to 'include' me. He asked me whether I thought I was being followed: otherwise how would people know I was going to the Shadow Lounge? I had no idea people would go to these lengths to try and ruin my reputation and career. Andy suggested that I install an alarm and a separate video entry system at my home – he was concerned that someone might break into the flat and plant drugs – and offered Michael and me anti-surveillance training. An expert in anti-surveillance came round to our home to train us in losing tails and we installed the recommended alarm and camera.

After this allegation had been made, a series of articles appeared in the tabloids about the fact that I went to the Shadow Lounge. The most memorable of these was the *Sun*'s effort where they claimed they had 'analysed' the club's six toilet seats and found traces of cocaine on five of them. I may be unconventional but sniffing toilet seats is not my thing.

Lambeth was going to be my biggest test. Relations between the police and the community were strained, and the borough was consistently placed at numbers one and two in London's crime league tables. For the financial year 2000–2001, Lambeth held the number one hotspot in London for muggings: 4,369 reported. Robbery was up thirty-eight per cent and the proportion of those crimes solved had fallen from twenty-one per cent to five per cent in the financial year that ended three months after I took over.

Drug dealers were selling crack cocaine and heroin on the streets and shooting each other to protect their turf and to enforce their deals. To make matters worse, the borough was one hundred officers short of its allocation of 923. Lots of officers were trying to transfer out of the borough, but no one was volunteering to join.

My first full financial year budget was £37,321,624. Lambeth was the third largest policing unit in England and Wales in terms of staffing levels, and the second busiest in terms of the annual number of emergency calls received. In November 2001 Her Majesty's Inspector of Constabulary described Lambeth as 'one of the most challenging policing environments in the UK, and possibly in Europe . . . Arguably, Lambeth Basic Command Unit is as busy and as challenging to run as many police forces.'

A lot of street crime was driven by the availability of high-value portable goods such as mobile phones. It was also driven by advertising. Young people had a very strong desire to own certain products, from clothing to electronics, and research showed that in our modern-day consumption culture, self-respect often depended on possession of desirable goods. Many criminals' life chances were limited and so, therefore, was their legitimate access to these goods. It didn't take much for them to override the moral issues associated with theft and robbery. Besides this, there was a culture of silence, CCTV footage was not of a very high standard, and mobile phones were easily unlocked and sold on.

The fact that many young people were living alongside lawbreakers resulted in a 'lawbreaker culture'. The perception was that the benefits of carrying out crimes outweighed the cons. There was a lack of positive role models and no consistent moral message, which might have discouraged criminal behaviour. Only forty per cent of young black men in Lambeth were in employment, and some were easily persuaded to take part in lucrative criminal activities.

Becoming a criminal at street level required some skill, and the most successful were often the fittest, fastest and smartest youngsters who knew how to manipulate those with weaker wills and less intelligence. Many young people joined gangs to escape being bullied. Street robbery involved thrills, bravery, danger and risk; it invoked power over the victim and rebellion against society, and contact with the victim was only fleeting and soon forgotten.

Burglary was a less attractive option as people now secured their homes with more sophisticated locks and alarms. While white-collar crime was not an option for these youngsters, a large number of white-collar workers were moving into the area as Lambeth began the process of gentrification. The newcomers supplied a rich source of victims. A thriving shopping area, combined with a major public transport interchange from British Rail to London Underground, meant that tens of thousands of commuters were passing through the borough on foot every day. Lambeth had become a twenty-four/seven cultural and entertainment centre.

If the external environment, the crime levels and the lack of resources were not daunting enough, staff management presented yet another challenge. I had responsibility for over a thousand employees – over eight hundred police officers, uniform and CID, spread over six operational bases, and over two hundred support staff; most of them working over a twenty-four-hour, seven-day time period.

The official line was that the borough commander should concentrate on external issues such as liaison with the Local Authority, the National Health Service and community groups, but I also wanted to be visible to my staff. I wondered how I was going to communicate with them all (my own Leadership Principles recommended communicating with staff face to face as much as possible).

I organised a series of meetings where I would get to meet all one thousand of them in their teams in my first month. I also spoke to the twenty members of my senior management in one-to-one interviews. I was pleased when I recognised a few members of the community who I knew from my time at Brixton as a chief inspector, and officers I had known since I was there as a sergeant. It was reassuring to see some familiar faces.

At the first round of meetings I asked them what could be done to make things better, and returned the following month with my responses. Some of the issues that they raised were relatively easy to resolve, giving me some early quick wins; others would require the agreement of my bosses. There were also a few suggestions with which I disagreed, and I explained the reasons for my disagreement in face-to-face meetings with those who had suggested them.

I learned that there are real benefits to genuine consultation. Even when I rejected ideas, by explaining why I showed that I was listening; and where I agreed, I demonstrated that I was prepared to act on what they were telling me. By the end of my first two months everyone under my command had met me at least once, most of them twice, and I was beginning to win them over.

In addition to my staff, I also had to see all the people outside of the police who, as borough commander, I needed to work with. These included the local Members of Parliament – Keith Hill, MP for Streatham and then Chief Whip; Tessa Jowell, MP for Dulwich and

West Norwood, and Kate Hoey, MP for Vauxhall. The first month was a whirlwind of meetings, names, faces and groups, all with their own agendas, issues and problems.

The most politically important group was Lambeth's Community Police Consultative Group (CPCG). Lambeth's CPCG had been the first of its kind; it was set up in the wake of the 1981 Brixton riots after the Scarman Report suggested that the local police chief should be more accountable to the local community.

The CPCG held a whole range of vigorous debates where we were ruthlessly held to account and often unfairly accused of misconduct. It was completely different from any other CPCG in London, and had become the focus for people from all over the capital who had a grievance against the police.

On 23 January I went to Brixton prison where I met the governor. He told me there were more drugs in his prison than there were in the streets of Brixton (which was going some). He explained to me just how futile his job had become, thanks to overcrowding and levels of drug abuse. I sympathised wholeheartedly. Like me, he simply did not have enough resources.

On 24 January I met Harriet Smith for the first time; she was the director of the Lambeth Crime Prevention Trust. As a leading Liberal Democrat activist, her influence on me would have long-term implications. I also met with people from the local press, including Mike Best who was then the editor of the *Voice* newspaper – 'The Voice of Black Britain' – which was based in Brixton. On 26 January I had a meeting with Lloyd Leon who used to be the chair of the consultative group and was a former mayor of Lambeth, and Vince Atkins, a convicted murderer who, having served his sentence and been reformed by the process, wanted to work with young people to talk about the dangers of guns.

Determined to keep up my early promise of being a visible and accessible leader, I attended the parades when officers reported for duty. These 'spontaneous' informal visits took careful planning and a lot of commitment; if you just went on parade when you had a spare moment, you were in danger of only seeing officers in Brixton, where

I was based, and seeing the same officers week after week while those on other teams never saw you at all.

During the first three months of dealing with the most demanding job I had ever experienced, both in terms of volume and seriousness, I was still waiting to know for sure whether I had contracted HIV. It was a tough time.

My predecessor had recently introduced functional rather than geographic responsibility for the policing of the borough. Under the functional plan, the borough commander and all the superintendents had been moved to Brixton from other parts of Lambeth. Rather than being responsible for a particular and identifiable area of Lambeth, all the senior officers now had responsibility for one aspect of policing, such as 'crime' or 'operations' across the whole borough.

Functional responsibility led to arguments and confusion over who was in charge and who was responsible for what, and the performance of the borough deteriorated as a result. No one, except for some of the superintendents who could avoid personal responsibility under the new structure, liked this arrangement. The staff no longer had a recognisable senior police officer they could identify as their local boss, and there was no longer any visible senior officer presence at Kennington, Clapham or Streatham.

Similarly, the community did not have a local police chief they could call their own. Moving all the senior officers to Brixton did nothing to reassure residents, or officers from other parts of the borough, that they were getting their fair share of police resources.

I wanted to change things back to geographic responsibility. Knowing how much time, effort and planning would have to go into such a major reorganisation, and wanting to involve the local community in the decision-making process (although I was pretty sure they would support it), I put off the inevitable until the end of 2001.

Every four weeks, I would spend four hours with the Late Turn at the end of my own working day, then parade with the Night Duty and spend four hours with them, either in the back of the area car or in the van. It was important for me to understand at first hand the pressures and challenges my officers were facing. It was also important that I was seen to be 'one of them', on their side – able to say, 'I understand' – and mean it.

CHAPTER SEVENTEEN

One of the teams had raised the case of a colleague of theirs who had been arrested by Internal Investigation (CIB) for finding cannabis and throwing it away rather than bringing it back to the police station. Officers had, up until then, routinely dealt with small amounts of cannabis in this way – throwing it down a drain in front of the owner and giving them a ticking-off before sending them on their way. As their colleague had been arrested, apparently for doing just this, they were adamant that they were no longer going to put their jobs on the line by taking this short cut and told me they intended to arrest everyone they found with even the smallest amount of cannabis.

My immediate reaction was, 'You can't do that! You must carry on putting it down the drain.' Indeed there had been a 'fly on the wall' BBC documentary some years earlier which showed a sergeant from Brixton stopping a car, finding cannabis and dropping it down a drain.

They told me, quite rightly, that 'As a senior officer, you can't tell us to do something which is contrary to police discipline.'

The real story was that some of the offending officer's colleagues had called the police whistleblower hotline and claimed that he was confiscating cannabis from people on the street and taking it home to smoke it himself.

Acting on this, Internal Investigation had launched a sting operation; lumps of cannabis resin (which had been chemically marked) were placed in a tobacco tin and left on the back shelf of a car. The car was then registered on the police national computer as stolen. All this was done under the utmost secrecy; a drug sniffer-dog and handler were brought in from Surrey Police to ensure the cat did not get out of the bag.

It took five attempts on five different nights before the officer checked the car, discovered it was stolen, searched it and found the cannabis. The chemical marking of the cannabis resin had made it go dry and the officer, realising it was therefore worthless, threw it away, rather than taking it back to the station as he should have done (or taking it home as CIB were hoping he would do).

He was arrested for stealing the commissioner's cannabis, and although the Internal Investigation officers could not find the resin he had thrown away, the offence of theft is complete if the thief disposes of the property in circumstances where the owner is unlikely to find it.

Having arrested him, officers searched his home but found nothing; they then searched his girlfriend's address, where, on top of a wardrobe in a spare bedroom they found a small amount of herbal cannabis in a plastic bag. The arrested officer said the cannabis had been left behind by some people who had come round for dinner; he had thrown it on top of the wardrobe, intending to return it to its owners, and had forgotten all about it. He took responsibility for the cannabis, even though it was in his girlfriend's home, in order to protect her. He was charged with:

1. Stealing cannabis
2. Unlawful possession of herbal cannabis
3. Misfeasance in a public office (which has a maximum penalty of life imprisonment)

He was sent for trial at the Old Bailey, and it was at this stage that I was appointed Lambeth borough commander and was confronted by his angry colleagues. Having heard the full story, I called Andy Hayman, who was then in charge of the Complaints Investigation Unit.

I asked him, 'Do you not think this operation against one of my officers over cannabis is disproportionate?'

Andy went ballistic. 'I'm the one who decides whether an investigation is disproportionate or not, not you!' and that was the end of the conversation.

After a long and expensive hearing at the Old Bailey he was found not guilty on all charges, except for possession of the cannabis that was found at his girlfriend's house, to which he had pleaded guilty. He was fined £50. At his disciplinary tribunal, the officer admitted smoking cannabis in the past, but only while on holiday abroad. The senior officer who sacked him told me he had done so because the officer was a habitual cannabis user.

This unfortunate sequence of events had left me with a real problem. If my officers did go ahead and arrest everyone in Lambeth who was caught in possession of a small amount of cannabis, it would be like Operation Swamp all over again. The memory of my time as a sergeant in Brixton came to mind: the time when the guy in Railton Road slammed the door in my face when I was after a smoker but who gave up the young man for stealing a handbag. Subsequent discussions with the community reinforced my view that many people would support a more tolerant approach to the policing of cannabis, provided the time saved was directed towards more serious offences in general and crack cocaine and heroin dealing in particular.

On the morning of 15 January I met Ken Hyder, a freelance journalist who interviewed me about becoming the new commander of Lambeth. I had met Ken before although I did not know him well. He said, 'All your predecessors in this role have failed. What are you going to do different?'

'Well, for a start I'm thinking of not arresting people for cannabis.'

Ken raised his eyebrows and said very slowly and sceptically in his Scottish accent, 'Riiiiight.'

We decided that we needed to keep this one to ourselves until we were ready, and began the process of trying to develop the arguments to support a different approach to cannabis. Ken played devil's advocate, coming up with all the negative arguments against such a change, and we tried to think of smart responses.

I drafted in my acting chief superintendent and a trusted friend and colleague of his, a detective inspector, to work on the practicalities of the scheme. I held meetings with the executive of the Community Police Consultative Group to discuss what their reaction and the community's reaction would be. While others were supportive, the chair was more cautious. 'It would be a brave move' was as much enthusiasm as she could muster.

Eventually, I was reasonably satisfied with our practical plans and with the answers Ken and I had prepared in readiness for the critics we were inevitably going to face. The arguments in favour seemed to me to be strong, and although I thought my plan would get the backing of the community, I couldn't be sure – not least because I didn't feel I could consult more widely with the community about this issue without alerting my bosses and the media before I was ready.

As a commander, and even later as a deputy assistant commissioner, the only way I could get ideas aired and discussed by the Met's commissioner and his top team was through my own assistant commissioner, at that time Mike Todd. And I was pretty certain that any proposal as radical as this that I made to the very ambitious and very conservative Todd would end up in the bin.

Ken and I adopted what is known in the trade as a 'high risk strategy'. We decided that the only way to bring the idea to attention was to put it on the front page of the London *Evening Standard*, which would only be possible if we did not tell anyone at New Scotland Yard beforehand. I was being driven to a meeting at NSY when I saw a placard outside a newsagent's which said 'Police Not to Arrest for Cannabis'.

My driver asked me, 'What's that about?'

'Oh, I think it might have something to do with me,' I said casually, although inwardly my heart was already pounding.

Although I knew my actions would attract a lot of interest, I hadn't realised the impact they would have nationally. The *Standard*'s front page was followed up the next day by all the nationals, along with national and local television and radio. I was pleased to discover that the initial reaction was almost universally either neutral or positive, although Anne Widdecombe told the BBC's *Today* programme I was usurping the authority of Parliament (in that Parliament had decided that cannabis was illegal and it was the duty of the police to enforce the law).

This was ironic as she had proposed at a recent Conservative Party conference that people who were caught in possession of cannabis should receive a fixed penalty of £100, rather than being arrested and taken to court, a proposal not too dissimilar from my own.

Sir John Stevens, our wily commissioner, kept quiet for two days to gauge the public mood. When he saw that it was generally in favour of my proposal, he asked me to produce a report on the mechanics of how the scheme would operate, along with supportive evidence to back it up.

We looked at the three hundred or so cases where people had been arrested and sent to court for possession of cannabis in Lambeth during the previous twelve months. Invariably the magistrate had imposed a conditional discharge, which meant there was no penalty unless the person was caught again, or they were given a small fine.

It was costing thousands of pounds in administration costs, incurred by the Metropolitan Police Criminal Justice Unit and the Crown Prosecution Service, and, on average, two officers spent four hours on each case. It was clear that arresting people for cannabis in Lambeth was using up a lot of police time and public money for only minor penalties imposed at court. This time, effort and money would be better spent focusing on reducing the high levels of burglary and street robbery, crack cocaine and heroin dealing, particularly when I was so short of police officers.

The commissioner was convinced and agreed to a six-month experiment in Lambeth, where officers were told not to arrest people for carrying small amounts of cannabis for personal use. I personally spoke to every police officer in the borough in an effort to convince them that this was the right thing to do. There was some opposition of course, and predictions of a drug-crime explosion.

The scheme was implemented in July 2001 on a six-month trial basis. We left it to officers' discretion to decide what was 'a small amount' rather than having to force them to carry around a set of scales. While it was difficult to control what the officers did on the street, the custody sergeants, who were tied to the station, were within easy reach and so had no choice but to follow orders. I gave them instructions to refuse to deal with anyone who had been arrested for a small amount of cannabis which was obviously for personal use.

This was another way of 'encouraging' officers to engage with the new policy and become familiar with the new process, which included confiscation of the drug and recording the offender's details on a local database. Once this process was established, I planned to allow officers to arrest for possession of cannabis or 'seize and warn' at their discretion.

An 'independent assessment' of the scheme was carried out by the Met's own internal consultancy group. Meanwhile, the Police Foundation volunteered to assess public opinion and commissioned a MORI poll which questioned a representative sample of 2,055 Lambeth residents. They found that the overwhelming majority (eighty-three per cent) approved of the cannabis pilot scheme, while only eight per cent disapproved.

One of the most popular parts of the new scheme (eighty-eight per cent approval) was that young people caught with small amounts of cannabis would have the drug confiscated and would be given a verbal warning. Parents did not want their children criminalised over possession of what was considered then to be a relatively harmless substance, when compared with the health consequences of crack and heroin.

As with crime figures generally, it is difficult to assess accurately what the effect of any one initiative is when there are always so many variables, but the cannabis pilot certainly seemed to contribute to the crime turnaround in Lambeth. More people were arrested for possession of crack cocaine (up fifty-seven per cent) and Class A drug dealing (up twenty per cent), while burglary fell by eighteen per cent and street robberies fell from 791 to 407 per month (forty-nine per cent) for the period of the pilot, compared with the year before.

The independent review estimated that every time someone was cautioned for cannabis, an average of three hours of police time was saved – the new procedure took about an hour – three hours in which the police officers were free to go after serious criminals. The official assessment estimated that we had saved 4,170 hours of police office time and 11,270 hours of support officer time.

Critics cited two main objections to the cannabis pilot: that more schoolchildren were using the drug, and that people were flocking to Lambeth from outside the borough to buy the stuff. Fifty out of sixty-six junior schools and seven out of the ten secondary schools in Lambeth responded to a survey carried out by the police about drugs. Junior schools reported no change in incidents relating to cannabis. Secondary schools reported a decrease in incidents, with fewer confiscations – a total of four cases – taking place.

Far from suffering from drugs tourism, the proportion of people dealt with for possession of cannabis from outside the borough fell during the pilot compared with the previous year. Arrests for cannabis dealing increased by eleven per cent, hardly an attractive incentive for out-of-borough dealers.

About three months into the pilot, the Home Affairs Select Committee began taking evidence on the government's strategy on drugs and called me, among others, to give evidence. They asked me about reclassifying cannabis from Class B to C. I advised them that the government had to be careful about the messages they were sending, whether they were talking about reclassification or decriminalisation of cannabis, or any other drug. It was very easy to give the impression that cannabis was harmless when it clearly was not, and stated that I was against reclassification

They asked me whether the system of seizing and warning could be applied to other drugs. I said that the difficulty with other drugs was that some people had died as a direct result of taking those drugs, so it was a completely different issue to cannabis; there appeared to be little evidence of people dying from taking cannabis. There were also few examples at that time of people having to commit crime to feed a cannabis addiction compared with hundreds of accounts of crack and heroin addicts committing thousands of crimes.

Emphasising the still-high levels of crime and inadequate police resources to deal with it, I said that my priority was to tackle those addicts who had to commit crime to buy drugs, and the dealers who fed them. To send my officers into nightclubs to arrest those who took ecstasy and sniffed cocaine at the weekend with money they had earned legitimately, and who would return to work on Monday with no serious ill effects, was not my priority. I thought it was a practical approach in difficult circumstances.

That evening, the headline plastered across the front page of the *Evening Standard* read, 'Cocaine OK at Weekends Says Police Chief'. Sir John Stevens was not very happy with me. By now I seemed to be always in trouble; it was only the depth that varied.

David Blunkett, the then Home Secretary, announced to the same Home Affairs committee that he was planning to withdraw the police's power to arrest people for cannabis by reclassifying cannabis from a Class B to a Class C drug. His officials spent months trying to convince and reassure the police service that removing the power of arrest would not be seriously detrimental. At the last minute, Mike Fuller, then a DAC in the Met with responsibility for drug policy, and Ian Blair, then deputy commissioner, went and saw Blunkett and convinced him to retain the power of arrest.

The drug was reclassified, but possession of all Class C drugs became an arrestable offence for the first time, and the maximum penalty for supplying a Class C drug was dramatically increased to fourteen years' imprisonment.

I believe reclassifying cannabis from B to C was unnecessary. All that was needed was to give borough commanders the authority to decide whether to place the emphasis on arrest or 'seize and warn', depending on what the local community wanted and on the level of the cannabis problem compared with other crimes locally. Reclassification was not necessary in order to save police time or to get officers to concentrate on more serious crime. As I told the *Independent* newspaper shortly afterwards, reclassification from my perspective was 'all pain and no gain'.

What people may not have realised was that I had been the borough commander in Merton for two years, where it never occurred to me to tell officers not to arrest people for possession of cannabis. We had sufficient police resources to be able to deal with almost all the law-breaking in that area. It was only when faced with a serious shortage of officers and rising levels of serious crime in Lambeth that I felt there was a need to ration policing in order to concentrate on the issues that were of most concern to the local community such as the dealing of Class A drugs and robbery. Of course the whole idea was sparked by the threatened 'work to rule' by officers who were going to arrest everyone they found with cannabis, gumming up the criminal justice system and possibly leading to another riot.

Looking back on it now, looking back at all the aggravation, looking back on how politicians intervened and how the whole thing ran away from me, clearly I would have done some things differently. For example, I would have resisted more firmly the extension of the pilot and the political interventions of Blunkett, but I would not have abandoned the idea of not arresting people for cannabis.

CHAPTER EIGHTEEN

Every eight weeks it was my turn to become the ACPO (senior officer) on call. That meant if any serious incident cropped up in the Met area in the middle of the night then it was my telephone that would ring. I was the ACPO on call for the first time on Saturday 3 March 2001, when I sat in for Tim Godwin who wanted to go to Twickenham to watch a rugby international.

That evening I was attending the National Domino Championship, a highly competitive event held at Brixton Town Hall. I was there in an official capacity to hand out the trophies. The event was supposed to finish at eleven p.m. but a series of particularly close-fought contests meant that I didn't get away until midnight. Just as I put my head down on the pillow the phone rang.

A taxi had exploded outside the BBC Television Centre in Wood Lane causing extensive damage. My first night on call and here I was, dealing with an IRA bombing. I lived ten minutes from Scotland Yard so I was quickly in command in the control room. My role was to coordinate, making sure there were sufficient resources on the ground, that the area was cordoned off, that officers from the anti-terrorist branch were en route and to deal with the inevitable press enquiries. At about two in the morning I phoned the commissioner, Sir John Stevens, and told him what had happened and that everything was under control.

The Met operates on a 'no surprises' principle; it was important for the commissioner to know what had happened as soon as possible rather than leaving him to wake up and hear it on the news. It happened to be one of the many weekends he spent in Northumbria, so he thanked me for alerting him and told me to phone the deputy commissioner, Ian Blair, and inform him, which I did.

Because Lambeth had a very high number of rape cases, we had a dedicated team of specially trained officers, Sexual Offences Investigation Techniques officers (SOITs). These uniformed officers led the rape victim through the investigative process, taking samples and statements. Unlike other boroughs, where nominated officers on each shift performed the role of SOIT when required, we had a full-time team working alongside the detectives who were hunting the rapists. Initially, our SOITs were female officers, but later a number of male personnel also became SOIT officers.

Our team also had the benefit of operating with a new and valuable innovation created by Assistant Commissioner Tim Godwin, who had set up a number of 'havens' – victim examination suites which were attached to local hospitals. Rape victims could 'self-refer' at any time (even months after the incident had taken place), be looked after in pleasant surroundings and, if they consented, could have samples taken from them. Even if they did not want the police involved, the samples could be stored confidentially in case they changed their minds, or could be used anonymously for intelligence (rather than prosecution) purposes. The medical staff also provided advice on sexually transmitted diseases and birth control. When a victim came to a police station, or was found by the police at the scene of a rape, she would be taken to the haven. It was an excellent system, a real breakthrough that made the trauma of rape and the consequences of police involvement a little easier for victims.

Channel 4 wanted to make a documentary about our SOIT unit, which would follow a number of cases. I agreed, with the proviso that we protected the identities of the victims. Overall, it was an excellent programme and gave the police some much-needed positive publicity – there was one small but significant problem, however. I went to a preview screening at the Channel 4 building in Horseferry Road at which some of the female SOIT officers were present, as well as the detective superintendent in charge and the Channel 4 team. When we were asked for our comments at the end of the preview clips I said, 'Am I the only one to have noticed that on the wall of the CID office there is a calendar of a woman with exposed breasts?'

This image should never have been on the wall and it would certainly have been very embarrassing if it had appeared in a documentary about female rape. Nobody believed me, so I made them rewind the tape. The picture was just visible in the background while a well-informed detective delivered a monologue to the camera. Channel 4 agreed to pixilate the image and the offending calendar was immediately removed from the wall in the office.

On 16 July 2001, we received an emergency call from a man who said he had seen someone with a small handgun enter the estate where he lived. In fact, it was a cigarette lighter in the shape of a gun being carried by Derek Bennett, a twenty-nine-year-old with mental health problems.

When the police arrived they chased Bennett towards a block of flats. As the officers closed in, Bennett grabbed a passer-by, fifty-three-year-old John Knightly, and held the 'weapon' to his head. The officers shouted at him to let go; Knightly was also convinced it was a real gun.

Knightly wriggled free, at which point Mr Bennett turned the 'gun' on the police and tried to take cover behind a pillar. As Knightly ducked into a doorway, the police opened fire, hitting Bennett four times in the back. When Knightly looked out, Bennett was lying on the ground, dead.

I had been away on holiday since before the shooting and was still away when, on 20 July 2001, a public demonstration about the shooting turned into a riot as night fell.

Officers in riot gear were drafted in from other parts of London and managed to quell the violence quite quickly. As soon as it was over an investigation was launched and a team of officers based at Kennington police station seized all the local authority CCTV footage in an effort to identify those involved in the rioting.

*

A week or so later, DCI Keith Gausden gave me a call. 'Boss, I've got some video I think you ought to see.' We watched it together in my office. The video was shot after dark in the pouring rain. In a gap in the shops, where Brighton Terrace meets Brixton Road, was a line of police officers in full riot gear. They were clearly visible in their flameproof overalls, along with their 'NATO' helmets and round plastic shields, stretched across the gap between two rows of shops. From the left of the screen I saw a young black man, being chased by yet more officers. He was going at such a rate that he actually managed to run though the line of officers before he slipped in the wet and crashed to the ground.

As he lay there helpless, the pursuing officers caught up and surrounded him until I could no longer see him. However, I could see the batons being raised high above the policemen's heads before they came down again; many blows rained down, time and again. At that point, a man and woman who were walking along Brixton Road together tried to intervene and attempted to pass between the line of officers. One of the officers pushed the woman away with his plastic shield (breaking her arm as we later discovered). I then briefly caught sight of the young black man as he scrabbled to his feet and dashed off into the darkness.

It was not quite as graphic as the Rodney King video, but it was close. After amateur footage of the beating King had received at the hands of the Los Angeles Police found its way on to the news in 1991, and the police officers were acquitted of assault the following year, the city had erupted into the worst rioting it had ever seen – leading to fifty-five deaths. I was extremely concerned as to what effect this video would have if it became public knowledge, especially as we had just had a riot after a contentious police shooting. I had visions of Lambeth going up in smoke. It was entirely my responsibility as to what I was going to do about this.

With DCI Gausden in my office I made three telephone calls. I called my boss, Assistant Commissioner Mike Todd, Andy Hayman, head of Internal Investigation, and Jennifer Douglas, chair of the Community Police Consultative Group. Jennifer and I agreed which trusted community leaders should be gathered together to be briefed on the incident. After making sure that none of them were witnesses whose evidence might be influenced by seeing the video, I sat them down and showed them the footage.

After it had finished, there was a stunned silence. I told them that I would ensure every possible effort was made to identify the officers responsible and prosecute them. What I needed from them now was to keep the matter confidential, at least for the moment, because I did not want the officers involved alerted. I had put all my cards on the table and they respected that; they trusted me.

When Sir John Stevens found out that I had told members of the community, he, according to Mike Todd, 'went ballistic'. Apparently, what I should have done was say nothing to the community until we had identified, arrested and charged the officers – which, in this case, was three months later – at which point I would have been able to give the community the good news that the matter had already been dealt with.

If I had waited to go to the community only at that point they would have asked, 'Why are you only telling us this now, when you knew about it months ago? . . . How many other incidents have happened, where you haven't been able to prosecute the officers, that you have not told us about?' What I learnt from that experience was that you *can* trust the community and be open and honest with them, even when it is in relation to something that is potentially devastating.

Only two officers were prosecuted over the events of that night. Although it was clear what was happening, the video quality was not good enough to identify most of those involved and the witnesses could not be certain that it was these men who had assaulted the young black man, who never came forward. Both officers were acquitted.

In 2004, an inquest into the original shooting, that of Derek Bennett, which had led to the rioting, recorded a verdict of lawful killing, much to the distress of Bennett's family. The decision was upheld on appeal in 2006.

Not long after this, Her Majesty's Inspectorate of Constabulary carried out an inspection of Lambeth. The HMIC inspections involved meetings of the inspectors with officers and support staff from the borough of every rank and grade, and with members of the community, as well as looking at the crime statistics, budgets and other information. I was interviewed by the chief inspector of the constabulary, Sir Keith Povey. The crime statistics for Lambeth, although improving, still did not make for very good reading, but when the report was published the recommendations were constructive rather than critical.

The report made clear that there was a need for the reinstatement of geographic command. This was the chance I had been waiting for to implement the changes I had wanted to make when I first took over in Lambeth. On 20 December 2001, I took my senior management team on a two-day away-day to the Union Jack Club in Waterloo. Through a series of presentations and discussions, I steered the team towards the inevitable decision that we had to have better accountability, and that meant geographic responsibility. Kennington and Clapham, Brixton and Streatham would each have their own superintendent with overall responsibility for their part of the borough and the CID officers at the various locations. My deputy, a chief superintendent, would have day-to-day operational responsibility, leaving me in overall charge. Not only did this system prove to be effective in Lambeth, it was later used as the template for other large failing boroughs across London.

While I had won over most of my staff, the various groups who attended Lambeth's Community Police Consultancy Group (CPCG) meetings tried to make my life as difficult as possible. One of these groups was Movement for Justice (strapline: 'By Any Means Possible'), an anti-police anarchist movement. Their leader, Alex Alowade, who had been one of the driving forces behind the protests that followed the shooting of Derek Bennett, seized on particular cases which he felt showed the police in a poor light. Often they would target people who had been arrested to try and get them to make an official complaint against the police.

One such incident involved a black couple who were driving through Streatham in the early hours when they almost drove over a very large, muscular and very drunk scaffolder who had staggered into the middle of the road. MFJ's allegation was that the scaffolder, without any provocation, had pulled the driver (who was much smaller) out of his car and had badly beaten him in a completely unprovoked, racially motivated attack.

They argued that the police had treated the black couple like suspects instead of victims; a sure sign of institutional racism. I promised Alex that I would get one of my senior detectives to investigate the incident. He managed to get hold of CCTV footage which showed us very clearly what had *really* happened.

The scaffolder was indeed very drunk and was stumbling up the middle of the road. The car had driven very quickly towards – arguably, directly at – him and had braked at the last moment, so the bonnet was almost touching his legs. The scaffolder, who was upset at almost being run over, shouted at the driver.

The driver climbed out of his car, went to the rear and opened the boot from where he took a knife. This action caused the scaffolder to sober up in record time; he wrestled the knife out of the driver's grip and chased his assailant down the road before throwing the weapon away.

The scaffolder had then assaulted the driver but the police had arrested both parties, the scaffolder for assault and the driver for possession of the knife. It was clearer now how the complaint that the 'victim of the unprovoked racist attack' had been 'treated like a suspect' by the police.

Alex Alowade refused to believe me and continued to present a distorted picture to the public meeting about what the police had done. At the following meeting, I set up a video screen and a projector connected to a VCR and announced that I had CCTV footage of the incident and that I intended to show anyone who was interested what had actually happened. Alowade protested that this was unfair, that the 'victims' had not had a chance to see the video first, and that it should not be shown. I told the meeting that it was quite clear from the CCTV footage what had taken place and that it directly contradicted what Movement for Justice were saying.

In the end, I didn't need to show the video and Alowade never challenged me on this issue again.

*

As a commander, one of the most difficult things to deal with is a 'death in police custody', a term that describes any death where the police might have had some involvement with the fatality. Not long after the tragic death of Derek Bennett, we had another. On this occasion the police had been called to a block of flats where immigration officers suspected an illegal immigrant was staying. On arrival, they knocked on the door and announced who they were before being let in. The flat was on a high floor and as they searched for the man in question they heard a dull thud.

When they looked out of an already open window they saw an apparently lifeless body lying on the concrete directly below them. It was not the person the officers were seeking, but another asylum seeker who, apparently fearing capture and deportation, had either decided to jump from the window or had tried to hide on an outside ledge, lost his footing and had dropped to his death. This led to another intense CPCG meeting where the question 'Did he fall or was he pushed?' was repeatedly asked. Local community groups were very critical; the feeling was that we could have done something to prevent what had happened, but I couldn't see what my officers could have done differently in the circumstances.

In a third tragedy, a young black man had been stopped by the police on suspicion of dealing in crack cocaine. They had seen him put something in his mouth and had taken him to Brixton police station to search him.

Believing that the suspect must have swallowed the drugs, officers called an ambulance. It took a while for the crew to arrive, during which time the young man consistently denied that he had swallowed anything and still appeared to be unaffected when he left in the ambulance. Five minutes after arriving at the hospital he suffered a massive heart attack and died.

The man's death was met with grief and disbelief by friends and family. Thanks to constraints put in place by the Police Complaints Authority, we were unable to give the family or the community any information. By the next CPCG meeting we still did not have the toxicology report, which clearly showed that the heart attack had been caused by a massive overdose of cocaine. As far as some in the community were concerned, Ricky Bishop, who was a fitness fanatic, was carted off in a police van, handcuffed and beaten to death.

Thankfully I was able to call in my trusted community leaders and show them some more CCTV. There was footage which showed Ricky sitting quietly and uninjured in the custody area, waiting for the ambulance to take him to hospital. There was also footage of Ricky sitting quietly and without a mark on him in the casualty department of the hospital waiting to be seen by a doctor. Within minutes of those latter images, Ricky was dead.

Of course nothing is ever straightforward and Richard Littlejohn's catchphrase 'You couldn't make it up' was never more applicable than at Lambeth. One of the officers involved in the struggle with Ricky asked his colleagues to cover for him since, among other things, he had an acrylic non-extendable baton in his locker that should not have been there. Although he was about to be public-order trained (which is why he had the baton), until he had completed the training, which included techniques on how to use the baton properly, he should not have had it.

Whenever there is a death in custody, Internal Investigation officers ask all the officers involved to hand in their protective equipment. Thinking his locker would be searched, the officer panicked and asked a colleague if he would take the acrylic baton and put it in his locker. His colleague immediately went to his inspector and told him what had happened; the inspector told me and I told Internal Investigation. The officer's panic reaction could have turned what was largely an innocent situation into a real problem for the police service. It was very interesting for me though, that this young officer had been reported by a colleague, because in the past officers would have closed ranks.

Unfortunately, the CPCG were not as generous in their assessment of what had happened, and at the next meeting I was under intense fire from angry members who barraged me with questions:

'Since July there have been three deaths in police custody. How many more are going to die?'

'Why have the names of the officers not been released? How can it be an independent investigation when it is being carried out by the Met's own internal investigations department?'

'What does it take to have an officer suspended?'

'There should be an independent post-mortem.'

'This is yet another death at the hands of the police.'

'Why do the police lie?'

A man in the back row, wearing a cap, said, 'Do you realise how people feel? People fear and hate the police with a passion!'

I had seen the CCTV footage so I was able to reassure the officers at an early stage that, as far as I was concerned, they had done their duty and there was no evidence to say otherwise. A subsequent inquest and post-mortem found the only force that had been used against the victim was reasonable and had no effect on Ricky's death; it was the high levels of cocaine in Ricky's bloodstream which had caused his heart attack.

The Police Complaints Authority had refused to release any information about the toxicology results, even though this was vital to reassure the community that the person had not died as a result of the police's use of force. The PCA claimed their refusal was on grounds of confidentiality and respect for the family. The fact that we might have had another riot on our hands did not, apparently, figure in the PCA's thinking.

The community's furious and outraged response to these deaths and incidents made what followed when I was removed as borough commander all the more remarkable.

CHAPTER NINETEEN

A major handicap in trying to stem the high levels of crime was that we were one hundred officers short of the minimum nine hundred that had been allocated to Lambeth.

When I addressed community meetings, I talked about the high levels of crime, explained our shortfall in officers, and told them that as far as I could see, because of the formula used to distribute police officers across London, there was no realistic prospect of the situation improving in the near future. What I could guarantee, however, was that we were trying everything we could think of to reduce crime and to provide the best service we possibly could.

Afterwards, people told me, 'Your predecessors would come along to our meetings and tell us things were going to improve and things would be better in a few months' time; they never did. Thank God we've got someone now who tells us the truth.'

A reworking of the Resource Allocation Formula that decided how many officers should be given to each borough suggested Lambeth should have one hundred officers less than the previous formula.

At a meeting with the chief executive of the local council, Mike Todd and Deputy Commissioner Ian Blair tried (and failed) to explain the RAF. Blair told the meeting that he understood the significance of Lambeth's problems, such as the scale of deprivation. 'We want to support the borough,' he said. 'For example, we've given you one of our finest officers as your borough commander.' It was not the last time that Ian Blair was supportive of me.

Lambeth council provided me with strong support in my campaign to at least maintain the allocation at the same level as the last formula. I argued that what counted most was local people's safety; no resident in London should be at any greater risk than any other resident of becoming a victim, no matter which borough they lived in, and police resources should be allocated so as to ensure this.

The Met carried out an annual survey to see how safe people felt across different boroughs. To my surprise, towards the end of my time in charge, people in Lambeth felt as safe as the residents of Bromley, where crime levels were half those of Lambeth. I think that people's fear of crime is not simply about the amount of crime happening around them, or even whether or not they themselves have been the victims of crime, but about lack of trust and confidence in their local police service and their local police chief.

As a result of the battle over the RAF (which we won after another statistical analysis revealed that Lambeth was an exception to the rule), a local BBC TV reporter called Penny Wrout, who regularly covered Lambeth in her reports, did a piece to camera from Brixton Road. She said, 'Every day Commander Paddick takes a step closer to the people of Lambeth and a step further away from his bosses at New Scotland Yard. Putting his loyalty to the people of Lambeth over his loyalty to his senior officers will not win him many friends in Scotland Yard.'

She was right, but I had achieved my professional ambition by becoming commander of Lambeth and all I wanted to do was spend the rest of my career there, doing the best for those who worked with me and those I worked for: the people of Lambeth.

This was never going to be an easy task and it was not just down to the numbers of police officers. While the borough of Westminster had money in the bank and other London boroughs had only small deficits, Lambeth was £1.2 billion in debt and had £1 billion in outstanding repairs to council properties to carry out. The government had decided that no additional financial aid should be given to the borough and it had got to the stage where a great deal of public anger was directed towards the council's apparent inability to deliver.

*

There was also a major problem with drug dealing in Brixton. It was centred on Coldharbour Lane between the junctions of Brixton Road and Atlantic Road. My predecessors regularly conducted lengthy large-scale surveillance operations, where undercover officers were videotaped buying drugs to secure evidence against the dealers.

These dangerous operations took months of evidence-gathering before officers would swoop and pick up twenty or so street dealers in what would be a spectacular raid with lots of media coverage. The trade was so lucrative, however, that there was no shortage of street dealers willing to replace those we arrested (who were considered expendable by their masters), and normal service was typically resumed within a couple of days. Infiltrating the higher echelons of the highly organised criminal network of drug dealers proved very difficult and was not always effective in long-term crime reduction.

Clearly, we could not just sit by and let the dealers carry on their trade with impunity, but without the help of specialist units at Scotland Yard, the National Criminal Intelligence Service (NCIS), and the expertise of the security services, we were never going to have much of an impact on drug dealing since we were unable to remove those who supplied the street dealers or those importing the drugs. Just taking out the street dealers was like cutting down weeds without taking out the roots.

The courage and enthusiasm shown by my officers as they engaged with the street dealers was extraordinary. On the rare occasions when they were assaulted I was amazed at how it made them even more determined to go back and carry on the fight. Many street dealers were kept in check by a fearless group of town-centre patrol officers. These were a small band of unarmed uniformed officers who were totally dedicated to making Brixton town centre safer. They worked with local authority camera operators, who monitored the CCTV and guided the officers to drug deals in progress. When my officers grabbed hold of the dealer, they would invariably have to extract the crack or heroin from his mouth by prising open the dealer's jaw – an activity which appeared very alarming to passers-by. While two or more officers wrestled with the dealer, a third would be engaged in explaining to the gathering crowd what was going on. This was no easy job; a WPC sustained a serious injury during one such operation.

The street dealers were often armed with handguns. Thankfully, none of them ever used their weapon to shoot or to threaten one of my officers. Guns were used to ensure that punters paid for their drugs and to ward off rival dealers trying to take over the patch. Usually the weapon was found in the course of the search, and sometimes they would throw the gun away while they were being chased by the police.

On one embarrassing occasion, Securicor arrived the morning after an alleged drug dealer had been arrested to take him to court. The Securicor staff found a handgun hidden in the underpants of the dealer who, with his gun, had been locked in a police cell overnight.

I believe that not many people in Lambeth realised just how often policemen and women risked their lives in an attempt to make life better for the people that lived there. I have talked a great deal here about the bad apples in the police, but the overwhelming majority of police officers are hard-working and courageous men and women for whom I have the utmost admiration. The majority do not deserve the almost daily criticisms which are levelled at the police by the media. Nor do they deserve the poor leadership they often have to suffer at the hands of senior officers.

While street robbery continued to be a major focus of my efforts in Lambeth and took up much of my time, I was given the occasional distraction, like the one provided for me by officers from Operation Trident, who mounted a significant operation on my patch without first telling me or any of my officers.

It started when police stopped a car at Heathrow. The vehicle had been linked to a series of shootings and a murder. The driver told the officers that it was his son's car and gave an address in Lambeth where he thought his son lived, or was at least where he was staying on a temporary basis.

Officers from Operation Trident quickly obtained a warrant to raid the address the driver had given them. I was blissfully unaware that a team of armed officers was racing into Lambeth, ready to stage a major raid.

From their limited observations when they got there, it appeared that there was some sort of party going on. Despite the fact that it was highly likely there would be a great many people inside, the armed officers were instructed to go ahead and raid the house. They stormed into the party, screaming at everybody to get down on the floor. One of the people present was already lying down.

It was the man in the coffin.

They had raided a wake. The suspect was not at the house and nobody there had heard of him. The alarm and distress caused to the grieving family can only be imagined and, needless to say, when I was finally alerted to what had happened I was incensed. Being used to following the horse with my shovel and bucket, I knew this was going to be another 'difficult' meeting. Whatever the operation was and whatever unit carried it out, if it was on my borough, I had to deal with the aftermath and face the community.

It was not until many years later that I realised how successful my intervention had been. I had gone for a swim at a local authority swimming pool in Camden when, in the changing rooms, I was confronted by a very muscular, heavily tattooed and scary looking black man, who had a rather menacing look on his face which was accentuated by the fact that one of his front teeth was missing.

His aggressive appearance was slightly tempered by his green Speedos and the swimming goggles strapped to his forehead. Nonetheless, being accosted by what was clearly a powerful individual whose opening words were 'I know you' was a little unsettling.

My unease only increased when he went on to explain that he knew me from Brixton, and turned to apprehension when he told me that he had been at that wake. Apprehension turned to genuine alarm when he added, 'It was my father's wake.'

I apologised and told him about my visit to speak to his mother about the incident; about how I had said sorry, and explained the reasons why it had happened.

'Yes, I know, I was there. My mum still talks about you, you know. You're the only police officer who ever showed any compassion.'

You never know when your past is going to catch up with you and in this case, I was glad that there was a happy ending.

I had benefited from those brave gay men and lesbians who had been open about their sexuality in the pioneering days when life was much more difficult for homosexuals. They had helped to change public attitudes and I now thought it was my turn to push the boundaries.

On the anniversary of the publication of the MacPherson Report into the death of Stephen Lawrence, the Met wanted to do a media piece about diversity, featuring interviews with three senior officers – commanders – from minority backgrounds: one black, one female, and one gay.

'Guess which one I am?' I asked colleagues when I told them about the plan, but the idea was too cheesy, even for *G2*, and it was dropped. From my days in Merton I had developed a good professional relationship with a journalist from the *Financial Times*, Jimmy Burns. He had known for a long time that I was gay and volunteered to be the journalist to tell the world. The then commissioner, Sir John Stevens, had wanted a 'managed outing' rather than lurid tabloid headlines when I was in the middle of some policing crisis, so everything was set.

I 'came out' in a Saturday edition of the *Financial Times*, in the middle of an article about the changing face of the Met, in a sentence which read, 'Brian Paddick, the UK's most senior openly gay police officer . . .' The world could easily have missed the announcement so, just to be sure, the subeditor had used the line as the caption for the photograph.

The reaction was positive – at least to begin with. I had no problems at work and no attacks appeared in the press. Some time later I received a call from Mary; the *Mail on Sunday* were trying to track her down but had just missed her as she had moved home a week before the journalists called. It sent a chill down my spine to know they were after me.

CHAPTER TWENTY

On Friday 21 December 2001, Movement for Justice planned another protest over the death of Derek Bennett. I decided not to allow the march to go as far as its planned destination of Brixton Town Hall, bearing in mind the last time that happened there was a riot.

That evening I was at a Christmas party with Michael and friends in Earls Court when I received a call from one of my superintendents who was leading the operation. He told me that the crowd had become hostile after they were prevented from turning towards the town centre and there had been calls from community leaders for me to intervene.

I immediately left the party and headed to Brixton. At the police station I bumped into Ivelaw Bowman, a black preacher and community leader and Nick Long, then the Metropolitan Police Authority member with responsibility for Lambeth and a former deputy chair of the Lambeth Community Police Consultative Group, and we went together to the top of Brixton Road where the crowd was being held. I took command of the situation and ordered that the protestors be released in groups of six. Apart from some unpleasant verbal abuse levelled at my officers who were holding people back, there was no violence.

When I returned to work after the Christmas break, my staff officer, a wonderful man called Noel Craggs, drew my attention to a community website called Urban 75 which was based in Brixton. Several people had posted messages saying they were at the demonstration and that the police had beaten them with batons. As I worked my way through the threads it soon became apparent there was a general tirade of allegations of brutality, all of which, from what I had witnessed, were untrue and unjustified. I asked my staff officer to keep an eye on the site to see if they were repeated or became worse. They were and they did.

In January I decided that I could not allow this anti-police propaganda to continue any longer; neither would I allow my officers to be libelled in this way. I decided to become a participant in the bulletin boards to put the police's side of the argument since no one else appeared prepared to do so.

I logged on as 'Brian the Commander'.

Was this a wise move? I was doing this at home in my own time, on my own without a press officer or advisor. I went on to the website to defend the reputation of my officers. I wrote about the demonstration and that from all I had seen, the crowd was well treated by the police.

This site gave me a unique chance to debate with sections of the community who the police would normally never get to engage with – people who would never have gone to the town hall or to the police station for a meeting with the police. While some were clearly activists and agitators, all sorts of other people took part, from doctors to local parents, who were simply concerned about issues relevant to Brixton.

One of the benefits of the Internet is anonymity, but there is also the potential for impersonation, so there was a healthy dose of scepticism from everyone, including the person who ran the site, as to who 'Brian the Commander' really was. At first nobody was willing to believe he really was their local police chief, but people gradually came to accept that it *was* me.

Once I'd established my credentials, a captivating debate developed which soon spread to drug issues. It was, shall we say, a 'free and frank exchange of views'.

In one often-quoted section, where I was giving my personal view that drug addicts are the victims of drug dealers, I posted 'Help the addicts, screw the dealers.' This was unconventional language for a police commander, but you have to talk to people in their own language.

Inevitably, with a number of anarchists on the bulletin boards, the discussion turned to anarchy. As far as the anarchists were concerned, the police were the lapdogs of their capitalist masters, a view I vehemently disagreed with. I was doing everything I could to help the ordinary people of Lambeth and to be described in these terms was both offensive and untrue. Thinking back over the previous year to the Resource Allocation Formula debacle, I posted 'Lapdogs sometimes turn round and bite their owners.'

At university, when studying philosophy, I had come across the concept of anarchism – as opposed to anarchy. I thought it a naively appealing philosophical theory, based on the apparent absence (since refuted) of evidence of violence between prehistoric humans. My understanding of what anarchists believe is that humankind is innately good but has been corrupted by society, government, laws, and the police.

To bring about the anarchistic version of paradise you had to eliminate all of these structures and only then would the innate goodness of man re-emerge, allowing us all to live happily ever after. As Lord Harris, former chair of the Metropolitan Police Authority, would have said, 'Interesting if true.' On one of the bulletins I said that the concept of anarchism appealed to me but I thought that there would always be bad people and mad people so you would always need laws and always need the police.

I joined in this sort of debate because I wanted to win the trust and confidence of those who had a completely negative, one-sided view of law and order in general and the police in particular. I was trying to demonstrate that I was not dismissing their views out of hand and, by the same token, I did not want them to dismiss mine.

Similarly, I believe the way to combat extremists who corrupt Islam or promote racism is not to ban them but to debate their ideas so as to demonstrate to all right-minded people how wrong and untrue extremist beliefs really are. I joined the debate to defend my officers, the process of law and order and the police, not to undermine them.

Throughout January and February, the debate on Urban 75 continued. Unbeknown to me, one of the people posting on Urban 75 was a journalist. Just before Michael and I were due to leave on a three-week holiday to Thailand and Australia, on Monday 8 February 2002, the journalist contacted me through the website to tell me that he was planning to write an article about what was happening in the *Big Issue*. Somewhat 'demob happy' after fourteen months of intense pressure and looking forward to the holiday, I naively said nothing about his proposal.

I left my deputy, Brian Moore (later deputy chief constable of Surrey) in charge, and before I went on holiday, I instructed him not to call me – unless my job was at risk.

On Wednesday 20 February, Brian Moore called me on my mobile phone. The *Big Issue* had published the story on Tuesday, and by Wednesday I had made the front page of the *Sun* under the headline 'The Odd Bill'. All the national newspapers were full of comments about my 'discussions with anarchists' on Urban 75. Thanks to some careful editing, my website posts had been transformed into the ravings of a pro-drugs sympathiser who thought that the breakdown of law and order was a good idea.

The *Sun*, as inventive as ever, used the problems Brixton had with drug dealing, combined with reawakened interest in the cannabis pilot, to christen me 'Commander Crackpot' – hurtful, but nonetheless quite clever, I thought. The press coverage did not go down at all well with Mike Todd or Commissioner John Stevens, but it was Deputy Commissioner Ian Blair who called me and told me not to speak to the press, just to wait until I came back to the UK when things could be sorted out. He was calm and reassuring and I respected him for the way he handled the matter.

My grandfather, PC Perkin, was a constable in the Metropolitan Police Mounted Branch.

Being held by my mother (right) next to my twin brother, John, May 1958.

Me (right) and John.

Wearing a sleeveless pullover
hand knitted by my mother.
You can see where I acquired
my taste for formal dress.

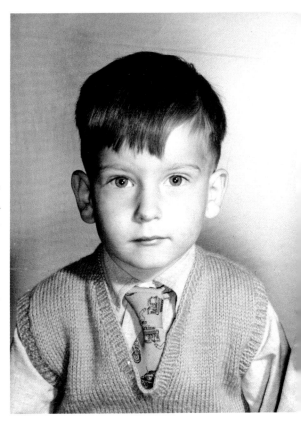

Sutton Manor High
School Swimming
Champion, 1976.

Playing rugby at the
Police Staff College
in Bramshill, 1981. I
am on the far right
of the picture.

In Inspector's uniform while at the University of Oxford, where I studied from 1983–86.

John and I posing for a photo accompanying an article in *Bankground*, the NatWest newspaper. The story followed my investigation of John's workplace, the International Trade and Business Services part of NatWest bank, as part of my MBA course at the University of Warwick.

Looking slightly chubby on holiday in the south of France with James Renolleau, 1999.

Making a statement outside Brixton Police Station on the day I was relieved of my command as Police Commander for Lambeth, 18 March 2002.

Marching with colleagues at London Gay Pride, 2004.

Speaking at the Liberal Democrat's Conference in Bournemouth, 2004.

With a fellow officer at my Passing Out Parade at Hendon, 17 December 2004.

With the pop group Queen at Hyde Park in 2005.

(Left to right) Frank Armstrong, of the City of London Police, me and Andy Trotter, of the British Transport Police, signing a book of condolence and laying flowers in Victoria Embankment Gardens following the 7/7 London bombings.

Boris entertaining Ken and I at the first TV debate of the 2008 Mayoral elections.

There I was, hoping to reward Michael for putting up with my late-night and weekend working, and instead I was on a tropical island surrounded by palm trees talking to the deputy commissioner on my mobile. On our last night in Thailand before moving on to Sydney, we were packing our bags when the phone on the bedside table rang.

'Is this Mr Paddick?'

'Yes, it is.'

'I'm a reporter from the *Daily Mail.*'

I hung up.

How do they do that? How was it possible for them to find out where I was staying?

The next call was from the head of the press department at Scotland Yard, who told me the media were waiting for me in Sydney and, if possible, I should alter my plans. Early the next morning we were waiting in reception for a taxi to take us to the airport when a reception-ist called me over. 'Mr Paddick, there's a call for you.'

On the other end of the phone was a reporter from *The Times*. As we talked, I could hear a strange echo. The reception was on a mez-zanine just above the restaurant where the waiting staff were busily collecting plates from breakfast and making quite a racket. I could hear the crashing around me and through the telephone, and at that point, I realised that the reporter was also in reception.

How do they do that?

It turned out he was a freelance reporter who worked for News International – essentially all the Murdoch papers in London. I refused to comment and we left for the airport. Instead of going straight to Sydney, we arranged to fly to Melbourne where we had some friends.

We arrived in the early hours and emerged from arrivals somewhat apprehensively but there were no reporters. Our friends were waiting and took us back to their place. We stayed the night there before con-tinuing on to Sydney where, to our great relief, there were no journalists waiting.

After checking in to our hotel, Michael and I unpacked and went to an early evening party. We returned to the hotel at about nine o'clock to find a note under the door which read, 'I am a BBC reporter and I'm waiting for you downstairs in reception.'

How do they do that?

I took pity on the poor chap who had been despatched all the way from London. I told him about the restrictions the deputy commissioner had placed on my talking to the media and I asked him how he managed to find us. Apparently a team of BBC researchers had worked through the night, phoning every hotel in Sydney until they found the one we were in: 'Can I speak to Mr Paddick please?' 'No one of that name staying here . . . We don't have a Mr Paddick . . . No Mr Paddick registered . . . No reply from his room.' Bingo!

When I complained to the staff at reception that they had handed out this information to a random caller without checking with me first, they told me I should have checked in as a 'silent guest'; the uniquely local term for remaining anonymous. They agreed to re-house us in a sister hotel as silent guests but not until the following day.

At nine a.m. the next morning, the BBC reporter confronted me with a tape recorder and I got out a few sentences before remembering I was under restrictions: 'I have been told that I cannot comment any further.' I then phoned the Yard's twenty-four-hour press bureau to explain what had happened.

While we were away, a friendly superintendent who had worked with me at Brixton, managed to ask a question on BBC Radio 4's *Any Questions* programme; he asked the panel what they thought about a police commander engaging with the public in the way that I had on Urban 75. The panel were unanimous in their support and one wag drew applause and laughter when he said, 'Times have changed. We used to have Dixon of Dock Green, now we have a Descartes of Dock Green.'

The reaction of people on Urban 75 was extraordinary. Back with our friends in Melbourne, we all gathered around their computer screen to look at the posts on the bulletin boards. There was strong support in the wake of the torrent of media criticism. The depth of feeling and the strength of support expressed in some of the comments brought tears to my eyes; it was a very emotionally charged time.

Geoff and Len had met James in London when we had been

together; indeed it was friends of theirs who lived in London, Allan and Brian, who had tried to persuade me to get back together with James when I decided to end the relationship. I talked to them about how there was a nagging doubt in the back of my mind that James might still do something to hurt me. I told them his favourite expression: 'Revenge is a dish best served cold.'

'Don't worry,' they said, 'he would never do anything thing like that.' How wrong can you be?

I was due back in the UK in the early hours of Saturday morning and had been told that I should be in Commissioner Stevens's office at nine a.m. on Monday to see him and Mike Todd about Urban 75. I was very anxious about what was going to be said at that meeting. I had never experienced such negative and personal criticism in the media before; I had featured heavily in almost every national newspaper in the UK every day for a week. A few newspapers had published balanced articles, but on the whole the coverage was overwhelmingly unfavourable.

After twenty hours of flying, Michael and I arrived, tired and jet-lagged, back at our recently acquired flat. What I was not expecting was an answerphone message from James Renolleau.

This unseen torpedo had been speeding towards me for some time, ever since a *Mail on Sunday* journalist, Fiona Wingett, had accosted James in an aeroplane as he flew to Miami on holiday. During the trip she said that, in return for his exclusive story about our relationship, he would be paid £25,000. James had asked to think about it and in the meantime he just wanted to enjoy his holiday.

Wingett continued to pester him while he was in Miami, in the baggage hall at Gatwick after his return flight landed, and then several times on the phone the following day, increasing the offer to £40,000. James hinted that he had a very interesting story to tell, that I had 'broken the law' and he would talk to a solicitor about striking a deal.

The newspaper's offer rose to £50,000, but James said he needed more as he would have to leave the country once the story was out.

He mentioned the sum of £100,000, hinting that there were many other salacious details. He had, meanwhile, also started talking to the *News of the World*, the *Mirror* and the *Evening Standard*. Desperate to secure the deal, Wingett told him that no other paper would take as good care of him as the *Mail on Sunday*; that they would take him out of London while the story broke. 'You know, the usual spiel,' as she wrote in an email to her editor.

As negotiations continued, James whetted the *Mail on Sunday*'s appetite with 'I smoke cannabis sometimes and, yes, Brian smoked with me sometimes . . . just a few puffs on a spliff, but that happened a few times.'

With the papers circling James, each of them vying with the others to snap him up for the exclusive, he hid in a quiet spot in Westminster Abbey from where he called Wingett and told her that he was leaving town to escape the journalists. Wingett told him that they would put him up in a central London hotel.

It was at this point that he had called me and left the message on my answering machine. When I called him back he told me he had 'done something stupid'. He said he had already done a tape-recorded interview with the *Mail on Sunday*.

He went into a long list of things he had told them, about our sex lives, about things that had happened before we had met, about me having to sell things in order to pay him what he was due when the relationship ended. 'And one other thing,' he said at the end, almost as an afterthought, 'I've told them about the cannabis.'

'What cannabis?'

'That you smoke cannabis.'

'But James, I've never smoked cannabis,' I replied angrily.

He told me he had been offered a large sum of money if he signed an agreement with the *Mail on Sunday*. He had employed a lawyer to draw up a confidentiality agreement but the newspaper had now told him that if he did not sign the contract, they would publish the story anyway because it was 'in the public interest'. As if trying to justify his actions, he said he had discussed it with some of his friends and they had told him the money would make a good deposit on a flat.

He also told me that he didn't want me to get into trouble or to

lose my job and he mistakenly thought that cannabis was now legal so
it was okay to talk about it. James appeared genuinely shocked when I
asked him whether he was prepared to go to court to back these claims.

Tired and angry, I suggested he took the money, 'go to France and
never come back'. At that time I had no idea about media law and it
hadn't even crossed my mind to take legal action; this was something
that celebrities did, not ordinary people like me.

Michael and I went into town and as we emerged from Goodge
Street underground in Tottenham Court Road my mobile rang. It was
James again. He told me not to worry because he was not going to go
ahead with the story.

We wondered whether to believe what James had just said. In fact,
he had already signed a £100,000 deal with the *Mail on Sunday*; he
would receive £50,000 on the Monday after publication, £30,000
eight days after the publication and £20,000 thirty days after publication. He never did move back to France.

After two weeks of defending myself from the media in relation to
my misquoted remarks on Urban 75, to find that James, who I had
loved and lived with for more than three years, was going to level
huge false accusations at me . . . well, it was my worst nightmare.

I was still trying to recover from being 'upside-down' for three
weeks and was already dreading the meeting at the commissioner's
office on Monday morning over Urban 75. The fear of what might be
contained in a forthcoming edition of the *Mail on Sunday* sent me into
a level of anxiety that was so high as to be unreal.

The *Mail on Sunday* flew James to Vienna to do the interviews. He
told them where we met, discussed our holidays, talked about himself
being on bail, and our meeting his family. He filled them in on trips
to Brighton, outings to bars and clubs, talked about the cannabis, and
alleged that we had sex in public places. He discussed my divorce and
coming out, my supposed extravagance, my family, other personal
relationships, and my ambitions. The drug-taking claims were false,
and much of the information about our life together should never
have been printed.

In the meantime, the anarchy comments needed to be dealt with. It was with much trepidation that I travelled into Scotland Yard on Monday morning to sit down with the commissioner, John Stevens, and Assistant Commissioner Mike Todd. The commissioner seemed quite relaxed, but Todd looked as though he was trying to keep his anger in check. He produced 'my' press statement and told me this was the only thing I would be allowed to say about the whole issue. I started to read it, much to the commissioner's irritation. The statement sounded as though I was admitting I had made a serious mistake and had brought all this upon myself.

'The trouble is,' I said, 'I don't agree with it.'

I saw the commissioner's eyes widen in an angry stare. He had a fearsome reputation for having a bad temper and, although he had never lost his temper with me, I could see from his eyes that there could be a first time for everything.

'If this is the only opportunity I've got to speak, then at least I should be able to agree the wording,' I said. The commissioner's eyes quickly returned to normal as he turned to Todd and said, 'He's got a point, you know.' Todd was furious.

Just before Mike Todd and I left to work on the wording, the commissioner said to me, 'Is there going to be anything else?'

'One of my exs has told me he was planning to do a kiss-and-tell story to a Sunday newspaper, but he's since said he's changed his mind.'

'Well, what was he going to say?'

'Amongst other things, that he had drugs in my flat.'

'What type of drugs?'

'Cannabis.'

'Oh, that's all right then.'

That was it; end of conversation. The commissioner seemed to have taken the whole thing in his stride.

The following week was relatively uneventful and I carried on as normal at Lambeth. Todd had given me strict instructions not to talk to the press. I thought that applied only to Urban 75, but on Thursday

I attended the launch of a local, Lambeth-based version of Operation Trident and, as I left Brixton Town Hall, I was doorstepped by the same BBC radio reporter who had confronted me in Sydney. I commented on the Trident Launch, but nothing else.

When Todd heard I had spoken to the BBC he went through the roof, saying that I had disobeyed his instructions not to talk to the press. I had had enough. I asked to see the commissioner. At the entrance to his office he was talking to his then chief of staff, Suzanna Becks, and said to me cheerfully, 'Come on in, Brian, you don't mind if Suzanna sits in on this do you?'

'Yes, Commissioner, actually I do.'

'Well . . . okay then, come on in.'

I told him that I thought Todd was being unreasonable and he saw my point. I said that perhaps Todd was concerned that he, the commissioner, would be angry that I had broken the embargo, whereas I had understood it to apply only to talking about Urban 75.

'The trouble is, Commissioner,' I said, 'your senior officers are afraid of you.'

'Afraid of me, Brian? Surely not?' He smiled broadly and winked at me.

CHAPTER TWENTY-ONE

On Saturday 16 March, Michael was at work when there was a knock at the door to my flat; not the locked door to the street connected to a video entry phone system but my own front door. I didn't answer. A voice shouted, 'Mr Paddick, I'm a reporter from the *Mail on Sunday* and I want to talk to you about what Mr Renolleau has told us.'

I ignored him and he went away. I then called a friend of Michael's who worked as a PR consultant. He told me that I ought to speak to them because they would then be duty bound to report my side of the story. I explained that James had smoked cannabis in our flat, even though I had tried to stop him. My PR friend said that by telling the paper this much, it would make my denial of smoking cannabis even more credible. If you are completely honest, he argued, then that is more powerful in terms of public relations.

I called the *Mail on Sunday* and spoke to the news desk who arranged for me to meet two reporters, Paul Henderson and Jason Lewis, in the lobby of the Mandarin Oriental Hotel, Knightsbridge at three o'clock that afternoon. We sat in a corner, and Henderson asked questions while Lewis took down what I said in shorthand. My first question was, 'Is this being taped?'

'No.'

They were lying. I eventually got hold of a copy of the recording.

None of the allegations they put to me in the interview were a surprise after the phone call from James the previous weekend. Sure enough, he said that I had smoked cannabis and that it was kept in our flat. I strenuously denied smoking cannabis or knowingly allowing him to keep it in our home.

I also asked them, 'What chance have I got of a fair hearing?'

'Very good,' Henderson replied. 'Whatever you say we'll print.' He then asked me if there was anyone else who might come forward.

'Depends how much you pay them,' I said, adding, 'I bet you're not going to print that.' Then I went on. 'What I would say is, I am a senior police officer and clearly some allegations are a matter of public interest. If there are allegations that I have broken the criminal law or I did not comply with regulations then I am very happy to answer for those allegations. When it comes to things that I said to James when I was in a relationship with him, they are not matters of public interest, they are very personal.'

That evening Michael and I went to have dinner with his brother and his wife, although I was not feeling at all hungry or very sociable. My stomach churned as I waited for the *Mail on Sunday* to hit the stands later that night.

On Sunday 17 March, the *Mail on Sunday* did a joint exclusive with the *People*. The *People* ran the story about our sex lives and did not mention the allegations about cannabis.

The *Mail on Sunday* headline was: 'Smoking pot, picking up strangers for sex in public, cruising swim pools for conquests . . . gay saunas and unprotected acts with AIDS victims.' In the *People*, James said: 'It's his character to do stupid things and I told him.' Well, the most stupid thing I ever did was get involved with him.

In the *Mail on Sunday* meanwhile, James alleged that I had smoked about a hundred joints (I did wonder wryly if they had offered him £1,000 for every one he was prepared to say I had smoked). When Fiona Wingett interviewed James in Vienna, she had probed him for details, dates, times, locations – things he was unable to provide. 'We need more detail,' she said, 'because obviously we're accusing a senior policeman of using drugs, and it's a big deal because it's illegal. What they want is to see if you can remember any specific times that you did it. You know, it was the World Cup football or the Olympics and you are sitting there and . . .'

James thought for a moment. 'At weekends. Saturday night . . . I can't remember specific times.' Needless to say, this part of the interview failed to make the paper.

During the same interview, when Wingett turned her attention to our sex life she got extremely personal, and James naively told her everything she wanted to know, adding 'I don't want to see this in the newspaper', as if that would stop them.

There were a total of nine pages of coverage in the *Mail*, including the front page. To fill out the columns they had included everything they could think of, from where we bought our TV (James said we got it from Harrods when in fact we bought it from Currys opposite Wimbledon dog track) to what skin care products I used.

After what had been the most dreadful weekend of my life, it took all my courage to go into work on that Monday morning. I was lucky enough to have a pool attached to the block of flats in which I then lived. I had decided to go for a swim before work to try to release some of the stress, only to find a journalist peering in through the window at me.

I knew that the blanket ban on talking to the media was about to be imposed again, and I also guessed that this would be the final straw for me as far as Mike Todd was concerned. My plan was to go on a seven a.m. visit to see the officers parading at Clapham police station. How on earth Penny Wrout from BBC London and her film crew knew I was going to be there on this unplanned visit at that time of the morning I will never know.

Having issued a brief denial of James's allegations to camera, I went to talk to the officers in the canteen at Brixton and asked them what they thought. Most had not seen the article, and those that had were sympathetic. However, they were concerned that people would believe the allegations of law-breaking, which would make it very difficult for me to carry on as the borough commander.

Then the inevitable call came to see Mike Todd who was at Imber Court, a police sports ground near Thames Ditton. He was with the commissioner, and the rest of the management board, for an away day. Ironically, this was where my grandfather had trained when he joined the police's mounted section.

When Mike Todd came to meet me he said he had discussed the issues at length with his management board colleagues. They had decided that it would be unfair for me to have to deal with issues arising out of this kiss-and-tell story alongside the many challenges I would face as borough commander of Lambeth. And he said I was not allowed to talk to the press. 'Change the record,' I thought to myself.

'I don't think that's a lawful order.'

'Well, we think it is.'

'Well, in that case, you'll have to add it to the list of charges.'

I asked him if I could talk to Ian Blair. 'I don't know,' said Todd, 'I'll ask him.' Sure enough, the next person to enter the room was Ian Blair.

I said, 'You've always been very supportive of me. I want to be able to put my side of the story.'

'Maybe at some point,' Blair replied, 'but not now.'

So that was it. Inwardly I was exhausted, and reeling from the events of the past few weeks.

'Do you think it would be okay if I took the rest of the week off?' I asked.

'I think that's a very good idea' said Blair quietly and reassuringly.

With allegations of drug taking and sexual impropriety against me published in the national press, I now faced the most serious challenge of my career. The one person at the Yard who I thought I could trust, who would support me and empathise with me, was Ian Blair. Only now, when recalling the events of the day, do I remember thinking that Blair was a like-minded ally, the only person on the management board that I wanted to see and speak to at my lowest moment. I truly believe that, deep down, Ian Blair is a good man – someone who, if left alone by his so-called advisors and taken out of the pressure cooker of the most demanding role in policing, is a genuine man – and a man who genuinely cares.

I was driven back to Lambeth where I had to fight my way to the back door through a throng of reporters and photographers. Once I made it into my office, I wrote out my resignation speech and then delivered it to the waiting reporters and camera crews on the front steps of Brixton police station. It is all a blur now, but it was recorded a hundred times: 'I'm very disappointed to be leaving Lambeth, albeit temporarily,' I said, more in hope than expectation.

Lord Harris, the chair of the Police Authority, issued a press release stating that a deputy chief constable from another force would investigate both the criminal charges and the allegations that I had breached police regulations. He then took the extraordinary step of praising the work I had done in Lambeth.

It is a cliché, but once back in my flat I was a prisoner in my own home, where I worried myself sick about what was going to happen. The doorbell was rung constantly by journalists wanting to talk to me, but I was gagged until the Thursday morning when my mobile rang.

'Hello?' I said tentatively.

'Brian, its Piers Morgan,' the then editor of the *Mirror* said to me in his characteristically bombastic manner. 'You can't just lie down and let them walk all over you; you've got to get your side of the story out.'

'The commissioner won't let me,' I said.

'Look,' said Piers, 'Stevens is a personal friend of mine.'

'Well, if he's a personal friend of yours, why don't you ring him?' I replied.

A few hours later I got a call from Dick Fedorcio, head of Public Affairs at the Yard. He said that Piers had spoken to the commissioner and I was allowed to speak to the *Mirror*, although strict limitations were placed on what I could say about the case. A journalist was already waiting outside the flat and we arranged to spend the coming Sunday at a hotel in Chelsea Harbour.

Mary, my ex-wife, called me during that difficult week to tell me she had been approached by the *Sunday Mirror* and she wanted to do a positive interview about me. I strongly advised her to keep her head down. Several calls later she told me she was going to go ahead. I said it was important that she was not paid for the interview (the thought had never crossed her mind) to show that she was motivated to speak only from concern for me and not for the money – unlike James, and someone else from my past.

The other mercenary was Fiona Pilborough. My former fiancée had since married and was now Mrs Fiona Chambers. The following Sunday there was another joint exclusive, this time between the *Mail on Sunday* and the *News of the World*. The article began: 'Gay police chief Brian Paddick told his shattered fiancée that he couldn't have any more sex with her because God had commanded him to stop.'

There were again photographs of me, this time from twenty years ago. One photo showed me and Fiona together, she in a dress and me stripped to the waist. ('I've seen more fat on a butcher's pencil,' was Michael's comment.)

Fiona entertained the readers with exaggerated stories about our relationship, which were almost entirely negative. She told them I was a 'religious nut', that I heard God speaking to me, and that in line with Baptist belief I thought 'God had left a copy of the Bible on the moon.' Here I should make it clear that neither I nor the Baptists believe in the divine moon-landing.

These 'revelations' were in stark contrast to the double-page spread in the *Sunday Mirror* in which Mary said what a wonderful person I was, how we had had a terrific marriage, and that I did not deserve to be sacked from Lambeth. This was a gracious and generous act of loyalty, and more than anyone could possibly have asked for.

Sadly, it had little impact on what was to come. The newspaper columnists of Great Britain, those piranhas of journalism, were by now savaging my character and my career.

My dear mother collected the articles and columns that featured me during this period in 2002 and I have dug them out for this book. I have a stack next to me the same thickness as London's Yellow Pages. Going through them now, some years after the event, it is amazing to read what the newspapers considered was in the public interest.

Melanie Phillips wrote in the *Daily Mail*: 'Paddick is an icon for our morally inverted, decadent times . . . The fact that such a man could be a senior police officer shows how sick this society has become. At its root lies a collapse of belief in morality and in the law by the political and intellectual class.'

Richard Littlejohn of the *Sun* did not pull any punches either: 'The Commander brings a whole new meaning to the expression "bent copper".'

The media campaign by the *Daily Mail* and *Mail on Sunday* was relentless and the big guns were also brought out to shoot down the cannabis experiment. Melanie Phillips, along with several other *Mail* journalists, wrote lengthy pieces along the lines of 'Metropolitan police analysis showed that drug users and dealers in hard drugs have been flocking to the area since last summer when the force launched its more tolerant approach.' Further on in the article they admitted that the evidence was 'anecdotal'. In fact, as we have already seen, it was completely untrue.

Typical of the misleading articles was one that featured a banner headline over two pages and an aerial photograph of a street, with arrows pointing to houses whose occupants had become victims of crime over the past twelve months. The headline read 'Proud of This Mr Paddick?' The street was not even in Lambeth, where the cannabis pilot was exclusively taking place, but in the neighbouring borough of Southwark where anyone found in possession of cannabis was arrested. It seemed as though I was being blamed for any increase in crime, anywhere in London.

The truth was, of course, quite different. As we have already seen, the doom-monger's predictions of anarchy and crime going through the roof failed to materialise. The official assessment of the first six months and the MORI poll revealed that we had achieved our objectives, allowing officers to concentrate on other crimes; and thousands of police hours were saved with no apparent negative consequences.

Then, suddenly, things began to turn around.

I went down to Vauxhall underground station to pick up a copy of the *Mirror* article I had done after Piers Morgan's intervention when I saw the front-page headline: 'Bring Back Paddick'. But it wasn't the *Mirror*; it was on the front page of the *Voice*, 'The Voice of Black

Britain'. The black people of Brixton, the so-called capital of Black Britain, the epicentre for anti-police rioting and a focus for poor police-community relations, were calling for my reinstatement as commander of Lambeth – their borough.

After Urban 75 had kicked off a public campaign, the *Big Issue* weighed in and started a series of petitions. On my birthday in April 2002, five thousand signatures were handed in to Scotland Yard demanding my reinstatement. Over forty MPs signed an Early Day Motion in the House of Commons which read that:

'. . . this House deplores the witch-hunt currently underway against Brian Paddick, until recently the Commander of the Lambeth Police Force; deplores the homophobic nature of many of the smears and innuendoes directed against him; finds it extraordinary the Metropolitan Police has taken action against him on the basis of a previous boyfriend once having committed acts the Home Office has now decided are no more serious than a parking offence; and congratulates Commander Paddick for having the integrity and bravery to speak his mind on policing issues and hopes this episode will not discourage other policemen from doing the same in the future.'

The Mayor of London, Ken Livingstone, and Canon Richard Truss, the Dean of Lambeth, along with some well-known journalists, wrote an open letter to Sir John Stevens. 'Paddick should be cheered rather than censured. He is an asset not only to Lambeth and to the Met, but to the entire police force.' They applauded my 'progressive response to the drugs crisis' and my 'imaginative and innovative use of the internet to communicate openly and honestly with the local community'.

Signatories to the letter included the editors of weekly magazines *Time Out*, the *Pink Paper* and the *Big Issue*, broadcasters Robert Elms and Mark Thomas, journalists from the *Voice*, the *Independent*, the *Guardian* and even the *Mail on Sunday*; MPs Brian Iddon and Paul Flynn and drugs agencies Lifeline, Release and Transform. Community leaders were also represented, including the CPCG for Lambeth, and Valerie Shawcross, Greater London Authority member for Lambeth and Southwark.

In the meantime, hundreds of letters and cards arrived at Scotland

Yard, mainly from people I had never met or heard of, from a grand-mother in Scotland to a retired chief constable of Devon and Cornwall. I cannot emphasise enough how these really sustained me through what was a very difficult time. I replied personally to every one who included their address.

The chair of the Lambeth Community Police Consultative Group called an extraordinary meeting at Lambeth Town Hall to demand my reinstatement as borough commander. I decided to make a surprise appearance.

Rumours had gone before me that I might attend. Determined to make my appearance a surprise, I approached the town hall on foot along Brixton Road, avoiding the Acre Lane entrance to the hall where the meeting was being held. I made my way through the corridors and into the hall, behind the TV cameras that were waiting for me to come in from Acre Lane. My sudden appearance caused an extraordinary reaction. The hall, which was packed with three hundred people, erupted in a standing ovation. I was worried that I would not be able to hold it together; it was already a very emotionally charged time.

Almost exactly twenty years before that meeting, I had stood behind a plastic shield as members of that same community had thrown bricks and lumps of concrete at me. Every month I had been given a rough ride by those in attendance at consultative group meetings, and I had fought battles with agitators who had attempted to undermine policing while I tried to uphold the best traditions of the Met. If someone had told me a year earlier that three hundred people, black, white, young and old, straight and gay, Liberal, Labour, and Anarchist, protestors and campaigners, would all be standing together in Lambeth Town Hall demanding their police commander be reinstated, I would have wondered what planet they were from.

It is only when you're on the ropes that you find out what people really think of you. The people of Lambeth were right behind me while my colleagues at Scotland Yard were nowhere to be seen. I had felt safer on my own in full uniform in the middle of Brixton than I ever did when I was at New Scotland Yard.

I think this unprecedented public response said something about what people want from the Met. I had tried to make sure the police were accessible and accountable.

Reverend Ivelaw Bowman was also on the platform and said, 'Commander Paddick has made a difference in policing in this community. Not only has he made a difference but he has also shown how this metropolis should be policed in the future.'

Mayor Ken Livingstone had sent a letter to be read out: 'There can be little doubt that Brian Paddick would not be in the position he is in today if it was not for his sexuality. Those who have waged a campaign against this officer are the real obstacles in the fight against crime . . .'

Thank goodness I managed to remain composed as I thanked everyone for their support. 'All I want to do,' I told them, 'is to serve the people of Lambeth.' I left the hall and marched towards Brixton underground, passing posters bearing my face and the caption: 'The Life of Brian – He's not a very naughty boy, he's the Messiah!'

I often walked to my local Sainsbury's in the Lambeth area of Nine Elms to do my shopping. More than once on these outings, I was accosted by silver-haired pensioners who said, 'It's terrible the way you're being treated; you're such a good commander.' And there, staring up at me from their shopping trolley, would be their very own copy of the *Daily Mail*.

Towards the end of that year, the *South London Press* ran a poll to discover who their readers thought the greatest ever South Londoner was, living or dead. In third place was a woman who was a spy in the Second World War and won the Victoria Cross; in second place was Charlie Chaplin and in first place was a certain former police commander of Lambeth who won by a considerable margin – I think my friends at Urban 75 may have had something to do with it!

Columnists like India Knight in the *Sunday Times* and Deborah Orr in the *Mail on Sunday*, were some kind of antidote to the poison of Peter Hitchens and Richard Littlejohn.

The London *Evening Standard*, whose editor had recently moved there from the *Mail on Sunday*, was gleefully joining in the onslaught. Then an opinion poll about London issues was published in the *Standard* which, among other things, showed that I was more popular with Londoners than Sir John Stevens was. The circulation of the paper was in decline and, belatedly realising London was nowhere near as right-wing as the readership of the *Mail on Sunday*, the editor commissioned a gay freelance journalist to do a 'sympathetic piece' on me.

About a week before this journalist made contact, I had another row with Mike Todd, this time on the telephone as he was about to leave to see the Trooping of the Colour. During our heated exchange, he described me as 'unpredictable and unreliable', a description of myself I had never heard before.

When the journalist called me and said that he had been asked by the *Evening Standard* to do a sympathetic piece on me, I was immediately suspicious. 'What do you mean a sympathetic piece?'

'We've been told that you're down and depressed and you're seeing a therapist.'

'Very interesting,' I replied. 'What else have you been told?'

'That you're unpredictable and unreliable.'

'That's strange, that is exactly the same phrase, the same words in the same order as my boss used when he spoke to me the other day. It wasn't Mike Todd who told you, was it?'

He said, 'We never reveal our sources, but perhaps we should meet up to discuss it.'

After a good lunch, he suggested that his choice of words when he spoke to me on the phone was not a coincidence.

What with the almost constant daily criticism of me that was in the papers anyway, I couldn't help thinking, perhaps wrongly, with a boss like that, who needs enemies, and I made a formal complaint to the commissioner.

John Stevens asked Sir Ronnie Flanagan, the former chief constable of the Royal Ulster Constabulary and by now Her Majesty's Inspector of Constabulary for the Met, to investigate Todd's alleged behaviour. Once Sir Ronnie concluded his investigations, he told me Todd had denied having said those things, and had gone even further, adding that he had never said anything detrimental about me to any journalist (which I found unbelievable considering how I had almost constantly tested his patience).

Having been told Sir Ronnie's conclusions, I still did not know who the journalist's anonymous source was.

CHAPTER TWENTY-TWO

The powers that be at Scotland Yard decided that I should be moved into an office at Territorial Policing headquarters on the Embankment at Canon Row. My job was so important that I cannot even recall what it was. It was something to do with a change in regulations and having to negotiate with the Police Federation, but I had more important things on my mind.

I had three personal staff members at Lambeth: my driver Keith, my secretary Sylvia, and staff officer Noel. Such was their allegiance to me, despite being *persona non grata* and with the threat of dismissal hanging over me, and despite the fact that they had been based at Brixton for many years, they came with me to Canon Row. I was deeply touched by their loyalty.

Michael, my partner, was amazing. He took the difficulties I was facing in his stride, always remaining positive with a witty remark or a joke, and encouraging me to go out with him to a party or event whenever I felt up to it.

Deputy Chief Constable Charles Clark of the Humberside Police was appointed by the Metropolitan Police Authority to investigate James's allegations. I was served with Regulation 9 notices, officially informing me what the allegations were and that they were to be investigated. The investigation was focused solely on James's claims about the cannabis, and the allegation that I had met him while he was on bail and that I had not reported it, allegedly contrary to regulations.

John Grieve, the Lawrence Inquiry mastermind, had recently

retired from the Met after one too many clashes with Sir John Stevens. John volunteered to act as my 'friend' – an official representative who is allowed to accompany you to any meetings and interviews relating to police discipline. From the beginning, I was very happy to follow his advice that, while members of the public have the right to remain silent when faced with criminal charges, police officers, especially senior officers, have a responsibility to account for their conduct. Police officers are public servants who hold important positions of authority in society and have significant powers – such as the use of force – and with such authority must come accountability.

From the outset, and with the agreement of my solicitor, we decided we would be completely open and honest and answer all of the questions put to me during the interview which would be in two parts: one criminal and the other in relation to police regulations regarding misconduct.

The interview took place at Jubilee House in Putney on 8 July 2002. Deputy Chief Constable Clark was waiting for us in what was quite possibly the smallest room in the building.

The proceedings began with the DCC saying, for the record, who was present in the room: his own detective chief superintendent, John Grieve, my solicitor and me. I was then cautioned: 'You do not have to say anything, but it may harm your defence if you do not mention when questioned something which you later rely on in court. Anything you do say may be given in evidence.' This was distinctly unnerving and brought back memories of the investigation at Lewisham.

I was facing two allegations with regards to criminal charges:

Possession of cannabis. Contrary to section 5(2) Misuse of Drugs Act 1971, and allowing my premises to be used for smoking cannabis, contrary to section 8 (d) Misuse of Drugs Act 1971.

James had told them that I had smoked cannabis and that I had only smoked when the two of us were there; there were no other witnesses. James had told them that we had smoked cannabis together 'most weekends'. He had also claimed that I started smoking when I was working on the tenure of post policy, and while I'm sure that such a job would have driven many people to drugs, all I required was the odd gin and tonic. I strenuously denied smoking cannabis and I became increasingly frustrated with Clark's tenacious, probing questioning. Ultimately though, it was a case of James's word against mine.

As far as allowing cannabis to be smoked in my flat was concerned, Section 8 of the Misuse of Drugs Act was designed to prevent the modern equivalent of opium dens, i.e. to prevent the owners of bars and clubs from allowing people to smoke illegal drugs on their premises. It was never in the minds of legislators that it should be used in relation to someone's home.

We made two points. Although my name was on the title deeds for the flat (along with the building society) there was a legal agreement drawn up by a solicitor between James and me whereby we both paid towards the mortgage. James was effectively 'in control of the premises' as much as I was; in practical terms he was a joint owner (no pun intended).

I also did everything I reasonably could to stop him smoking, and so had not 'allowed or suffered' the smoking of cannabis in my flat. As I have said before, I argued with him, I shouted at him, I complained bitterly about how he was putting my job on the line, and he responded to my complaints, at least until the next time. What else was I expected to do?

Was I supposed to telephone my colleagues and have my partner arrested? Should I have ended the relationship with the person I loved? Should I have thrown him out despite a legally binding agreement? What was the reasonable thing that I was supposed to have done that I did not do to stop him smoking the drug in our flat ever again?

There was a break in the interview. Criminal and police discipline issues have to be dealt with separately, although you have the option to allow the answers you give in the criminal interview to be used in the misconduct investigation.

We were satisfied that we had given a full, detailed and honest account in the criminal interview, so we agreed that the answers I had given could be used in the misconduct investigation. Instead we could move on to the other issue – James's bail.

It was three weeks after James and I had met that he told me he was on bail. (He told the police it was a week.) The instructions regarding the reporting of meetings with people who were on bail were ambiguous. The rules in place at the time were designed to prevent the sort of corruption that had occurred many years before when a tiny minority of corrupt Flying Squad officers would arrest and charge armed robbers, then meet them afterwards to 'lose' vital evidence in return for cash. As a result, police officers who wanted to meet people on police bail were required to obtain prior authority; if they had a chance encounter, they had to report the event to their DCI. The rules did not apply to 'neighbours and family members'.

At that time, I *was* a DCI, and although I could have had a word with myself, I decided that the rules were never intended for the scenario I found myself in. I classified James as falling somewhere between a 'neighbour' and 'a family member'. It seemed clear to me what the rules were driving at – the difference between genuine friends and contrived corrupt relationships – and James and I were already in an intimate relationship by that stage.

Besides this, the allegations against James were, as far as I knew, very minor: that he had stolen a tennis racquet and a bird bath as mementoes of his dead lover. In any event, within a short space of time he was released from police bail with no further action taken against him. Not only had I not interfered in the case, but the investigating officers never knew that I was involved with James in any way.

Having said all this, if I were to be entirely beyond reproach, if there was the slightest chance that I might get caught by the regulations (as I now had been), perhaps I should have told my superintendent. Of course, that was the superintendent who I had a difficult time with at Notting Hill, and he would have been the last person I would have told about my private life.

After the interviews, an agonising wait followed while the Crown Prosecution Service decided whether or not they were going to press criminal charges against me.

The decision when it came was extraordinary.

The issue of possession was straightforward. They concluded, in the absence of any admission on my part, in the absence of any witnesses and in the absence of any cannabis, that there was insufficient evidence to prosecute.

On the issue of allowing my premises to be used, they decided that there was sufficient evidence to prosecute but they had decided that it was not in the public interest to do so.

John Grieve, my solicitor, and the QC we had employed on the criminal case, all believed that there was insufficient evidence to prosecute. For the CPS to say that a prosecution was not in the public interest did not make any sense at all. Surely, if it was ever in the public interest to prosecute someone, it would be when the accused is a senior police officer, someone charged with upholding the law. What would have been more in the public interest? In what circumstances would it have been in the public interest to prosecute if the evidence was there?

It was now 9 October and it had taken the CPS nearly seven months to draw a blank – and this was only half the story. All the matters were then referred to the Metropolitan Police Authority for them to consider whether to institute formal misconduct proceedings against me. On 12 November 2002, some eight months after the *Mail on Sunday* story, the MPA issued a press release:

> Members of the Police Authority's senior officer conduct sub-committee have announced today their decision in respect of allegations against Commander Brian Paddick. The case will not be referred to a tribunal hearing. The MPA has provided feedback and comment to Commander Paddick. The matter is now closed.

The MPA had concluded that, even if a misconduct tribunal found that my behaviour had fallen below the standards expected of a police officer, the failure was so minor that it did not warrant any formal penalty, and that even if I was found guilty, my misconduct would not have justified even a reprimand, the lowest form of formal sanction.

What was not made public was that the MPA, in their conclusions, said that I should have a constructive discussion with the commissioner during which it would be emphasised that, if I found myself in similar circumstances again, I should tell the commissioner or another senior officer what was going on. In the meeting I had with John Stevens, together with John Grieve, the 'constructive discussion' with the commissioner was, 'There we are, then. It's over. Time to move on.'

John and I raised the point with the commissioner that there was no guidance for officers who caught their partner smoking cannabis and he acknowledged this. He said he would get Mike Fuller, the deputy assistant commissioner who handled the Met's drugs policy at the time, to address this.

It never happened. Fortunately, the culture in the Metropolitan Police has since improved, and I genuinely believe that a gay officer finding him or herself in a similar position today could go to their line manager and get a sympathetic hearing.

The result of the investigation was announced just days before Michael and I were due to take a planned holiday to South Africa; it was fortuitous timing as we were able to enjoy a really good break.

During the investigation, the commissioner had been asked on a number of occasions by a tenacious journalist, Tim Donovan from BBC London News, whether I would be allowed to return to Lambeth if exonerated. To start with Stevens said that I would, but over the next few months he avoided the question.

Early on in the investigation, Stevens had hired a consultancy firm to evaluate what the rank of officers in charge of boroughs should be, whether his new 'big ships, little ships' approach was the right one. At that time there were several different ranks in charge; a deputy assistant commissioner was in charge of Westminster, a chief superintendent was in charge in most other boroughs, while a commander ran Lambeth.

The consultants concluded that officers belonging to the Association of Chief Police Officers (ACPO) should be responsible for the strategic direction of the force as a whole, while superintendents were responsible for service delivery. Therefore, each borough should be headed by a chief superintendent rather than an ACPO officer. The commissioner used the findings from the report (which despite numerous requests was never published) to justify downgrading the rank of the officer in charge of Lambeth from commander to chief superintendent, but he retained an ACPO commander in charge of Westminster.

As a consequence there was no way I was ever going back to Lambeth, as I was a commander and therefore too senior. Obviously I was devastated to have lost the job I felt that I was best qualified for. Although I was only at Lambeth for fifteen months, an inspection by Her Majesty's Inspectorate of Constabulary supported my belief that I had made a positive difference. They compared April to September 2001, shortly after I had taken over, to the same period in 2002, just after I had left. They found that there had been a five per cent increase in the proportion of all crimes solved, a twenty-one per cent reduction in burglary and a thirty-eight per cent reduction in street robbery, the crimes that most affected the people of Lambeth. Our return to geographic responsibility had enabled officers to focus on these and other priority areas.

This change was unequivocally supported by all the staff, who also confirmed to the inspectors that they were positive about improvements in the leadership style. The inspectors found tangible examples of a much-improved relationship between the police and many of the partner agencies with whom the police worked. Lee Jasper, the Mayor of London's advisor on policing and diversity, said at the time, 'Brian Paddick has revolutionised the face of police and community relations. He is a tremendously effective officer . . .'

CHAPTER TWENTY-THREE

There was no time for me to dwell on the fact that my career in Lambeth was over. I was transferred to the Serious Crime Directorate where my new boss was Assistant Commissioner Tarique Ghaffur, the most senior Asian officer in the country.

I officially started on 6 January 2003, and arrived at work at seven-fifteen a.m. for a breakfast meeting with Tarique. My new responsibilities lay with that part of the organisation which dealt with murder, kidnap, child abuse and other very serious offences.

I was given what was more or less admin work, looking at things like performance indicators, and during my time there I had a collection of different and unglamorous responsibilities such as working on the implementation of the National Intelligence Model. This was a complex but reliable way of ensuring intelligence was shared within the Met and with other agencies such as the National Criminal Intelligence Service. Among other things, I was responsible for crime policy and a unit designed to check whether the rules around police use of surveillance were being adhered to across the Met. This was an important collection of responsibilities, but it was not my thing.

While I was there, Commissioner Stevens, who had been a detective for most of his police career, came up with the idea of revitalising and relaunching the detective training school at Hendon as a centre of excellence with an international reputation. Stevens's idea was to restore the reputation of the CID but the centre's new name was somewhat unfortunate: 'Crime Academy' had echoes of the *Police Academy* comedy films. Prisons were often referred to as 'Academies of Crime' in the press, and Crime Academy seemed to be a cross between the two.

It was my job to turn something that was in decline into a beacon of excellence and, although it was dull after Lambeth, it showed early signs of success.

At the school's launch, to which journalists were invited, I spotted Steven Wright, the crime correspondent for the *Daily Mail*, who had written a constant stream of misleading and damaging pieces about me over the previous year. I went up to him and said, 'Hello, Steven, I don't think we've met.'

'Ah, Brian, erm . . . I just want you to know that it's nothing personal.'

After putting up with the *Mail*'s vitriol day after day, I felt like kneeing him between the legs and telling him that that was 'nothing personal' either.

'I'm sure you're the same,' he added, 'I just do what my bosses ask me to do.'

I stared at him and thought to myself, 'Come to mention it, no – actually, I have the opposite problem.'

I missed Lambeth terribly. I felt that I belonged there and, all other things being equal, would still be there today if it had not been for James and certain tabloid newspapers. It was now time for justice as I began the arduous process of suing the *Mail on Sunday*.

While the kiss-and-tell story had had a devastating impact on me both professionally and personally, there were wider issues involved. Should a former partner who had been involved in a serious long-term relationship (in my case almost four years) be allowed to reveal the intimate details of that relationship to the world at large? If nothing was done, then other such stories would surely follow involving other high-profile public figures.

There was no legal right to personal privacy established in British law at that time, although the enshrining of Article 8 of the European Convention on Human Rights in the Human Rights Act provided a right to 'respect for private and family life, home and correspondence'.

(The situation later changed with the case of Naomi Campbell v Mirror Group Newspapers.)

I contacted the head of Stonewall, the prominent gay and lesbian pressure group, who put me in touch with Bindman and Partners, Solicitors, a firm of civil rights lawyers who were prepared to give me their first three hours free of charge. I was introduced to a young lawyer called Tamsin Allen, who told me that there was no established right to personal privacy in British law, but it was a situation that needed to be challenged. Although speculative and on the margins of established law, she suggested that there might be the potential for suing for breach of confidence, in that when you enter into a serious personal relationship there is an implied duty to keep personal matters personal – interpreted in the light of Article 8.

Certain things – from my sex life to my state of health – that James had revealed and the papers had published, were so intimate that only he could have known them, and then only because he was my partner. Although there was no precedent for such action, Bindman's felt that there was merit in bringing the case, and there was a possibility I could win.

There was no financial support forthcoming from the police or from Stonewall, but after the first £4,000 of work had been completed both the solicitor and the two barristers, Matthew Nicklin and Desmond Browne QC, one of the top five libel lawyers in the country, said they would work on a conditional no-win, no-fee agreement. In his long and distinguished career, Desmond Browne has only done two conditional fee agreements – one when I sued the *Mail on Sunday* over the kiss-and-tell story and the other when I sued the *Daily Mail* over another article. I am so very grateful to Desmond.

'No win, no fee' only applies to your own legal team, not to your opponent's. If you lose the case, you are liable to pay the other side's costs, unless you can get insurance to cover these. If you win, you usually do not have to pay your opponent's costs; they have to pay yours but there is often a shortfall for which you become liable. My advice: think hard before you embark on such an enterprise and, if you win, don't spend all your award until the final legal bill is settled.

After about twelve months' work on both sides, and having told

Associated Newspapers we were taking action, no one was prepared to offer me insurance. By this time it would have cost me just as much to pull out as to carry on. If I had gone on and lost I would 'only' have had to pay the other side's lawyers, but if I had pulled out at this stage, I would have had to pay both sides' costs (no win, no fee only applies if you see it through to the bitter end).

The estimated costs, whatever I decided to do, had risen to about £350,000. I did not have £350,000. Michael and I discussed the possibility of being forced to sell our home, which would have only covered a portion of this bill. The eight months of worry about possibly losing my job was now replaced with eighteen months of worry about possibly losing everything I owned.

The managing editor of the *Mail on Sunday* asked for a meeting and we went along more in hope than expectation. He told us that he was definitely not paying me anything and he was not apologising. He suggested that the only way I could get any money out of them was by writing articles for his paper, an offer I wasted no time in rejecting. In fact, a little unprofessionally perhaps, Tamsin and I couldn't help ourselves and laughed out loud at the suggestion.

The gloves were off. Associated Newspapers started a series of applications to the judge about one thing and another. Each hearing, where we had to be represented, brought the concern that if we lost the application, I would, there and then, have to pay the costs of the hearing. We won all of them.

Finally, after eighteen months, a date was set for the trial in February 2004.

As the date of the court case approached, both sides had to disclose all the information they had relating to the case. Initially the *Mail on Sunday* refused to hand over the transcript of the interviews they had done with James. They said it was too expensive to have them transcribed and we had to make application to the court to force them (more costs for me if I lost). Once we got hold of the transcripts, almost every page had the word 'inaudible' on it in place of James's answers to questions, so we demanded they hand over the tapes. After much argument we finally got our hands on them.

Amazingly, what had been described as inaudible was all-too painfully clear. One of the most important parts previously marked as 'inaudible' were two arguments between Fiona Wingett and James.

At one point Fiona said to James, 'Well, you're lying. You've already proved you're a liar, James.'

Then, when they continued the interview on the following day, Fiona said, 'James, you're lying to me now.'

'I'm not lying.'

'You're lying to me now.'

'I'm not lying just to get more money.'

Part of the *Mail on Sunday*'s case was that James was a credible witness and yet, in their own tape recordings, their own journalist called him a liar. A chink of light glimmered at the end of the tunnel.

Another section of the tape involved the journalist pressing James into saying he bought his cannabis in Brixton where I had become the police commander, because that would suit the article very nicely. James laughed at the suggestion but it still appeared in the article as being true.

The full, horrible intimate extent of the interview was also revealed. James was asked repeatedly about our sex lives ('What does Brian say or do when he climaxes?'). James also said positive things about me, that I was considerate, caring and thoughtful. Funnily enough, the *Mail on Sunday* decided that these matters were not in the public interest and did not share them with its readers.

I also discovered that James and the paper's journalists had recorded our phone conversations and the interview in the Mandarin Oriental without telling me. Another very telling fact was that James was not being called by Associated Newspapers as a witness for their defence; their only witnesses were journalists. Shortly after this material was released, Associated Newspapers offered a paltry sum to entice us to settle out of court. After some tough negotiation, we reluctantly accepted a substantial five-figure settlement.

By the time the costs were settled, it was October 2004; two years and seven months after the whole thing had started.

I was lucky because I had a public profile and this was an important case. If it had come to court and I had won, it would have established significant precedents in law, so I was fortunate that an excellent legal team was prepared to operate under a conditional fee agreement. Most people who either have their privacy invaded by the media, or who are libelled by them, have little if any access to justice because of the enormous up-front costs and financial risks involved. Justice in the UK is often only available to those who can afford it.

This experience had been as nerve-racking as the criminal and disciplinary investigation and had lasted three times as long. Michael and I had had to put all our plans, our lives, on hold while we awaited the outcome of the case.

The battle with Associated Newspapers was not over, however. The next action we took was a straightforward libel against Melanie Phillips. Shortly after Ian Blair became commissioner he asked me to do a comprehensive review of the way the Met dealt with rape investigation. Phillips, in a long diatribe under the title 'When is a man guilty until proved innocent? When he's accused of rape', wrote 'you'll never guess who Ian Blair has got to do this review – Brian Paddick, the author of the disastrous turn-a-blind eye to cannabis policy.' She also mentioned 'allegations made by a former lover', and that rather than being punished I had been promoted; Phillips said '[Paddick is] wrapping himself in the flag of a gay martyr'.

My mother's neighbours have the *Mail* delivered and she would scan their copy of the paper, looking for references to me. I have her to thank for finding this libellous piece by Phillips. Associated's lawyers tried the usual approach of pulling every trick in the book to get me to throw in the towel before they caved in with another eleventh-hour out-of-court settlement.

Once the suing of Associated Newspapers was over and the general furore had died down somewhat, I invited Peter Hitchens to lunch at the Royal Academy of Art. It has to be said that, while I did not agree with a lot of his views, we had an interesting and engaging lunch where, it probably pains both of us to admit, we enjoyed each other's company.

Encouraged by this success, I then invited Richard Littlejohn for dinner at The Ivy. One of the managers who knew me well came up to me when Richard went off to the loo and said, 'Tell me that *isn't* Richard Littlejohn!' I did well enough in convincing Littlejohn that he had been wrong about me for him to insist on paying the bill at the end of the evening.

The point I was making with these overtures to 'the enemy' was to show them I was a real person, and that some of the things they had written were hurtful, unhelpful and a distortion of the facts. Littlejohn said that he did not expect anyone to take anything he wrote seriously; my reaction was, to use his own catch phrase, 'you couldn't make it up'.

Neither Hitchens nor Littlejohn have said anything negative about me since, except when Richard claimed I was writing this book while I was still a serving police officer. When I told him this was not true (as I write this I am hovering dangerously close to my publisher's deadline at the very end of 2007) he published a correction and emailed me, saying, 'I guess the Milky Bars are on me again, Brian.' Well, I'm still waiting for my Milky Bar, Richard!

Who would have thought things would have turned out the way they did with Hitchens and Littlejohn – or the *Mail on Sunday* for that matter. Maybe Stephen Wright was right: perhaps it *is* nothing personal. It just feels like it at the time.

PART FOUR

CHAPTER TWENTY-FOUR

My 'celebrity' life really started after I had sued the *Mail on Sunday* but it was Michael's connections that really took me to the stars.

The tenth anniversary of *Attitude* magazine was held in the Atlantic Bar and Grill in Soho in 2004. This was after I had got to know David Furnish who sent Michael and me tickets for the party and the opening show. Once there, we found David in the VIP area and when I sat down I was surprised to find myself next to Cilla Black. This was at the time when Cilla was still hosting *Blind Date* – a programme that James and I used to watch avidly. We chatted about this, that and the other, and after about ten minutes, I thought I had better introduce myself. I said, 'I'm Brian Paddick, the policeman.'

'Oh! I'm sorry,' said Cilla, 'I thought I knew you!' After a little more conversation we were joined by Lulu, but the person I was most keen to meet was Elton John. When I did finally get to meet him, he walked up to me without saying anything, kissed me on the lips and said, 'Hello, Brian, I'm a great fan of yours.' I had bought a double cassette tape of *Goodbye Yellow. Brick Road* when I was a PC at Hendon, and I remember the lyrics were a point of some discussion when I was still at school. I was awe-struck on meeting Elton. He was surprisingly tall and his large frame made him an imposing character.

We were taken through the kitchens of this club, around to the back of the crowd to watch the entertainment. It was a new and then rarely heard of group called the Scissor Sisters. David, who had heard them play before, wanted Elton to hear them, which is why he had come along. Elton liked them so much that he subsequently used them as his support band for a series of summer concerts in the UK and set them on the road to fame and fortune.

Elton, Lulu, Cilla, David, my partner Michael and I were in the back of the room where there were semicircular bench seats. To be able to see properly, we sat on the backs of the seats. When I noticed I was rubbing backs with someone I recognised, full of champagne and self-confidence I said to David, 'I haven't met this young man before.' David made the introductions: 'George, this is Brian,' and I met George Michael for the first time.

After I had won my case against the *Mail on Sunday*, I told David that I wanted to treat Michael and to give some of the money to charity. A good way to do this was to take Michael to one of Elton's white-tie-and-tiara balls. These amazing charity events are held in the grounds of their home in Windsor where Elton and David welcome every guest personally. The whole affair is sponsored by commercial companies and all the money spent on tickets and auctions goes to the Elton John AIDS Foundation. At the one single event we attended, Elton and David raised over £10 million for charity. As well as fellow guests George Michael, Lulu, Kylie, Stephen Gately, Rod Stewart, Sting and others, the cabaret was provided by Bryan Adams and Mary J Blige, sometimes accompanied by Elton. This was followed by dancing, where you could literally rub shoulders with the rich and famous, all under an enormous marquee in the grounds.

Some years later I was surprised and delighted to receive an invitation to Elton and David's stag night, to be held at a nightclub in Soho called Too2Much, as well as an invitation to the reception following their civil partnership ceremony.

The stag do was an amazing night, with many stars putting in special performances (the guests were sworn to secrecy as many of the star turns were doing things out of their comfort zone). But nothing I had experienced before compared with the main event which took place a few days later. We arrived reasonably early, but when we got to the entrance we were asked by security to drive around the block as they were having trouble fitting in all the cars. We drove round the corner, only to hit a terrible traffic jam; it took us an hour to get back to the entrance. The paparazzi's dream had come true: all the celebrities were trapped, stationary in their cars; forced to sit and smile as the photographers picked them off one by one.

The unrelenting pressure from being under investigation, the hounding by the media and the long and difficult process of suing the *Mail on Sunday* took its toll on my relationship with Michael and it did not survive the onslaught. I was sad that it was not Michael accompanying me to the event but I reassured my companion for the evening that we were not going to merit much attention, given that the people who were caught in the jam included Victoria Beckham, the stars of *Little Britain*, Ringo Starr, Sting, Fergie, Prince Andrew and Boris Becker, amongst many others. What I did not account for, of course, was the *Daily Mail*, which published a picture of us both.

George Michael was also at the reception and introduced me to Ronan Keating and his charming wife while James Blunt was on stage. Janet Street-Porter was unique among the guests in that she had been present at Elton's marriage to Renate Blauel in Australia many years before.

Having been introduced at the stag do, I went over to say hello to Sharon Osborne. I remembered that an article about her breast enlargements had just been published in which it was said that she was thinking of having them downsized.

'Sharon, I don't know what you're worried about, they look fantastic to me!'

She glared and then smiled at me. As we started chatting, we were joined by Ozzy. When he found out who I was he said in his broad Brummie accent: 'I'm usually trying to get away from you lot!'

It had been an unforgettable evening, but the next day I heard from Dick Fedorcio, director of Public Affairs at the Yard. He said he had had a query from the *Mail*: 'Is it true that Mr Paddick used his official police car and driver to take him to Elton John's wedding reception?'

Irritated, I said, 'Tell them to print it and then I'll sue them again.' I had employed a retired officer who had his own Mercedes.

CHAPTER TWENTY-FIVE

In July 2003 I was posted back into Territorial Policing and it was around this time that Assistant Commissioner Tim Godwin from the Met and Chief Constable Denis O'Connor from Surrey came up with the idea of 'reassurance policing'. Despite a downward trend in reported crime, fear of crime was increasing. Their idea was to design policing tactics not simply to prevent or reduce crime, but to provide a more visible reassurance – something which was now considered as important as actual crime reduction.

Commissioner Sir John Stevens had gone to New York where he recognised the success of the NYPD in crime reduction, which was in part due to the Big Apple having a lot more police officers per head of population than London did. After he pointed this out to the mayor, Ken Livingstone agreed to a significant increase in funding for the Met but insisted that money was not for 'more of the same' but for 'something different'. Tim Godwin suggested reassurance policing was the 'something different' the Met needed.

When Ian Blair was chief constable of Surrey, he had created the idea of police community support officers (PCSO's). These were people employed by the police service who were not police officers but who wore a uniform and patrolled the streets, becoming 'the eyes and ears of the police' while reassuring the public. They were cheaper to employ than ordinary officers, but had few powers, much less training and less equipment.

The promised funding increase would not produce a noticeable increase in visible policing if it was all spent on regular constables;

PCSOs appeared to provide the answer. With some additional savings from other parts of the Met, there was just enough cash to provide one Safer Neighbourhood Team of one sergeant, two constables and three PCSOs for every ward in London. On my return to Territorial Policing I was given responsibility for PCSOs across London.

The mayor approved and, just before his re-election, Safer Neighbourhood Teams were rushed out ahead of schedule with a promise they would reduce crime in London over the next four years by fifty per cent. They didn't.

Safer Neighbourhoods were supposed to end the swing from a performance culture based on fast cars and plain clothes squads to neighbourhood policing and back again. While the performance culture produced good crime reductions, it also drew complaints that the police were no longer in touch with their communities. Neighbourhood policing was popular with the public but was ineffective in reducing crime. The additional resources put into the Safer Neighbourhoods initiative were supposed to provide neighbourhood policing in addition to, rather than instead of, the fast cars and squads.

There was understandable concern expressed by the Police Federation that PCSOs were policing on the cheap. Although PCSOs were given the power to detain someone for up to thirty minutes, thus allowing time for regular police officers to arrive, they often found themselves powerless to prevent people running off. They were also powerless to act in other situations that demanded a prompt response, particularly in terms of physical restraint and emergency rescue; they were trained to avoid violent confrontation for their own safety.

Their limitations quickly became apparent. Some PCSOs had to be rescued from Stratford Shopping Centre in East London when some local youths deliberately targeted them because they had no powers. In a recent and more serious case, two PCSOs looked on as two members of the public tried to rescue a young girl and boy from a pond; by the time a real police officer arrived and jumped into the pond to help a family friend recover the boy, it was too late.

I now believe the whole concept of the PCSO to be flawed. Police officers are supposed to be 'citizens in uniform' who are given the powers, equipment and skills. The distinctive police uniform enables officers to stand out as those who can do the things the community would want to do if they were able, like breaking up a fight or marching a burglar down to the local police station.

PCSOs stand out in their uniforms, too, but they do not have the ability to act for the community in potentially dangerous situations, the whole purpose of the Police Service. If we have to pay people to be the 'eyes and ears of the police', rather than relying on the public, then something has gone terribly wrong with British policing.

We currently have fully trained, fully equipped police officers spending up to half their time performing administrative tasks in police stations while PCSOs patrol the streets. Surely this is the wrong way round? If we could spend the money currently spent on PCSOs on professional keyboard operators doing the admin tasks for regular officers, we could significantly increase the amount of time each fully trained, fully equipped police officer spends on the street.

Some at Scotland Yard felt everything was being funnelled into Safer Neighbourhoods to the exclusion of everything else. Whereas other parts of the Met had a proven track record of success, the effectiveness of Safer Neighbourhoods in reducing crime and reassuring the public was not yet established.

Nonetheless, the rollout of Safer Neighbourhoods began with a massive recruitment drive. It was 2003, and we were approaching another 'bulge' in terms of thirty year service officers who were approaching retirement; the need to start recruiting thousands of PCSOs as well as police officers was only going to increase the pressure on the Met. In 2004, the Met had a total of thirty thousand officers and the plan was to recruit another five thousand as soon as possible.

As well as responsibility for PCSOs, I was also responsible for the Metropolitan Police Special Constabulary. Special constables are 'volunteer' police officers who perform their duty for love rather than money. Most have a day job and perform their police duties in their spare time. These people have my utmost respect and admiration. I have had to deal with some difficult situations during my career but I was getting paid for it. Specials receive nothing in lieu of the insults and the danger they face, working alongside regular officers. Unlike PCSOs, Specials have all the powers and all the equipment of full-time police officers. Unfortunately, Special constables were often, and unfairly, treated with disdain by their full-time colleagues and given the derogatory title 'hobby Bobbies'.

Part of the explanation for this is the fact that the Met is the country's biggest police service by a long way (25 per cent of the UK total in fact), and the media's microscope keeps us very much in the public eye. This resulted in a quite strong 'siege mentality' in which many officers distrust anybody who 'isn't one of us', i.e. a full-time police officer. Most officers did not like being sent on a paired patrol with a Special, even though the best of the Specials are just as useful as regular officers. It was with genuine respect and pride that I often represented the commissioner at attestations where they are sworn in as constables, even when I was no longer directly responsible for them.

In addition to these London-wide responsibilities, I had to oversee the boroughs of North West London – Hillingdon, Ealing, Brent, Harrow, Barnet, Camden and Islington. There were some interesting characters among the borough commanders, such as Martin Bridger in Ealing, out of the same mould as John Stevens and a friend of the commissioner's, who was later selected to lead Lambeth; Andy Bamber headed Brent and had previously taken over from me as the DCI at Notting Hill, and Tony Brooks in Camden had been one of my sergeants on my first team at Holloway, except that this time I was his boss.

I had also worked with Barry Norman, now the borough commander of Islington. I had been his inspector at Deptford when he was a sergeant. Norman was about to become more famous than he would have wanted when his role as the senior investigating officer in Operation Helios, the multi-million pound investigation into Ali Dizaei, turned into a fiasco.

As I had done at Lambeth, I had regular meetings at Scotland Yard with Assistant Commissioner Tim Godwin, who had taken over from Mike Todd. The first meetings concerned the issues surrounding PCSOs, in particular the breakdown in discipline which was occurring at a much higher rate amongst PCSOs compared with other 'police staff', as support staff were now to be called. Despite my own reservations about the PCSOs, I was responsible for their recruitment and training and I immediately ordered a review.

Another aspect of the portfolio was taking responsibility for the Met on restorative justice (RJ). This programme had been sponsored by Deputy Commissioner Ian Blair after a previous Home Office-funded pilot scheme had shown some initial promise. Ian Blair had been told by the Home Office that, although his introduction of PCSOs had been progressive and modernising, he needed to keep on innovating and the Met should volunteer to sponsor the next restorative justice pilot.

Police officers were trained as 'restorative conference facilitators' and with their agreement, the victim and the perpetrator would meet. The perpetrator would be told what effect their offence had had on the victim and, at some stage, the perpetrator would – hopefully – apologise and, where appropriate, offer some sort of reparation for what they had done. The offender would already have been convicted in the courts and the conference would take place before the judge passed sentence. The pilot scheme worked with cases of robbery and burglary, so the majority of offenders were still sentenced to a term of imprisonment after going through this process. The judge was given a record of what had happened at the conference but this provided little relief when it came to sentencing. Sometimes judges handed out a heavier sentence than usual, as the conference probably brought home to them how badly the crime had affected the victim.

Restorative justice had a profound, positive effect on the victims of crime, who were much less fearful of becoming a victim again after realising that, in most cases, the criminal had just picked them at random. Once they understood it was nothing personal and had seen that the offender was not some kind of monster, they were much reassured.

The effects on the perpetrator were less clear, especially in this pilot project where they were all behind bars. Evidence from other countries had shown that RJ had reduced repeat offending. I was sceptical about the Home Office scheme because any beneficial effects on the offender were likely to be undone by the brutalising effects of a year or two in Wormwood Scrubs. Besides this, the cases were selected randomly, and in many instances either the offender or the victim refused to take part, often backing out at the last moment of what was an expensive process, taking about eighteen hours of police time for each case. While I'm convinced RJ and community-based sentences do work, this particular pilot appeared to be set up to fail. The only gauge of the effect on offender behaviour was whether they committed offences in prison – not a good indicator.

We should have been using restorative justice in combination with community-based sentences for first-time and young offenders. The punishments given to young offenders tend to be very minor and the deterrent effect of being caught, charged and prosecuted was minimal. In addition, the court process is divorced from reality. While the offender sits in the dock, usually not required to say much, if anything at all, solicitors, barristers and judges perform an alien ritual in front of them. With RJ, meeting their victims at this early stage of their criminal careers, and seeing the effect their criminal behaviour has had, might make some of them think twice in the future.

I was also responsible for youth issues across London. There was at this time a bewildering array of government initiatives aimed at reducing youth crime; youth-inclusive projects, youth intervention supervision programmes – all sorts of exotic, uncoordinated and ad hoc initiatives set up in a vain attempt to reduce youth offending. There did not appear to be any coherent government strategy or uniform application. I was invited to one of these programmes in Lambeth. It was a regular evening of football practice, supposedly aimed at youngsters who were involved – or were in danger of becoming involved – in drugs. In fact it was a general kick-around for anyone who wanted to turn up. The youths were happy, the organisers were happy as they got paid, but was this really an accurately targeted government intervention for young people at risk?

An area which took up a lot of my time was anti-social behaviour (ASB). Here too, the government had launched a bewildering number of initiatives in an effort to curb its seemingly unstoppable rise. An 'academy' was supposed to help educate local authorities and other agencies about how to tackle anti-social behaviour; this was coupled with a telephone 'action-line' and a website containing advice and guidance.

Since only fifteen per cent of houses are burgled from the front, most burglars preferring to approach via an alleyway, alleys that ran between and behind houses were going to have gates installed in a scheme known as 'alley-gating' to cut down on burglaries. There were going to be anti-graffiti operations and anti-begging initiatives. Specialist ASB advocates from the Crown Prosecution Service were to be appointed, and there were to be new sentencing guidelines for magistrates. This approach was supposed to demonstrate how enforcement and prevention went hand-in-hand, but addressing anti-social behaviour with this scatter-gun approach and multiplicity of ideas sowed only confusion.

There is much to be said in favour of the police taking anti-social behaviour seriously. Understandably, significant resources are put into rape and murder investigations because these are very serious crimes – but they affect relatively few people, a tiny proportion of the UK's population. Anti-social behaviour, such as aggressive begging outside train stations, can affect hundreds if not thousands of people every day. Behavioural misdemeanours like these increase people's fear of crime and their general feeling of unease. It remains a dilemma as to where the police should allocate their limited resources.

The most notorious ASB initiative remains the Anti-Social Behaviour Order (ASBO). Their use in London has been variable, with some boroughs throwing ASBOs around like confetti while others refused to use them at all. Despite there being only one Met, there are thirty-two boroughs with thirty-two different attitudes towards ASBOs.

Some boroughs took the controversial step of publishing photographs of young people against whom ASBOs had been issued. Normally in criminal proceedings the media are prevented from identifying suspects under seventeen years of age, at least until they are convicted. ASBOs were also controversial in that they could be imposed based on the balance of probabilities as opposed to 'beyond reasonable doubt' in a criminal case. To grant an ASBO, the court merely had to be satisfied that what they were being told about an individual was more likely to be true than false. Once an ASBO was issued against that individual, any breach could result in a prison sentence.

I believe ASBOs are a useful weapon to have in the police armoury to deal with anti-social behaviour, but it is one of a whole set of different tools that are available and should only be used in appropriate cases. An alternative and effective device is an ABC (Acceptable Behaviour Contract), formulated by a Met police officer called Paul Dunn. This is a voluntary contract between the parents of an unruly youth and their social landlord, i.e. the local authority or housing association. Once the parents sign an ABC, if their offspring continues to behave in an unacceptable fashion, they can be evicted.

The difficulty with the young is that they are less responsible than adults. In addition, some of them suffer from learning difficulties or behavioural disorders which make their continuing compliance with an ASBO difficult. It is only in those cases where a young person makes a complete nuisance of him- or herself and is clearly responsible for and aware of the consequences of their actions, that an ASBO should be used. There is clear evidence that this is not always the case.

CHAPTER TWENTY-SIX

A major recruitment problem emerged when, in the wake of the Macpherson Report, the Home Office decided to set targets for recruiting ethnic minority police officers. These targets were set in proportion to the number of black and minority ethnic people in each police force area, which, in London, was much higher than in any other part of country. It is of course a good idea that a police force reflects the make-up of the community it is serving, but there were a number of problems with these government targets. They were set on the basis of the black and minority ethnic population as a whole whereas, in some of these communities, the proportion of people under eighteen was much higher than the white population but under-eighteens were ineligible to join the police because they were too young.

Also, particularly in London, a proportion of the black and minority ethnic population were recent immigrants, visiting overseas students, or others who were in the UK temporarily, all of whom were ineligible to join the police. The eligible pool from which the Met could recruit was a lot smaller than the total black and ethnic minority population upon which the Met's targets had been based.

Despite this, the powers that be decided that visible ethnic minority and female candidates should be fast-tracked through the recruitment and selection processes, with other high-calibre male candidates having to wait three or more years before they were able to join the police, simply because they were white.

To try and prevent these high-calibre white male candidates from giving up while they were on the waiting list, it was decided to hold

'keep warm' events at the weekends, when those who had been waiting two or more years to join after having completed the selection
process, were invited to Hendon training school to see presentations
given by the specialist departments such as the dog section, the
mounted branch and the armed police and air support units – none of
which they could have joined for at least two years after they had finished their training but they were considered 'sexy'.

Having reluctantly agreed to give a morale-boosting speech at one
of these events, I met a black female recruit in week twelve of her
training. She told me it was embarrassing for her to meet a white male
who had gone through the same selection process as she, yet had to
wait at least another eighteen months before he started training while
she was already three-quarters of the way through hers. At a Scotland
Yard briefing on 28 July 2003, the head of Personnel told us there
were eight thousand application forms waiting to be processed, mostly
from white males.

I do not agree with mandatory quotas delaying the entry of white
candidates in order to fast-track black recruits. What I do agree with
is taking significant action to ensure racism is eradicated so that more
high-quality black and minority ethnic candidates are attracted to a
career in the police. Just as importantly, we also need to improve the
way in which existing ethnic minority officers are treated by the
organisation in an effort to reduce the high rate of black and minority officers leaving prematurely. There is simply not enough emphasis
on making the police service somewhere where black and minority
ethnic people feel safe and can thrive once they have joined.

A major part of achieving this is to root out racist officers at an early
stage, something the police had clearly failed to do by November 2003
when the BBC screened the controversial documentary 'The Secret
Policeman'. Since the Lawrence Inquiry, the Met in particular and the
Police Service generally had been congratulating themselves on the
progress they had made in tackling racism in the ranks. That was
until undercover journalist Mark Daly was recruited into Greater
Manchester Police, went to one of the national police training centres,
and recorded the experience using hidden microphones and cameras.

Among other things, PC2210 Daly found, on day one, that the

training instructor listed words that recruits were not allowed to use because they were racially insulting, but didn't give any explanation as to why. Once off duty, and after a few drinks, some of Mark's fellow recruits exhibited astonishingly overt racism, including one now famous sequence where one of the recruits used a pillowcase to impersonate a member of the Ku Klux Klan. This man's views on ethnic minorities would not have been out of place in such an organisation.

When Chief Constable Mike Todd found out, he had PC2210 arrested for obtaining a pecuniary advantage by deception (failing to declare he was employed as a journalist when he filled in his application) and causing criminal damage to a police uniform (Mark had made a hole in his stab-proof vest for the camera). This, I thought, was an interesting reaction from the chief constable, although Todd did subsequently take steps to address the issues raised in the programme.

I had been part of a minority of police officers who had complained that the two-day community and race relations training, the Met's sole response to the Macpherson Report in making a direct attempt to change attitudes, was a bit like the philosophical arguments for and against the existence of God. If you are a believer in equal opportunities, then the two days did much to boost your belief, whereas if you were not, there was nothing in the two-day training that was going to make you change your mind.

The claims that, since Lawrence, the police service had been transformed were, in my opinion, only true in relation to the police approach to victims of crime. Nothing had been done about the racial stereotyping of black people as criminals and the resultant disproportionate number of black people who are stopped, searched, arrested and charged compared with white people. At last, thanks to PC2210, there appeared to be incontrovertible evidence that, at least among those being recruited into the Police Service, racism was still present and was still a problem.

The lessons from the tragic death of Stephen Lawrence also appeared not to have been learned. In 2003 I chaired a Police Disciplinary Tribunal held for the officers who investigated the death of Roger

Sylvester. Roger's parents sat at the back of the tribunal room for the duration and listened intently to the proceedings.

On 11 January 1999, officers had found Roger naked in the front garden of a house in Haringey. A police officer has the right to detain someone under Section 136 of the Mental Health Act if they are in a public place, and once Roger stepped onto the pavement and after a bit of a struggle, the officers managed to get him into a van and drove him the short distance to St Anne's Psychiatric Hospital. He was placed in an examination room where he was waiting to be assessed by a psychiatrist when another struggle ensued, during which Roger collapsed and lost consciousness. He never woke up again and his parents, on medical advice, asked for his life-support machine to be switched off a week later.

Those on trial before me were the detective superintendent in charge, his detective sergeant and the senior forensics officer. The senior investigating officer had never visited the original scene where Roger was picked up by the police, even though the local uniformed inspector had cordoned off the area and preserved it for forensic examination. The police van that conveyed Roger to hospital was similarly preserved, as was the examination room at the hospital. The police van was subsequently examined only by torchlight in the middle of the night while it was *in situ* at the hospital and was then released back into service – usually suspect vehicles are taken to a special facility where they are carefully examined under cover and under strong light.

Roger's clothing, rather than being placed in special reinforced paper bags with one item in each bag – standard practice for potential exhibits – was placed in one large plastic bag. Paper bags were used because the moisture which is present in recently worn clothing causes the clothing to rot if sealed in plastic. Paper, on the other hand, allows material to 'breathe'. None of the medical equipment used to try and revive Roger was seized and, in our opinion, the examination of the room where the struggle took place was cursory. None of the officers' protective equipment or uniform was seized, which was also standard practice in cases of 'death in police custody'.

The potential seriousness of this case in terms of community relations was clear to the borough commander and the uniformed officers of Haringey where the incident took place, although those facing the discipline board were unaware of the effect of their apparent complacency. An active campaign was launched by Roger's family, supported by local pressure groups and the local press, and feelings were running high – this in an area that had suffered similar rioting to Brixton in 1985 when the Broadwater Farm riots led to the death of PC Keith Blakelock.

The detective superintendent's mitigation, that he had not yet been on his advanced senior investigating officers' course, we considered to be an indictment of the organisation. How could someone who was not trained be given such a case? On the other hand, none of the three of us who were judging his case had been on such a course either, but we knew what steps should have been taken. We unanimously agreed that all three officers were guilty of neglect of duty in that they had failed to investigate Roger's death properly; not only had they potentially deprived Roger's parents of a clearer explanation of what had happened, but they might have overlooked evidence which could have proved that the officers involved in the incident had acted entirely properly.

As a result of this case, a review of the methods used by the Met to restrain people was begun with a view to finding the safest possible way someone could be physically held against their will. When people struggle violently over a long period of time, some of the metabolic process becomes anaerobic. They don't take in enough oxygen and this creates an 'oxygen debt' which the body tries to pay back as soon as the exercise has ended. This is why we continue to breathe heavily for some time after we've stopped exercising.

Also during violent struggle, high levels of lactic acid are built up and if the officers, as they sometimes did, end up sitting on the person or holding them down in a way which constrains their breathing, they are unable to take in enough oxygen to pay back the 'debt' and the point is quickly reached where the person loses consciousness and cannot be revived. This condition is sometimes known as 'positional asphyxia'.

Obviously, it is very difficult to control people who are struggling violently – especially in a safe way. As a result of Roger Sylvester's death much research has been carried out, and the methods of restraint used by the Met (and the police in general) are being modified to keep people as safe as possible. New techniques range from trying to defuse the situation by talking to the person calmly, to holding people in a way that does not constrain their breathing.

Around the time of 'The Secret Policeman' documentary, the Met was being subjected to a review, this time by an academic from the London School of Economics sent on behalf of the Home Office to gauge progress post-Lawrence. She had visited a number of police stations and operational bases across London and had reported back to the then deputy commissioner, Ian Blair, in a meeting immediately prior to my seeing him over an unrelated matter.

When I entered the room, Blair told me it was the most depressing day he had ever experienced in his service. The academic had found widespread evidence of sexism in the force. One of the many examples she had given was of finding inappropriate pin-ups of scantily clad women in almost every police station and building she visited (as I had in the CID office at Streatham). Blair had the opportunity to address the issue that afternoon as he was meeting with borough commanders from across London. He simply told them to ensure that all the pictures were taken down. Unlike the one-off example I had discovered in Lambeth, what had been discovered was widespread institutional sexism, a failure to respect people who were different from the straight-white-male majority. Rather than accepting the message given to him by the academic, that radical cultural change was needed to address the underlying attitudes manifested by these soft-porn images, at that time Blair simply addressed the symptoms rather than the causes.

I fully understand the dilemma faced by senior police officers in relation to racism, sexism and homophobia; to be open and honest about these difficulties within their own ranks could undermine public confidence in the police. On the other hand, simply ignoring them is not in anyone's interest and failure to address them is, in my opinion, a dereliction of duty by the leaders of the Police Service.

I am reminded of my experiences as a sergeant at Brixton, either side of the 1981 Special Course, when I returned to find my colleagues 'had become' racist. The sad fact is, in an organisation where the majority are straight white males and led by straight white males, racism, sexism and homophobia might even go unnoticed by many at the top of the organisation.

I was asked to chair a Gold Group in a case which, because of what had happened, could severely harm the reputation of the police and our relationship with the public.

It involved a female officer in her twenties who was at the end of her first two years of service. She had attended her first CID Christmas lunch, having just moved on to the crime squad. She alleged that, when she went to the toilet, her superintendent had followed her, and when she went into a cubicle in the female lavatory, he pushed the door open and raped her.

She was seen by officers from Operation Sapphire, the Met's expert team in rape investigation, who interviewed her on videotape where she repeated in graphic detail exactly what had happened to her. At the very end of what was an extensive and detailed description, she said that she didn't want to take the matter any further because she felt that making a complaint against such a senior officer would end her police career. Bearing in mind this was the twenty-first century, that the officer should have felt so constrained was itself an indictment of the organisation.

The meeting in my office at Canon Row included two female officers from Operation Sapphire and a middle-service ranking detective from Professional Standards. Throughout that meeting, the officer from Professional Standards expressed his doubt about the female officer's account. One of the female officers and I frequently stared at each other in disbelief; I was concerned, as the detective appeared to me to be an unreconstructed chauvinist from the same school of chauvinism as the detectives from *Life on Mars*.

The policy developed by the officers from Operation Sapphire was that the wishes of the victim were paramount, and while they resolved to keep in touch with her to ensure she was okay, at that stage nothing more could be done. A few months later, one of the officers from

Operation Sapphire who had dealt with this case told me that the officer who had alleged rape had changed her mind. Although she did not want to go through the ordeal of a criminal case, she now believed that her senior officer should not be in a position of power and she was prepared to support disciplinary action against him.

Although by this time I had moved on and was no longer involved in the case, I made sure I received regular updates. Discussions were held at the highest level about this dreadful and potentially very damaging incident. The accused officer, who already had more than thirty years' service and therefore qualified for a full police pension, was allowed to retire with no action being taken against him.

In another case, a very high-ranking officer who was to retire was accused by a female officer of propositioning her. Being an assessor for the police promotion assessment centre, he allegedly offered her the answers to the written part of the examination in return for sex. As he was so senior, the matter went to the highest levels, where the whole thing was apparently covered up.

I cannot adequately express how angry these sorts of cases make me feel. How can the public have confidence in the police when senior officers allow this kind of behaviour to go unpunished? It is not as if we are short of recruits waiting to replace the 'bad apples'. I said to Ian Blair that it seemed strange that the Met should be making sure a senior male officer accused of raping a junior female officer was able retire on a full pension. Ian Blair told me it was 'a lot more complicated than that'. I'm not sure whether it was more complicated because of the politics surrounding the case or more complicated than the facts I had been privy to.

Operation Helios was the name given to the multi-million-pound police operation which was set up to investigate Superintendent Ali Dizaei, who was finally cleared in 2003. He was acquitted in a jury trial for allegedly attempting to pervert the course of justice, and misconduct in a public office. He had told colleagues that his car was parked somewhere other than where he said it was when he reported the fact that it had been damaged. In another trial against the same officer concerning alleged false mileage claims the Crown Prosecution Service offered no evidence.

Dizaei is an interesting individual whom I first got to know on the three-day extended interview process, when we both attempted to qualify to become members of the Association of Chief Police Officers (ACPO). This was at a time when, although neither of us knew it, he was under constant surveillance by his colleagues.

During the 'leaderless discussion', one of the assessed exercises carried out in groups of six, the topic we had been given was 'Is it ever justified to tell lies?' In the light of what subsequently happened to Ali and me, this was an interesting topic. Ali asserted that it was never right to tell lies and the man who later became the deputy chief constable of Devon and Cornwall replied: 'Come off it, Ali, surely you've told your kids to believe in Father Christmas?' To which the Muslim Ali replied, 'I don't believe in Christmas.' As I predicted, although I thought he was relatively inexperienced at that time, Ali was selected, but his place on the Strategic Command Course was deferred until the following year.

Ali was a powerful character, who some would say was 'inappropriately assertive', a polite way of saying he was aggressive. He was very keen on weight-training and he had the rather disconcerting habit of rolling up his short-sleeved shirts to expose a pair of impressive biceps. With the reputation I had established for being a champion of equality, and race in particular, we got on very well.

When it was my turn to appear before the selection panel for commander a year later, I sought Ali out in his office in Kensington to discuss with him the police attitude to race. All Ali's phone calls and meetings, including those between him and me, were being recorded by internal investigations as part of Operation Helios (a conservative estimate put Helios's cost at about £4 million, while some have suggested £7 million).

In his book *Not One of Us*, Ali explained in great detail how the Met spent these millions trying in vain to come up with evidence that he was corrupt, including attempting to draw him into a sting operation while he was in Canada and recording 3,500 of his telephone calls. He was variously accused of spying for Iran, taking bribes, using drugs and sleeping with prostitutes.

In the end, the only offences for which the police and the CPS thought there was enough evidence to support a prosecution, was claiming false mileage expenses and lying about the location of his car when it was vandalised. Helios resulted in two criminal trials, two acquittals, and Ali being paid £80,000 in damages in an out-of-court settlement. Even more extraordinary, part of the settlement was that he should be allowed to write a book about the whole thing.

In my opinion Ali Dizaei is a highly intelligent, very able and extremely ambitious man who is determined to get what he wants. From what I know, I would place him firmly in the category of 'real character' rather than 'corrupt criminal'.

On 24 November 2003, Commissioner Sir John Stevens held a meeting with the borough commanders about the Dizaei case where, in an amazing theatrical performance, he leaned on the lectern and stared intently at his audience before saying: 'I want to make it clear to everyone in this room. Ali Dizaei has been found not guilty. Understand? Not guilty.'

Barry Norman, whom I had known since 1986, was one of the borough commanders I had responsibility for, and as a detective chief superintendent before his borough commander posting, he had led the Helios investigation. At the operation's end, Norman was facing 120 separate complaints against him, made by supporters of Ali about the way he had conducted the investigation. Significant decisions in such a large, complex, costly and high-risk operation into one of the Met's most senior and high-profile ethnic minority officers should not and could not have been left solely to a chief superintendent.

For a start, a decision as monumental as to arrest and charge Dizaei was bound to have been referred to Andy Hayman, then head of Professional Standards, if not to the then deputy commissioner, Ian Blair. Barry Norman felt that he was being made a scapegoat for what was an organisational failure rather than an individual one. Responsibility was being pushed down to the lowest possible level rather than the officers in charge taking responsibility themselves.

Ali, however, was still intent on continuing his police career and hoped to become an ACPO officer, so it looked to me as though he avoided casting aspersions in the direction of those who could well be in pivotal positions in the future – Hayman and Blair. Ironically, some years later at the end of 2007, Hayman was to resign from the police, immediately leaving his post in the wake of allegations about his own conduct, but being allowed to take four months' unpaid leave in order to qualify for his police pension.

In the space of a few months I found myself having lunch with Barry Norman, trying to ensure that he was supported in what had become a very difficult situation for him, before having dinner with Ali and talking about the best way for him to be reconciled with the Met. I really saw no conflict in looking after both individuals and keeping both of their confidences; as far as I was concerned, they had both been victimised by the organisation.

CHAPTER TWENTY-SEVEN

It was while I was a commander in North West London that the government became concerned with 'narrowing the justice gap' – the difference between the number of offences committed and the number of offences that were successfully solved. Successfully dealing with an offence such as 'violent disorder' meant either arresting, prosecuting and convicting someone in court, or issuing a fixed penalty notice (issuing these on-the-spot fines were by far the easier, cheaper and faster option).

During Condon's time as commissioner, police effort was concentrated on those criminals still at large and committing further offences. Before then, a rich source of clear-ups had been provided by convicted prisoners who the police took out of prison for a day or two so they could point out the premises of burglaries they had committed but not previously admitted to. Provided the premises had indeed been burgled and the offence had been reported, and the prisoner was able to provide some corroborating evidence (describe the colour of the curtains in the lounge, for example), then this was considered to be a clear-up.

Needless to say, such a system, coupled with the intense pressure to achieve results, led to some dubious claims. Prisoners were only too happy to have a couple of days out of jail, where they would be well fed and well looked after, safe in the knowledge that there would be no additional penalty as a consequence of their 'confessions'. In many cases they were happy to admit to several hundred offences. Condon's assistant commissioner, Ian Johnston (now chief constable of British

Transport Police), stopped this practice of 'post-sentence visiting', but it still carried on outside the Met. As the Labour government started to focus on 'narrowing the justice gap' and created league tables which showed the Met was at the bottom, the practice of post-sentence visits was reinstated.

The pressure put on the police to increase the number of cases successfully solved meant that some officers were given targets for the number of clear-ups they should achieve every month. One practice that I personally witnessed gave me cause for serious concern.

I was in Camden on patrol with the area car when officers were called to an argument in the street between a man and his estranged wife. The man had been drinking and was certainly very angry, but when we arrived his behaviour could, at most, be described as drunk and disorderly – an offence not serious enough to qualify as an offence brought to justice. In my opinion, the behaviour of the police officer significantly contributed to the winding-up of this man until he cracked and exhibited behaviour sufficient for the officer to issue a fixed penalty notice for disorderly behaviour, which does count.

I told the borough commander and my boss that officers might well be 'goading' people to commit more serious offences in order to increase the clear-up rate, but my concerns fell on deaf ears.

One of the main problems with the government wanting more cases successfully solved was that there was no weighting given dependent on the type of offence or the amount of police time that had to be invested. A complex murder investigation taking six months to investigate and several months at trial counts as one case successfully solved (and only then if the person is convicted). Issuing a fixed penalty ticket for disorderly behaviour also counted as one case successfully solved, so an ambitious borough commander might well be tempted to encourage officers to issue more fixed penalties.

To make matters worse, Assistant Commissioner Tim Godwin successfully argued that the Met was being penalised for doing just what

the Home Secretary wanted – issuing formal warnings on the street
for possession of cannabis; the argument being that this would save
time so the police could focus on more serious crime. Warnings did
not count towards narrowing the justice gap; formal cautions, handed
out by other forces after they had arrested someone for cannabis possession, did count.

The Met eventually managed to get the Home Office to change
the rules so as to count formal warnings for cannabis as a successfully
solved case. We now have a situation where the quickest and easiest
way to narrow the justice gap is to issue a formal warning for cannabis,
since it counts for the same as a murder conviction. Rather than getting the police to concentrate on more serious crime, the Home
Office have created a situation where forces are rewarded for dealing
with minor offences.

In another recent controversial development, the use of fixed
penalty notices has been extended to people stealing from shops. One
has to ask whether all these fixed penalty notices are being issued in
appropriate cases or whether police forces are simply chasing government targets.

Deputy Commissioner Ian Blair always seemed to be unfortunate in
having to deal with serious issues whenever John Stevens was away on
annual leave. On one occasion, when I was posted to the Specialist
Crime Directorate under Tarique Ghaffur, I was asked to look after
Gurpal Virdi.

Gurpal had complained that he, as well as some of his colleagues,
had been subjected to a campaign of racist emails. The ensuing investigation suggested that Gurpal himself, along with a white female
officer, might be a suspect. While the leads suggesting Gurpal were
followed up relentlessly, those against the white officer were pursued
with little enthusiasm and the investigation into her was eventually
dropped. Gurpal was eventually charged with sending the emails himself and faced a full disciplinary tribunal.

It was the national story of the day when Gurpal was successfully
convicted. John Stevens sent a message to the chair of the discipline

tribunal, asking him to let his office know when they were nearing a conclusion. The chair duly called to tell Stevens that Gurpal had been found guilty, but it would be a few hours before they had written up their judgement and before they publicly delivered the result. By the time the result was announced, Stevens was on a flight to Belfast, with Blair left to deal with the fall-out from the Virdi case. In Stevens's absence, Blair was left with little choice but to toe what seemed to be the appropriate line, although he left it to Mike Todd to proclaim on BBC's *Newsnight* that justice had been done, now that Gurpal had been convicted.

Not only was the verdict of guilt overturned on appeal, but Gurpal won his employment tribunal, which was very critical of the way in which he had been victimised by the Met.

Gurpal's treatment by the Met appeared to me to be an example of the police's double standards, something I had also been a victim of. When allegations were made against me in the *Mail on Sunday*, a formal investigation was launched within hours and yet, when I was falsely accused of corruptly using a police car and associating with a drug dealer in the Shadow Lounge, no attempts were made to take action against those making what were known at the time to be malicious allegations.

Once I had been exonerated, I saw Ian Blair and talked to him in general terms about how allegations against some people were dismissed out of hand while allegations against others, such as myself, Gurpal and Dizaei were investigated to the nth degree.

Blair reluctantly agreed to have my complaints of inaction by the Met when I was the target of malicious allegations investigated by Deputy Assistant Commissioner Barbara Wilding (now chief constable of South Wales) who was at that time head of Internal Investigation for the Met. I had originally complained to the previous head, Andy Hayman, before the kiss-and-tell story (in fact the day before I went on my holiday to Thailand and Australia during which the Urban 75 case erupted), and provided him with a formal written statement outlining the complaints I was making. Hayman said that he would refer the matter to the Department of Legal Services for advice as to whether a hate crime had been committed. If they agreed, then he would make sure there was a proper investigation. I had heard nothing since.

Wilding's investigation established that my file was never sent to Legal Services. She also established from the head of Legal Services that if the file *had* been forwarded to him, he would have advised that a hate crime had been committed. Barbara Wilding concluded that I had been seriously let down by the Met. Eventually, having rejected Ian Blair's first so-called letter of apology, he wrote a second letter detailing the Met's neglect in the face of my complaints and apologised for letting me down.

It was in the course of meetings about this topic that he said to me: 'The trouble is Brian, when we've got a senior [ethnic minority] officer [presumably the suspect although I could only guess who he was referring to] and a senior gay officer involved, we don't know what to do.' The correct response is, of course, that it should not matter what colour somebody is or what their sexuality is; if you are having trouble with the concept, you should look at the case as if both parties are straight, white male officers and make a decision on that basis. In my case, someone had tried to damage my career by making unfounded and malicious allegations. On that basis alone, something should have been done. This was a measure of how political correctness appeared to be undermining the whole process of officers being held to account on the one hand and achieving justice for those who were victims on the other.

Equally, many police on the ground didn't know what to do when a gay or ethnic minority officer was the victim of a hate crime. Two gay male PCs, one of whom I knew from Lambeth, were walking hand in hand one evening near their section house in Kennington when they were subjected to homophobic abuse from a man on the other side of the road. When the officers took exception to the abuse the verbal taunts turned into a physical assault and one of the officers dialled 999.

Colleagues from Southwark arrived and started taking details. The victims of the attack explained they were serving policemen. When the officers who were taking their details kept referring to them as 'mates' one of the two said, 'He's not my mate, he's my partner.'

When I met the two of them the next morning, they described how the PC literally took two steps backwards when he realised this was a homophobic attack and, having told his colleagues, the officers' attitudes towards them changed completely. It was only when officers from Lambeth, on whose patch the assault had taken place, appeared, that the pair felt they were dealt with appropriately. This incident was symptomatic of the situation the Met had got itself into. Rather than ensuring that officers are confident in the way they handle minorities, a climate of fear had been created where, when faced with a gay man or a person from an ethnic minority, many officers froze – not necessarily because they were homophobic or racist, but because they were terrified of putting a foot wrong.

We had created a situation where our colleagues, when faced with a man wearing a turban were thinking, 'Oh my word, is this guy a Sikh or a Muslim? Is he allowed to carry a knife or does he think bacon is unclean? Is it my left or my right hand I should not touch him with, and will he mind if I keep my boots on when I go into his house?'

Community and race relations training should have been designed to give officers the confidence to say straight out, 'I want to respect your values and traditions, so please let me know if there's anything I do that you find offensive.' If our Kennington colleagues were not sure how to handle a homophobic attack, they should have had the confidence to say, 'I know I should know about this but I haven't dealt with a homophobic attack before, so let me know if I go wrong.'

I have to say that some of the political activists from minority groups have not helped the situation, many of whom say police officers *should* know what to do in every instance of hate crime. Until we get to the situation where police training becomes a three-year degree course (as in many other countries), we have to make allowances and we have to tell officers they will *not* be disciplined if they do not know every aspect of every different culture they are likely to encounter in London. Instead, they should treat every person they meet with the same dignity and respect; listen carefully to the needs of that person and treat them accordingly. There is a world of difference between a genuine mistake based on ignorance and deliberate discrimination based on prejudice; we need to establish whether a particular case is one of a genuine mistake or one of malice, and deal with it accordingly.

CHAPTER TWENTY-EIGHT

Thanks to events that have dominated the news since, it is all too easy for people to forget the Asian tsunami that happened on Boxing Day 2004. The Foreign and Commonwealth Office initially issued a helpline number for friends and relatives who thought that their loved ones had been affected by the catastrophe. Within hours the helpline was overwhelmed with its own tidal wave of calls and turned to the Met for assistance. There was no other body or organisation able to come even close to dealing with a tragedy on this scale.

They asked us to open our casualty bureau; this was a call centre in Scotland Yard where specially trained officers recorded the details of missing persons and attempted to match that information to those who had been found, dead or alive. The casualty bureau uses a major enquiry computer system known as HOLMES2 – but it was never designed to handle the numbers of missing being reported in this tragedy.

We received an average of 17,000 calls an hour and were able to deal with a creditable sixteen calls a minute. But it was obviously not enough, and although the system couldn't cope, everyone valiantly attempted to maintain some kind of control. There were five hundred police officers and support staff involved in the overall operation, forty-three of whom were overseas, where body recovery and identification teams had been immediately despatched to the worst-affected areas in Thailand and Sri Lanka.

By 3 January, I had taken over responsibility as Gold commander (the Gold commander has overall responsibility for the strategy of a major operation; Silver and Bronze commanders manage tactical and operational decisions respectively) to give Assistant Commissioner David Veness a break for thirty-six hours. At this point there were 198 grade one missing persons – people reported missing who were confirmed as having last been seen in the areas devastated by the tsunami. There were six thousand grade two missing persons, that is, persons who were known to be in the general area, and forty British nationals so far confirmed dead. All the families of grade one missing persons had been allocated a family liaison officer.

Apart from chairing the Gold Group meeting during my time in charge, I dealt with visits from the Home Secretary, Jack Straw, David Davis, the Shadow Home Secretary, and the chair and chief executive of the Metropolitan Police Authority.

It was anticipated, and it turned out to be the case, that the operation to deal with the missing person inquiries and body identification was going to last for between nine and twelve months. It was expected that many of the missing would never be found. There were reports every day of stacks of bodies being piled up in various parts of Thailand. British police officers were there trying to identify UK citizens, but it was impossible to tell which bodies *were* British, and so they simply helped local officials to identify every single body they found, British or not.

It was agreed that live casualties would be flown into Gatwick and bodies into Heathrow. This in itself was a massive undertaking, and despite some initial problems the Met showed itself to be an amazing organisation at being able to respond very quickly and effectively to such an enormous disaster.

CHAPTER TWENTY-NINE

During the run-up to Ian Blair's appointment as commissioner, our professional relationship appeared strong. As part of the selection process, Ian had to write one side of A4 on why he wanted to be commissioner and what he would do if he got the job. He asked me for advice on what he was proposing to submit. At the top of the three pages of feedback I handed to him, I said that I believed he could not successfully answer the question without using the word 'I', a word that had not appeared in his draft.

Once appointed, but before he took over, Ian Blair held a series of meetings with a handful of his trusted colleagues so he could bounce ideas off them and discuss his plans for the Met. I was one of the few of our 47,000 employees he included in this process.

On his first day as commissioner he was going to make a speech to the top three hundred police officers and police staff in the Met. He confidentially circulated a draft of his inaugural speech to a limited number of trusted colleagues (including me) and I again gave him feedback on what he was proposing to say.

In the summer of 2004, before his appointment as commissioner, Ian had invited me to have lunch with him at the Tate Britain gallery on the north bank of the Thames. During our lunch on the lawn outside the gallery, he asked me what job I would like if he were to become commissioner, as it would then be within his gift.

Apparently, he was having a series of these lunches with some key allies, and asking them the same question. I told him I would like to head up Internal Investigation. That department had suffered much criticism, culminating in the Morris Inquiry set up in the wake of Operation Helios to look at the Met's complaints and discipline system. With my equal opportunities experience, I told Ian that I would ensure complete fairness in the future. Having been subjected to investigations myself, I would also be in a good position to make balanced decisions.

When Ian became commissioner, he called me into his office and told me that he had had to give up a deputy assistant commissioner post in exchange for an additional assistant commissioner, and the DAC post he had decided to do away with was head of Internal Investigation. This was becoming a habit. First the ranking system had changed after I had left Lambeth, so I couldn't go back there; now it had happened at the Yard. I told colleagues that if they were not happy with their current posting to let me know; I would tell the commissioner I was interested in doing it and he would abolish it! With hindsight, I don't think Ian wanted an additional assistant commissioner or to reduce the rank of the officer in charge of Internal Investigation; I'm sure it was nothing personal.

I was then told that I was going to be taking over from Suzanna Becks as head of security in Specialist Operations, and would be in charge of diplomatic and royalty protection. As we were waiting to file in to hear the new commissioner's first speech, the head of Human Resources called me into a quiet corner and told me I was staying where I was, the second in command of Territorial Policing.

This was arguably the best role for a DAC in the Met, certainly the one with the greatest resources, so while it was a surprise it was also a very good consolation prize. Apparently Suzanna Becks had convinced Ian that her experience in the role was essential to ensure the safety of the capital, and having been concerned about the possible consequences, he kept her in post.

While he was still commissioner, John Stevens had introduced an innovation whereby he would deliver a morale-boosting speech every four to six weeks to about two hundred members of staff from across the Met. This would be followed by a question and answer session.

Stevens came to the Met having been the chief constable of Northumbria, where he had a reputation for decision-making on the hoof. The story goes that, while visiting a police station, officers suggested to him that they needed an additional fast response car. Quick as a flash, without any consultation with the local commander or consideration for his budget, Stevens replied, 'You've got one!' Old habits appeared to have died hard at these meetings and Stevens sometimes appeared to relish the role of 'miracle-worker'. The stories about these question and answer sessions became legend. In one famous case, a member of the support staff told the commissioner how he was very keen to be a police officer but had been told that his height-to-weight ratio made him too heavy to pass the physical. This might be considered a trivial issue by some, but people who are overweight tend to suffer more from joint problems and diabetes – both conditions which could severely limit a career in the Met.

Stevens, however, leant forward over the platform and, from a distance, looked the man up and down. He said, 'You look fit enough to me. You're in!' to rapturous applause. Stories of such instant responses to people's grievances led to rumours that invitations to one of his audiences were changing hands, between those invited and those not invited, for large sums of money.

These were Stevens's personal audiences. If he were unable to attend that month, then it was cancelled. Ian Blair was not allowed anywhere near them until, in the run-up to his retirement, the commissioner allowed him to conduct a practice session, restricted to those officers involved in the Safer Neighbourhoods teams. I was in the audience, being responsible for the initiative at that time. Ian did remarkably well, delivering an effective speech and then taking questions which he deftly answered. I went up onto the stage afterwards and said to him, 'That went well; you're very good at this.'

'Yes, I am,' he replied immodestly, 'I wanted to be an actor, you know.' His arrogance was unappealing.

The new commissioner held his first 'get together', as he called his version of Stevens's audiences, on 12 April 2005. He told us how, on his first day as deputy commissioner, everyone was miserable, and how since then the organisation had been revitalised with forty per cent more resources than it had on that day five years ago. Targets had been hit across the board, he said. We were highly successful in counter-terrorism and had high public and victim satisfaction levels, and at 47,000 strong we were London's biggest employer. All the while, however, our mission was widening; we were being asked to do more, there were no 'ors', only 'ands'. Officers who had transferred into the Met found it operationally brilliant but a bureaucratic nightmare. He pointed out what a public opinion survey had found – that Londoners were largely satisfied with the Met until they had any dealings with us.

He said we were excellent at the big set-piece (like the tsunami) but not so good at the day-to-day; what was routine for us, was not so for victims. Overall, he told us, we had improved compared with our own past performance, but it was still poor when compared with the other big police forces; if we doubled the number of offences brought to justice, we would still be behind them. Ian then said there was a need to improve communication and a need for real honesty.

The main difference between Stevens's sessions and Ian's get-togeth-ers was that Ian got every member of his top team to sit 'together' on the stage with him. He would deliver a shorter speech and then two of the other members of the team would follow to talk about their areas of business. I regularly deputised for Tim Godwin and neither of us were terribly enamoured with this part of the job, especially when we were forced to listen to the commissioner and then two colleagues saying more or less the same thing each time. We faced a constant struggle to stay awake for the two hours that the speeches would go on for, under full stage lighting and facing the audience, but things livened up when we were involved in answering the questions Ian was unwill-ing or unable to answer.

'Together' was Ian's watchword. In the run up to the takeover, he decided to repeat something he had done when he was chief constable of Surrey. He had come up with a new slogan for the Surrey police, which had been 'Making Surrey safer'. Ian changed it to '*With you*, making Surrey safer'. He left shortly after this for the Met and his Surrey officers informally renamed their slogan '*Without* you, making Surrey safer'.

Not having learnt from his previous mistake, and arguably lacking in imagination, Ian Blair announced that his addition to the Met police service slogan, and the name for his major change initiative was 'together'; from 'Working for a safer London' the Met strapline became 'Working *together* for a safer London'.

Under John Stevens, the phrase had been written on police vehicles in a stylised handwriting script but Ian's slogan was written in a plain font. When it was shown around for consultation I gave the feedback that it was good but the font was not as interesting or exciting as the previous one. I was told by the Department for Public Affairs that the change had been made to make it easier to read by those who were visually impaired and despite the 'consultation' the change of font went ahead. When the word inevitably got out (not from me) that Ian had spent a small fortune redesigning the slogan and making it easier to read for those who were visually impaired, the Yard strenuously denied it.

An issue which caused me much greater concern was how political Ian Blair appeared to be becoming; in particular, what appeared to me to be his apparent support for the Labour government. I think there are real issues here with the so-called political independence of the police.

Few people realise that the Home Secretary can delete the name of any applicant for any of the top posts in the police service (ACPO posts) throughout England, Wales and Northern Ireland from a selection shortlist. Probably more widely known is that the top two police jobs in the whole country, the commissioner and the deputy commissioner of the Met, are ultimately appointed by the Home Secretary. It would therefore be unwise for any ambitious senior police officer to do anything that might upset the Home Secretary or the ruling government (unless a change was imminent). One has to question to what extent senior police officers can declare themselves completely independent in light of the power the Home Secretary holds over their futures.

At the time of the 2005 General Election, a risk assessment was carried out on Prime Minister Tony Blair and it was decided it would be too dangerous for him to travel around the country on the campaign trail in anything other than an unmarked, armour-plated police Range Rover.

Number Ten complained that other party leaders were travelling on campaign buses in the party colours with a 'vote for my party' slogan on the side. The PM's office said this gave the others an unfair advantage over Tony Blair. Ian Blair (no relation) agreed that a Labour rose and 'Vote Labour' sign should appear on the side of the police Range Rover. The commissioner was apparently surprised when this decision caused some controversy.

Ian Blair also became involved in the politics of the debate around the proposed change in legislation to allow detention of terrorists for up to ninety days without charge. Whatever the merits, clearly Ian and Andy Hayman, by this time head of Specialist Operations, including terrorism, had convinced the PM that detention for this period of time was necessary. There should of course be no objection to the police setting out clearly the evidence to support such a change, which the government can then use to support the desired legislative change.

It is the role of Parliament to consider the case presented by the government, supported by the police, against the other considerations such as the erosion of civil liberties and human rights. That Ian Blair allowed Andy Hayman, the head of Specialist Operations, the overall head of the anti-terrorism command, to go into the House of Commons to try and persuade dissenting Labour MPs to vote with the government was, I believe, a totally improper blurring of the distinction between law makers and law enforcers, between the legislature and the servants of the law. Similarly, it is totally wrong for government to use police officers to try and influence the parliamentary decision-making process in such a blatant and direct way. The debate in Parliament should be restricted to that between the government and the opposition rather than directly involve police officers.

Around this time, I was asked to deliver an after-dinner speech to the McWhirter Foundation, a right-wing organisation. It was to be given at their annual dinner and prize-giving, where members of the community who were prepared to stand up bravely for their fellow citizens were honoured. The Foundation was named in honour of

Ross McWhirter (twin of Norris and co-founder of *The Guinness Book of Records*) who, having failed to persuade the government to offer a reward for information leading to the conviction of an IRA hit squad that was then terrorising London, went to a number of business leaders to establish his own £50,000 reward fund. As a consequence, he was assassinated on his doorstep by that same hit squad, who were eventually captured after the infamous Balcombe Street Siege.

At the Foundation dinner, I spoke about the freedom of speech and the freedom of the individual. This was at about the time Parliament was to debate the ninety-day pre-charge detention as put forward by the commissioner. I said that the government had to be careful to explain to the Muslim community exactly why the police needed to detain people for ninety days, because there was a real danger of alienating them. It was John Grieve, the Met's former anti-terrorism head who said 'It is communities that defeat terrorism' and not the police acting alone. It was important to take the Muslim community with us when enacting what some would call Draconian legislation.

The following Sunday, an *Observer* journalist made an oblique reference in her column to what I had said. This was picked up by Andrew Gilligan in the *Evening Standard* who claimed that I had said I was against ninety days detention (which was not what I said at all). Within an hour of the Gilligan article being published, I received a call from Moir Stewart, the commissioner's staff officer, who told me: 'As you've now been reported as being against the ninety days – the commissioner's sure that isn't what you said by the way – you have to issue a statement in favour of ninety days.'

'Can you tell the commissioner that there's a slight problem with that? I *am* against ninety days,' I replied.

After ten minutes, the phone rang again and Moir said, 'The Commissioner says you are a DAC in the Metropolitan Police and one of his senior officers, and as such you will support ninety days detention, and you will issue a press release to that effect.'

Thus began a process of negotiation between myself and the Met's media machine where we tried to find a form of words which reconciled my personal beliefs with what the commissioner considered to be my professional duty to him. Being a subordinate in a disciplined organisation and with my work not yet done in the Met, he gave me no choice but to issue the statement, which read: 'As a professional police officer and a senior member of the Metropolitan Police, I support the view that an extension of detention to ninety days is necessary in difficult, complex and sensitive terrorism cases where it would not otherwise be possible to carry out a full and proper investigation and to bring terrorists to justice. We must however be mindful of the impact this may have on the Muslim community from whom we can expect to get valuable information that might lead to arrests and the detention of terrorists.'

Thankfully the media saw the statement for what it was. The *Financial Times* reported that 'While the ninety-day limit had strong backing from a majority of senior police chiefs and rank-and-file officers, some police commanders felt that insufficient consideration was given to the implications for human rights and to the proposal's unpopularity within the Muslim community. Brian Paddick, Deputy Assistant Commissioner of the Met, warned last week: "Communities are an important source of information about suspect terrorists and it is important to maintain public confidence."'

On another occasion I was told that Commissioner Ian Blair was angry with me (again) and I had been summoned to his office to see him with Tim Godwin. I cannot recall now what it was I was supposed to have done to annoy him, but the meeting itself was unforgettable.

For a start, Ian Blair seemed to be more nervous than I and the rebuke he issued was so mild that I almost missed it. Obviously as relieved as I was that the ordeal was over, Ian looked across at me, smiled, and said, 'There you are, Brian; you see it wasn't a trousers-down session after all.'

Not believing what I had heard, I looked back at him in disbelief; this was hardly the most appropriate thing to say to the most senior openly gay officer in the UK. What the commissioner had meant to say (I think) was that it was not a 'book down trousers session', as in the old schoolboy trick of protecting oneself from the cane.

Tim Godwin was already straining to control a snigger when the commissioner, realising his gaffe said, 'Er . . . I mean it wasn't a pockets in trousers session.'

This made even less sense. Realising the poor fellow really had lost the plot, and in an effort to pre-empt any further Blairisms, I just said 'Yes, Commissioner' with a dead-pan face, then got up and left . . .

Godwin later told me it took him some time to stop himself laughing enough to explain to the commissioner exactly what he had just said.

CHAPTER THIRTY

Roger Graeff's fly-on-the-wall TV documentary about the rape investigation unit in Thames Valley had been seen by many as a catalyst for dramatic improvements in the way the police investigate rape.

Not long after becoming commissioner, Ian Blair summoned me to his office. He was waving a copy of a slim tome on rape investigation, called *Investigating Rape: A New Approach for Police*, and published in 1985 by the Police Foundation.

Ian told me that, as the author of this book, he could not preside as commissioner over a Metropolitan Police Service that was not the best in the county for rape investigation.

He pointed out the dramatic differences in the proportion of rape cases solved in different parts of London and said that such variations, which he assumed were the result of differences in police performance, were unforgivable. He wanted me to conduct a review of rape investigation in the Met, to look at the anomalies in performance, and to come up with recommendations to ensure that every borough performed to the best possible standard.

What became apparent was that at least some variations in performance were driven by external factors as much as by the competence and dedication of the officers involved. The clearest example of this was the borough of Westminster. Most cases in the West End and central areas were solved, whereas far fewer were successfully concluded in the Paddington area. This was despite the fact that it was the same team of officers who investigated offences in both places.

In the West End, offences tended to be of the 'date rape' kind where women had agreed to meet with someone they knew for a date, so it was easy to identify the perpetrator and make a quick arrest. There was also extensive, good-quality CCTV coverage within and outside licensed premises, which meant that there was a good chance of identifying a perpetrator even if it was someone the woman did not know.

In Paddington there were high levels of prostitution, and a number of rapes were reported by prostitutes when a client had gone beyond the services he had contracted for or had run off without paying. There were also a high proportion of cases involving women with mental health issues in Paddington. Indeed, I found that across London women with mental health issues figured disproportionately amongst victims of rape.

While some of these cases might have been false claims, i.e. people suffering from delusions, this could not account for every case. The fact is that women who had had too much to drink, as well as people who were users of mental health services, were the most vulnerable to attack. Importantly, these categories of victim tended to be the least able to convince the CPS or – if the case ever got that far – a jury that they were reliable witnesses. This is a fundamental dilemma facing the criminal justice system; those who are most likely to become victims are also the most likely to be unconvincing witnesses.

More worrying and more controversially, black and ethnic minority women were disproportionately identified as victims of rape. This had been highlighted a year or so earlier by Ken Hyder (the freelance journalist I had worked with on the cannabis pilot) who had suggested that there were very high levels of rape amongst young black women.

Two possible explanations were put forward in the review:

1. Young black women are disproportionately involved in violent and risk-taking behaviour.
2. Black women were more likely to report rape to police as the support network available to white victims among friends and family was less likely to be available to black victims.

Clearly some of the variation in the results achieved by the police appeared to be the result of the level of commitment from individual officers, and the willingness of senior officers to put resources into rape investigation as opposed to other crimes. Overall, the report concluded that the Met was a beacon of excellence for rape investigation compared with other forces, but the report was still controversial in highlighting the difficulties with certain categories of victim and the fact that improvements could be made in some parts of London.

That it highlighted inconsistent approaches across the capital was seen by the Met's media machine as potentially damaging for the commissioner, whose first year in office had been dogged by unrelenting media criticism. I was asked to water down the findings and recommendations while the Met stalled publication, trying to quell the media interest. The press officer in charge of launching the review told me she had been instructed to try and ensure it was *not* reported in any newspaper.

This was an example of a very serious issue that required urgent attention but which, because of politics and concerns about the reputation of the Met in general and the commissioner in particular, who was having a hard time in the press, ended up being suppressed.

To see this review submerged for political reasons was galling – not just because my team and I had put an enormous amount of effort into conducting the review, but because rape victims in London were not receiving a high enough level of service. This was not some academic exercise. We were trying to make sure that rape victims stood a better chance of achieving justice while protecting some of the most vulnerable people in society from attack.

CHAPTER THIRTY-ONE

On 7 July 2005, London was revelling in its own success. Wimbledon had just finished, the Live 8 concert in Hyde Park had welcomed a crowd of 200,000 and we had won the 2012 Olympic bid, leading to a triumphant party that started in Trafalgar Square and spontaneously spread up through the West End and beyond. 'London seems to be the hub of the world . . . fun, big-hearted and spontaneous' wrote one journalist. On 6 July even the terrorist threat level had been reduced from 'Severe General' to 'Substantial' (which was level three out of six) by the Joint Terrorism Analysis Centre.

The four men who were last seen together at London's King's Cross railway station on 7 July 2005, must have looked ordinary enough to the thousands of commuters rushing to work. Three were British born – a thirty-year-old teacher with a baby daughter and a reputation for dedication to his learning-disabled students; an eighteen-year-old described by friends as a 'gentle giant', dressed in denims and loose jacket; and a twenty-two-year-old cricket fan who worked in his family's fish-and-chip shop in Leeds. The fourth was a nineteen-year-old Jamaican who had become a British citizen, married a British woman and had a young son. All four were carrying military-style backpacks. Closed circuit television footage showed that, after several minutes of calm conversation, the men fanned out in different directions. They all knew they were about to meet their deaths.

*

That morning I was chairing a meeting in my office at Scotland Yard with representatives from the National Health Service. I had spent months trying to schedule this meeting and I was not best pleased when Susie Bragg, my staff officer, burst into the room. 'Sorry to interrupt, Brian, but there's been a major incident,' she said.

Hoping it was a false alarm, or at least the kind of incident that would not merit my personal attention, I replied, 'Thanks very much for letting me know; keep me updated.'

'No,' Susie replied insistently, 'I think it's serious.'

I apologised to my guests and immediately left for the second floor and the public order control room of Scotland Yard where the Gold commander for that day, Commander Chris Allison, was in control. Allison had been in his office on the Embankment when, at nine-fifteen a.m., he learnt that 'a number of incidents' had occurred on the underground. He raced to Scotland Yard in his car, sirens on, texting his daughter who lived in Aldgate East to check she was okay.

The Met did not usually have a Gold commander on standby, but this was the time of the G8 summit in Scotland and the Met had sent a large number of officers to help local police deal with anti-globalisation protestors. We also had several Serials (a unit of officers with one inspector, three sergeants and eighteen constables) on standby in central London in case there were any local protests.

I asked Allison what had happened and he told me there had been a power surge on the underground in three separate locations, resulting in trains becoming stuck in tunnels. I asked him whether we suspected terrorism. No doubt thinking the same as I, Allison replied that, at the moment, the latest information from London Underground was that it was a power surge.

As we continued to monitor the situation, the first call came in that a bus had exploded in Tavistock Place. 'Chris,' I said. 'You don't get power surges on buses.' We were under attack.

Forty people attached to the Gold Coordinating Committee met around a table in a conference room at Scotland Yard. They agreed on a strategy statement and had it typed up and circulated. The priorities were obvious, but having them on paper brought them into focus: first, save lives and treat casualties; second, start the criminal investigation; third, reassure the wider community; fourth, get London back to normal.

Having had a lot of experience with the media, I said to Chris Allison, 'I'll be your talking head.' It was established practice that a senior officer dealt with the press, leaving the officer in command of the operation to deal with the incident free of distraction.

I left Allison to it and went up to the thirteenth floor of the Yard, home of the Met's media machine. I spoke to Chris Webb, the deputy head of Public Affairs, who readily agreed I should handle the media. We went together to the eighth floor to speak to the commissioner. Webb explained what had happened and added, 'Brian is going to do the media.'

The commissioner replied, 'No he's not, *I'm* doing it.'

Webb became agitated at this and told him that this was a bad idea, at least until we knew exactly what was happening. The commissioner needed to keep out of the media spotlight while information was still sketchy. In the middle of this discussion, Moir Stewart, the commissioner's staff officer, came into the office and delivered a message from Cabinet Office Briefing Room A (COBRA). 'The commissioner is *not* to do the media.'

To which Ian replied, 'Tell COBRA I'm doing it.'

Chris Webb managed to negotiate with the commissioner that I would take over once he had done the initial round of TV interviews at eleven a.m. We travelled the short distance to Millbank where the BBC, ITN and Sky have their Westminster studios.

The first reports suggested that there were five or six devices on the underground. This confused picture resulted from victims coming out of Edgware Road, King's Cross, Russell Square, Moorgate and Aldgate East stations. What had actually happened was that the bombs had gone off on trains when they were between stations and victims had fled to stations in front of and behind the train.

The reason nobody wanted the commissioner to take part in the first set of press conferences was because, as expected, the situation was confused and there was a risk he might end up looking as if he didn't know what was going on. Fortunately, he did an excellent job, and people now recall how in control the commissioner seemed more than the fact that he got the number of devices wrong – although, as we shall see, the *New York Times* and Sky News both picked up on this and other errors when they criticised Ian Blair in the wake of the Stockwell shooting.

After that it was down to me. As media spokesperson it was essential that I had the latest information from the emergency services, and the others involved in the incidents. At these huge press conferences I was very happy to be sat alongside Andy Trotter, by now deputy chief constable of the British Transport Police. An excellent policeman and a good friend, Andy was one of the two DACs I had reported to as a commander of Lambeth. Like me, he was a rugby-playing divorcé (although the similarities ended there) and we worked very well together, which made all the difference at this time of crisis. We continually gave briefings on Thursday and Friday, working twelve-hour-plus days.

It is in times of crisis that I appear to perform at my best. Despite a constant stream of updated facts and figures, and knowing that I was being watched by the world's media at one moment and then talking to some of the UK's most respected journalists on a one-to-one briefing the next, I felt completely in control.

The Gold Group set up incident commanders at each of the scenes. The City of London Police took control of Moorgate and Aldgate East while the Met took command of the other scenes, working closely with the British Transport Police. By 10.10 a.m., London Underground had suspended all services. The initial picture was that there were two dead and nine seriously injured reported by the City of London Police, while the London ambulance service was reporting a hundred and fifty serious casualties at various sites and a total of over one thousand injured people overall. The fire brigade were already at the scene of all the incidents, as were London ambulance teams.

The fire brigade was considering calling in fire officers from neighbouring areas but, as far as the Met was concerned, while all of our resources were being mustered it was decided not to call in any off-duty officers. The repercussions of the attacks – and we were not sure that there were not going to be more – were likely to continue for some time, and we needed to keep officers in reserve to ensure resilience over the period. All of the emergency calls to the police were still being answered with no problem.

The line I was asked to deliver to the world's media was that there had been a series of serious incidents, and to provide reassurance to Londoners that the emergency services were in control of all of them. I urged people to stay where they were and not to call the emergency services unless it was life-threatening. I also had to explain that there was no way to travel around central London because both underground and bus services had been suspended, although buses were running in outer London.

Each press conference consisted of making a statement and then fielding a whole raft of questions. There was a rumour going around that the Israeli Secret Service had been tipped off that London was about to be bombed and I was quizzed about this by a journalist from the *Sunday Herald* (no evidence exists that this was the case, and it could not be tracked beyond a rumour started by the Associated Press who quoted an 'anonymous source'). Nothing indicated that this was a failure in our intelligence and I said that at the moment there was need for calm and a little less speculation.

Over 104,000 calls were made to the casualty bureau that morning. I asked people to call again if they found people they had already reported missing, and I urged people who had been near the blasts to get in touch with their family and friends as soon as they were able, to let them know that they were all right.

We were still not sure how many explosions there had been or what type of improvised explosive devices were used. There were obvious concerns that there might be other devices planted around London, and controlled explosions were carried out on some vehicles throughout the day. All of them proved to be false alarms. We did know that damage was confined to a relatively small area around where the explosions had taken place. We were unable to confirm the number of casualties, although later that day I was able to confirm that three hundred and fifty people were treated at the scene and another three hundred and fifty were taken to hospital. At that point we knew there were fifty-plus confirmed dead, but we didn't know how many bodies there were yet to be discovered.

Andy Hayman informed the press that 'the best possible people' with a proven track record (having dealt with Irish Republican terrorism) were already investigating the matter; that they were gathering as much evidence as possible and were committed to a successful prosecution. Of course, he did not yet know that the underground bombers had all died in the process, since there was nothing at this stage to suggest a suicide attack.

I made the point that we needed the help of London's communities. We needed them to tell us about people who had been behaving suspiciously; people who had hired garages and lockups (this was how the IRA had worked; they came over to the mainland and hired lock-ups to store bomb-making equipment).

As the day progressed, I spoke of the Met's admiration for the way in which Londoners had reacted to the attack; that we had support from all communities and faith leaders and the whole of London was united against the terrorists. We also paid tribute to London's emergency services and I stressed our implacable resolve to track down those responsible.

Not everything went smoothly of course; the bus and the Russell Square crime-scenes were proving very difficult to deal with. We had been told in a Gold Group meeting by DAC Peter Clark, the national anti-terrorism coordinator, that there were thousands of body parts, and nobody knew how many people that signified. We needed to be able to explain why we couldn't be certain about the number of dead, but at the same time we had to be as sensitive as possible.

During a briefing with an officer from the anti-terrorist branch, I suggested that he should only tell me things they wanted made public so that when I was asked a question about something they wanted kept confidential, rather than lying I could honestly say I didn't know.

They did tell me something that they didn't want me to give away in my statement but thought I ought to know in case journalists had heard about it from another source and asked me a question about it. Three British citizens from West Yorkshire had been arrested at Toronto Airport in Canada after leaving Manchester at midday on 7

July. As it turned out, these arrests were completely unrelated to the bombings and the anti-terrorist branch didn't want me to mention them in the briefing as they were not relevant – if asked, however, I was to say that arrests had been made.

Having kept silent about the arrests for the whole of the press conference, Stuart Tendler from *The Times* asked, 'Have you made any arrests?'

I turned to Andy Trotter and said 'Here we go' before turning back and telling the assembled press that three people had been arrested in relation to terrorism offences. This led to uproar. 'Why didn't you tell us before? This is outrageous!'

My reply was clear: 'I've been told that these arrests have nothing to do with the bombings on July 7th and I have no further details.'

There were some other difficulties. We inaccurately reported that the first bomb exploded at 8.51 a.m., the second bomb exploded five minutes later, at 8.56 a.m. on a train at Russell Square station, and the third was detonated on a train at 9.17 a.m. as it approached Edgware Road. On the evening of 8 July, a video aired by the BBC showed that the bomb at Edgware Road had exploded at 8.51 a.m. – not at 9.17 a.m.

By the morning of Saturday 9 July, we knew that the bombs had exploded within fifty seconds of each other. The initial estimate of the times that the bombs exploded was mistakenly matched to the first emergency calls made from each underground station. By Saturday, we had seen Tim O'Toole, head of London Underground, who explained how they knew from electronic monitoring of the railway tracks exactly what time the bombs detonated. We took some time, with Tim's help, to explain this complicated issue to journalists on Saturday. The journalists who work on daily newspapers usually have Saturday off and so on the Sunday we had the daily hacks back who had missed the explanation around the timings. When we repeated that all the bombs had been detonated at the same time, one American reporter said, 'Hang on a minute, you said one went off twenty minutes after the others', which created a bit of confusion and even longer to explain than it had on the Saturday.

On Saturday evening I finished the last press conference of the day and travelled by tube to West Hampstead. People were looking at each other nervously while I tried to carry on the good work by smiling at people if they looked in my direction. I had arranged to go to an open-air music concert at Kenwood House on Hampstead Heath. It was a glorious summer evening and here I was with twelve friends, listening to (admittedly popular) classical music and sharing a picnic. It was an extraordinary feeling. As I looked at the thousand or so people of every nationality enjoying the sunset and the concert, one of thousands of events this marvellous city offered every day, it could not have been clearer that terrorists would never achieve their objectives.

It was of course back to work first thing on Sunday. One of my interviews was with BBC Radio London, held in the back of a radio car outside the QE II Centre. I repeated much of what I had spent the day saying: warning people to be careful, not to leave packages or bags anywhere, and to go back to work as normal – but to be aware that sections of the tube would not be working. Everyone needed to stay vigilant as the eight million people who travelled on London's transport system every day were our best weapon against terrorism. By this time, out of 1,700 calls to the anti-terrorist hotline, ten per cent had yielded useful information. I said it was essential that communities should stick together while all our efforts were being directed at protecting the community. We were by this time already receiving reports of a number of attacks on ethnic minorities, including attacks on buildings.

The journalist asked me what I felt personally about the bombings. Up until then I had been wholly professional; I was the voice of the organisation and had wanted to sound authoritative and reassuring to the public. My personal reaction as a Londoner was quite different; by then I had been going flat-out for nearly four days and emotion was beginning to surface.

The most personal memory I have of 7/7 was of visiting police stations all over London from where officers under my command in territorial policing had rushed to the aid of those caught up in the bombings. Some of them had walked along the tunnels and gone into train carriages where the dead and injured were, and had helped to bring out the living, the dying and the dead in what was the most gruesome of circumstances. Many were young officers who had just finished their initial training at Hendon and had just joined the station at West Hampstead to take part in six weeks of training on their street duties course.

I knew from my personal experience that some of these officers could have been seriously affected by what they had seen. I was very keen to meet with them and see that they were getting all the support they needed, particularly following the experiences I had had during my service of the Met sometimes failing officers in such circumstances. In particular, I remembered the sergeant who shouted at the young female PC to pull herself together after dealing with the traumatic car accident, and my own experience at the Notting Hill carnival. I wanted to be certain that nobody was being treated like that today.

These young officers had all done so many heroic things on that day and yet very few appeared to me to be badly affected by what they had seen. Some of them, who looked to be in shock and sat in total silence, gave cause for concern, but I did my best to reassure them. It was good to see that they were receiving the best possible support from their colleagues who had shared the same experiences – the only people who really understood what they had been through.

I travelled to Sutton where officers from that station had tended casualties from the bus bomb in Tavistock Place. Then I went to Croydon police station and headed for the canteen where I was due to meet a supervisor who would introduce me to other officers who had worked in central London that day.

I was taken aback when I spotted Steve, the PC whose father had been killed by the boy racer twenty years earlier when I was an inspector and who I had not seen since. The feelings and memories I had experienced then came flooding back to me: how we had cried on each other's shoulders when I told him the sad news; the moment when he said 'You're just like the rest of them, you don't care about us' because I had been forced to restrict overtime. These events were taking more of a toll on me than I thought.

Steve stood up and said, 'Hello, Sir.'

'For goodness sake, Steve,' I replied, 'how long have we known each other? Call me Brian.'

I started to explain why I was there when he interrupted me. 'Don't worry, I've told them all already.'

I looked at him, puzzled.

'I'll never forget the help and support you gave me when I lost my dad. I've told them you're absolutely genuine; that you do really care.'

From Monday, it was decided that the situation was under control. The investigation had by now taken over from the emergency response and DAC Peter Clarke (head of the Anti-Terrorist Branch, SO13 and national coordinator for Terrorist Investigations) was able to take over the press conferences as life, in the Met and in London, attempted to return to something near normal.

On Tuesday 12 July at 4.30 p.m. I was in a meeting with Andy Hayman where he gave a briefing that the bombings were commit-ted by Al Qaeda. He already had CCTV pictures of four young men who were at King's Cross, having arrived from Luton at 8.20 a.m. They had at that stage identified three of them and were pretty certain who the fourth one was; the three were all British. One of the bodies they had recovered was completely shaved, an indication that he was a ritual suicide bomber. Hayman told us there was link-age with 'nominals' (terrorist suspects who might have helped them) and they had found the bomb-making factory in the Midlands.

Community issues were rapidly moving up the agenda. The National Front had been ringing round their members, trying to scrabble together a protest outside Finsbury Park mosque, and they were also planning a march in central London on the Saturday. Combat 18 were advocating violence against prominent Muslims. Assistant Commissioner Tarique Ghaffur spoke to national faith lead-ers to provide some reassurance that we would protect them.

Meanwhile, the commissioner told us he was going to ask the gov-ernment for another five hundred counter-terrorism staff. He also said that the London Olympics were now in a fundamentally different position from where we had been on 6 July, and the Crime Reporters' Association was planning to turn their focus onto new terror legislation. At the same meeting, Deputy Commissioner Paul Stephenson wondered whether the Met was vulnerable and whether we could we have prevented 7/7.

By 20 July, other than thanks being passed on from the Home Office for the Met's efforts in relation to 7/7, our discussions had moved on to other areas such as the performance of the Met against crime in general, and how far the Home Office should be allowed to intervene in police matters. This was the first meeting since 7/7 that was not dominated by those events.

Despite the attacks, the Met was enjoying high regard. The emergency services response to the bombings had been magnificent and the investigation was making rapid progress. The Met and Londoners were united in adversity, and the courage and dedication shown by our officers meant that public attitudes towards the police were very positive. In the immediate aftermath of the bombings, even the local Pret a Manger sandwich shop was not charging officers for their sandwiches (something never seen before or since!).

But all of that was about to change dramatically.

CHAPTER THIRTY-TWO

On 21 July 2007, two weeks after the first bombings, another attempt was made to explode devices on the London transport system; again, three devices on underground trains and one on a bus. This time the explosives failed to go off and the would-be bombers fled. The search was on to catch them.

On the following morning, Friday 22 July 2005, a surveillance team was watching a three-storey block of flats in Tulse Hill. They had been led there after finding a gym membership card in a rucksack left at Shepherd's Bush station.

They were looking for a man called Hussain Osman who had tried to detonate his bomb at Shepherd's Bush. In addition, the number plate of a vehicle spotted at a suspected terror training camp in central Wales had been linked to the Tulse Hill address.

The suspect address was number twenty-one on the third floor of the block; Jean Charles de Menezes, a Brazilian, lived a few doors away at number seventeen. On 22 July, the communal entrance was being watched by one surveillance officer, armed with a video camera. It was considered too dangerous to enter the block.

That day, the cameraman, codenamed Tango Ten, was a soldier who had been on secondment to the police for about a year. He began watching De Menezes's block at 6.30 a.m. His task was to take footage of anyone who left the address and compare it with pictures of the suspects involved in the failed attacks the previous day.

At 9.33 a.m. De Menezes emerged from the communal entrance. He was on his way to North London to help a friend install a fire alarm. Tango Ten was caught off guard because he was 'relieving himself' as De Menezes walked into the street.

The surveillance officer wrote in his logbook: 'I observed a U/I (unidentified) male IC1 5′8″ dark hair beard/stubble, blue denim jacket, blue jeans and wearing trainers exit the block, he was not carrying anything and at this time I could not confirm whether he was or was not either of our subjects. As I observed this male exited [sic] the block I was in the process of relieving myself . . . At this time I was not able to transmit my observations and switch on the video camera at the same time.'

The cameraman had described De Menezes as IC1 (light-skinned European). Hussain was IC4 (South Asian). Nevertheless, the surveillance officers followed De Menezes for the next thirty minutes as he travelled north on a bus towards Stockwell, still trying to establish whether he was Hussain. Their observations and radio transmissions were being reported to Gold Command where the officer in charge was Commander Cressida Dick.

Cressida had to decide whether the man sitting on the number two bus heading towards Stockwell was a potential suicide bomber on the basis of information being fed to her by the surveillance officers. At 9.47 a.m. De Menezes got off the bus, waited for a few moments and boarded it again. To the officers who were following him, this looked like an anti-surveillance measure and their suspicions increased. In fact, De Menezes had tried to get onto the tube at Brixton but the station was closed, so he decided to carry on towards Stockwell on the bus and get on the tube there.

It became clear to the officers that De Menezes was heading for Stockwell station, from where three of the suspected bombers had left on their mission the previous day. De Menezes entered the station and picked up a copy of the *Metro* newspaper. He put his Oyster card on the ticket reader and descended the escalator. About halfway down he began to run as he heard the sound of an approaching train, just as any commuter might do and as I have on many occasions. He sat down with a glass panel to his right, two seats in. The surveillance officer, codenamed Hotel Three sat on his left. There were three members of the public between them. Hotel Three suddenly saw plainclothes officers arriving on the platform. He quickly leapt to his feet, placed his left foot against the open carriage door and shouted 'He's here!' pointing at De Menezes.

The armed officers had been briefed since the 7 July bombings that under the terms of Operation Kratos they could be ordered to shoot a suicide bomber in the head, without warning, to prevent him detonating a bomb.

It was obvious to De Menezes that something was up, and with the other passengers in the carriage, he stood up and moved towards the doors as the armed officers piled into the carriage. The surveillance officer grabbed hold of De Menezes in a bear-hug, pinning his arms to his side and tried to force him back into his seat. At that moment there was a gunshot and the officer was pulled away; he shouted 'Police!' and held up his hands. As an armed officer dragged him out of the carriage, another six gunshots rang out. Terrified commuters scrambled out of the train onto the platform. The officers checked De Menezes – there was no bomb. Among the dead man's possessions were his wallet and mobile phone. It was 10.06 a.m.

THE INQUIRIES

The shooting of Jean Charles de Menezes led to two inquiries, Stockwell 1 and Stockwell 2, both carried out by the Independent Police Complaints Commission (IPCC). Stockwell 1 has two parts. The first, known as Stockwell 1A, deals with the circumstances of the death of Jean Charles de Menezes. The second, known as Stockwell 1B, deals with complaints by the family of Jean Charles de Menezes concerning the treatment they received from the Met immediately following his death.

Stockwell 2 is the report on the investigation into complaints about the Met's handling of public statements following the shooting of De Menezes. This second investigation followed allegations from De Menezes's family that Commissioner Ian Blair and others had knowingly made public inaccurate information or had failed to correct inaccurate information placed in the public arena, specifically:

The complaint alleges that, following the shooting of Mr de Menezes, you [the Commissioner] alone or together with other officers of the Metropolitan Police Service knowingly or negligently made public statements, or concurred with public statements made by officers or employees of the Metropolitan Police Service, concerning the circumstances of the death that were inaccurate.

The misinformation included statements that Mr de Menezes had failed to stop when challenged by police, had leapt over a ticket barrier, was wearing a heavy jacket with wires protruding from it and other indications his behaviour had alerted suspicion.

The complaint also alleges that no steps were taken to correct the misinformation that had been released into the public domain prior to requests from the IPCC to the Metropolitan Police Service to avoid further comment on the circumstances of Mr de Menezes's death. If proven the alleged conduct could amount to a breach of The Police (Conduct) Regulations 2004, Schedule 1, Code of Conduct, Code 1 in relation to Honesty and Integrity.

Stockwell 2 was about whether there had been a cover-up at the highest levels at New Scotland Yard: whether the commissioner had lied or whether he had been misinformed or left ignorant by his most trusted senior staff. If the leader of the Met is to retain the confidence of the public, he cannot lie to the public whom he serves; the job is all about trust and confidence and the man at the top has to be beyond reproach. As the commissioner himself said, 'If I had lied, I would not be fit to hold this office.'

Stockwell 2's remit had been expanded after an article in the *News of the World* quoted the commissioner as saying something about the shooting which I believed to be untrue: that Ian's advisors did not believe that we had shot the wrong man until the next day. He later repeated this in an interview with the *Guardian*.

There were concerns that Stockwell 2 might not only bring the commissioner down but other highly ranked officers based at Scotland Yard as well. Senior journalists at the BBC became so convinced that the commissioner would be forced to resign that the BBC prepared the news item well in advance (they called me to see if I would be prepared to comment on 'when the commissioner goes'; I refused and told the Met's press office what the BBC was up to).

When the report was published in August 2007, it was to the dismay of the De Menezes family. They could not believe that the commissioner had been cleared while only one man, Assistant Commissioner Andy Hayman, the head of Specialist Operations, was found to have misled his boss and the public.

My own feeling is that the information contained in the report does not dovetail with many of its own conclusions. What follows is my own personal account of events based on my recollection of what happened at New Scotland Yard in the wake of the shooting (which I also gave in evidence to the IPCC) and on the findings of the Stockwell 2 report. Others' accounts differ; the Stockwell report gives the official conclusions. Although not everyone will agree with what I say, this is my honestly held recollection of a sequence of remarkable events which I will never forget as long as I live.

22 JULY 2005, NEW SCOTLAND YARD

At 12.30 p.m. on Friday 22 July 2005 Commander Rod Jarman (responsible for community engagement) gave me an update about the public reaction to the shooting. Some community groups were already outraged; there was talk of a 'police execution', and the question, 'Were the police going to keep shooting black people?' had already been asked more than once. At that time, I knew nothing about the identity of the man who had been shot.

At 3 p.m., back at Stockwell underground station, a detective superintendent logged the details of a wallet that had been found on the dead man: 'The wallet examination suggest(s) that the deceased is Jean Charles DE MENEZES, b 7.1.78, a Brazilian born in St Paulo. Urgent enquiries to be undertaken by SO13 to establish if he is linked to their investigation and if they can find a next of kin by examination of the phone.'

This information was relayed to Detective Superintendent Stephen Kavanagh who, at 3.08 p.m., passed it on to his boss at Scotland Yard, Assistant Commissioner Alan Brown, the Gold commander with overall responsibility for the police operation to capture the terrorists. Kavanagh was his staff officer.

'A wallet had been recovered from the carriage where the man had been shot. The wallet contained bank cards, a temporary Inland Revenue card and a driving permit.'

According to the Stockwell 2 report, Kavanagh then briefed Caroline Murdoch, the commissioner's chief of staff and Chief Superintendent Moir Stewart, the commissioner's staff officer, about the contents of the wallet.

Shortly afterwards, I went to see Moir Stewart to see if there were any developments I needed to be made aware of. My boss, Tim Godwin, was on leave and as acting assistant commissioner I had full responsibility for the twenty thousand police officers and support staff who worked in Territorial Policing, so I wanted to ensure I was kept tightly in the loop. At about 3.15 p.m., I was in the office occupied by the commissioner's staff officer and his chief of staff, his two closest aides, when the commissioner walked past me in full uniform, tunic and commissioner's cap, on his way to a press conference.

Stewart, whom I had known for years, and was a larger than life character, said, 'You never guess what we've done now?'

'No,' I replied, having no idea what he was about to tell me.

'We've shot a Brazilian tourist.'

'You're joking,' I said in complete disbelief.

'No he's not,' said Caroline Murdoch, a petite woman, utterly charming with a hard edge, just as a chief of staff should be, 'We found a Brazilian driving licence in his back pocket.'

What I recall them telling me is entirely consistent with what they had been told by Detective Superintendent Kavanagh (apart from the assumption that he was a tourist, which I took simply to indicate that he was innocent). Stewart has subsequently denied that this is exactly what he told me and Murdoch has said she still believed at that point that the dead man was a suicide bomber.

Realising the enormity of what I had just been told, I went up to my office to watch the press conference, thinking 'This is going to be interesting!' What was the commissioner going to say in the light of what his staff had just told me?

The conference started at 3.39 p.m. The commissioner, who was appearing with Assistant Commissioner Specialist Operations Andy Hayman, said: 'As you are aware there is a lot of police activity going

on today in relation to the underground and bus incidents of yesterday. This is a very, very fast moving investigation.

'As I've said before, this is the greatest operational challenge ever
faced by the Metropolitan Police Service. The MPS and its sister services
are doing a magnificent job, but officers are facing previously unknown
threats and great danger.

'We need the understanding of all communities, and the coopera-
tion of all communities, and we need calm. We know that there are
rumours sweeping London, and I really do appeal for people to listen
to the facts as they emerge.

'The most important message we have other than this appeal is that
this operation is targeted against criminals. It is not targeted against any
community, or any section of the community.

'I can say as part of operations linked to yesterday's incidents, Met
police officers have shot a man inside Stockwell Underground Station
at approximately 10 a.m. this morning. London Ambulance Service
and the air ambulance both attended and the man was pronounced
dead at the scene.

'The information I have available is that this shooting is directly linked
to the ongoing and expanding anti-terrorist operation. Any death is
deeply regrettable. I understand the man was challenged and refused to
obey.'

After Andy Hayman had spoken about the failed bomb attacks on
the tube the previous day (not mentioning the shooting), the commissioner reiterated 'the need for calm and the need to understand
that rumours will sweep around about what is happening.

'At the moment the situation is under control and the investigation
is proceeding. The scenes are under control and the house being
searched is under control and the second crucial message is that we can
only defeat this form of terror by working with communities, by getting the communities' support in to everything that we are doing. We
will try and explain everything that we possibly can – but it is a very,
very fast moving scenario and we can only do that from time to time.'

From what I knew, this did not make sense. I had just been told
by his staff officer, a chief superintendent no less, that we had shot a
Brazilian tourist, dead. In what way was he 'directly linked' to the

ongoing terrorist operation? Well, I thought to myself, the man had emerged from a building which was linked to a suspect in the failed bomb attacks the day before, and the building was under police observation. In that sense, although some might say it was a little economical with the *actualité*, strictly speaking, the commissioner was correct to say the shooting was linked to the terrorist operation.

The commissioner had also used a phrase that senior police officers learn during media-training sessions: 'The information I have available', similar to 'on the basis of what I know now' or 'I have been given to understand'. These important phrases are designed so that, if the information given is later shown to be wrong, you can say 'Ah yes, but I said that on the basis of what I was told at that time' or 'on the basis of the evidence available to me then', as opposed to 'what we know now'.

The commissioner had also said (twice) that rumours were sweeping London; I wondered whether he could have been referring to the 'rumours' that were now sweeping through Scotland Yard, that we had shot the wrong man. Although it turned out that I was wrong, at the time I believed the commissioner had been told what I had been by his own staff.

After the press conference had concluded, I went to a Gold Group meeting being chaired by Assistant Commissioner Alan Brown in the fifth floor conference room. He was the Gold commander for the Met with overall responsibility for the police operation for both the shooting and the failed bombings the day before. When Brown said to one of my commanders, Alf Hitchcock, who had taken responsibility for community issues, that there might be some community issues arising out of the shooting, I leant forward and said quietly to Hitchcock, 'Especially if he is a Brazilian tourist!' Hitchcock looked at me in disbelief and wrote down what I had told him. This was at 3.45 p.m.

At about 4 p.m., I joined a smaller sub-meeting in Brown's office with Hitchcock. Also present was Rob Beckley, the Assistant Chief Constable of Bedfordshire who had the lead on community tension. Alan Brown told us the Brazilian's name, Jean Charles de Menezes, adding that he was connected to the inquiry because he came from an address relevant to the investigation but that he was not believed to be one of the 21/7 bombers. (Brown later denied that he had given us the name but both Hitchcock and Beckley wrote the name down and recalled how Brown had described De Menezes was linked to the operation.)

This made sense. The man we thought would emerge from the flats was one of the bombers, an Asian guy called Osman. If the person we had shot was not Osman, the chances of him being linked to the bombings were slim.

Of those in the meeting, Beckley, Hitchcock and I had all written down De Menezes's name. Hitchcock told the IPCC that he left the meeting thinking that there was a strong possibility that an innocent man had been shot. Beckley told the IPCC that he left with the meeting with the impression that De Menezes was not one of the four bombers and that it was likely that he was not involved in the attempted bombings.

Brown also told us that he did not want the press to know that the person shot was not one of the four bombers. He later told the inquiry that he was unsure at the time that de Menezes was an innocent man, and that identity checks continued until the morning of 23 July. I pointed out that it would not be long before the media worked that out for themselves. At the press conference Andy Hayman revealed that there were four bombers and he had asked the public to help us identify who these people were from CCTV images. If there were four bombs, four bombers and we were still looking for all of them, then the person we shot was clearly not one of them.

'You have a point there,' he admitted.

One of the reasons for this meeting was to prepare a Community Impact Assessment (a CIA is undertaken to assess community concerns and to come up with appropriate strategies to deal with them). While I was under the impression that this was because everyone believed the person we had shot was innocent, Brown later told the IPCC that he thought this was simply an appropriate contingency plan in case the deceased man's identity turned out to match the documents that had been found on him. That Community Impact Assessment document, as shown on the police computer system, was created minutes after 5 p.m. on that Friday afternoon of the shooting.

Shortly after this, I learned that the commissioner had made the decision not to allow the Independent Police Complaints Commission to start their investigation until Monday (the IPCC are bound by law to immediately start investigating every police shooting). Delaying the IPCC for this length of time was bound to raise questions and suggest a cover-up was underway, undermining public confidence in the police at what was arguably one of the most crucial times in its history, a time when we needed public support more than ever.

On Friday 22 July, I went home convinced we had shot an innocent Brazilian and I assumed the commissioner must have been briefed outside the meetings; surely if his staff officers had been told, and Brown had told us the dead man's name, then that would have been shared with the commissioner?

SATURDAY 23 JULY

Shortly after I arrived at the Yard at 8 a.m. on Saturday morning to take up my responsibilities for community issues, I received a visit from Commander Jim Smith, the senior designated officer for Operation Kratos for that morning.

'Take a look at this,' he said, showing me his briefing folder, 'this is very interesting.' He showed me four photos of the four suspects being hunted for the failed 21 July bombings. These were not grainy CCTV images; they were instead sharply focused surveillance photos. These people had been under surveillance before they tried to bomb the tube network.

This meant that the senior officers at the scene must have had these photographs and would have known almost immediately that the man they had shot was not one of the four bombers. De Menezes's face was still intact after the shooting, so they could match it to the photograph on his driving permit. Sure, his documents could have been false, but his face would not have matched any of these crystal-clear surveillance pictures we had of the bombers we were hunting.

At 11 a.m., I met with Ken Jones, chair of ACPO's Terrorism and Allied Matters Committee and Superintendent Steve Swain, the Met's expert on Operation Kratos (whom I had first met while we were at Hendon training school). We discussed the events that led up to the shooting. I asked Steve, 'What was the codeword to authorise the armed officers to shoot?'

'There isn't one.'

This seemed crazy to me. 'So if an armed team are after a suspected suicide bomber they will shoot to kill unless they are called off?'

'I guess so.'

So when Cressida Dick told the armed surveillance officers that the man they were following must not be allowed to board the train, she was signing De Menezes's death warrant.

It was clear to me that the armed officers, once they had been told to pursue this person and had been told it was a Kratos operation, they were going to kill him, unless Cressida Dick gave a clear and unequivocal order not to shoot.

According to the policy, the firearms officers were instructed that if there is no doubt that the person is a suicide bomber, they should be shot in the back of the head without warning. If there was any doubt, they should challenge the suspect and then react as the situation develops.

Here was a man dressed in jeans, T-shirt and lightweight denim jacket carrying nothing except a newspaper. The surveillance officer who saw him leave Scotia Road had said he was not carrying anything although the firearms officers who shot him described De Menezes denim jacket as 'bulky', which it clearly wasn't. He was being held in bear-hug by a surveillance officer when the armed officers entered the carriage. All of these things, you might think, would at least give rise to some doubt that he really was a suicide bomber about to detonate a bomb.

The first official press release that announced we had shot an innocent man came at 4.52 p.m. on the Saturday: 'We are now satisfied that he [De Menezes] was not connected with the incidents of Thursday 21st July 2005.' In the same press release it also said: 'His clothing and behaviour added to their suspicions.' This was the fourth press release to containing this incorrect and misleading information.

Another press statement released at 6.13 p.m. reiterated this 'fact' again. By now it was being widely reported in the press that although innocent, De Menezes had vaulted the ticket barrier, was wearing bulky clothing, had run from the police and had refused to obey police instructions (this last 'fact' was first mentioned to the world's press by the commissioner himself during the 3.39 p.m. press conference the previous day: 'I understand the man was challenged and refused to obey').

These press releases insinuated that De Menezes had given the armed officers cause to shoot when he had in fact done nothing of the sort; he was not wearing bulky clothing, he had not vaulted the barrier and he had not run from the police. None of the seventeen passengers in the carriage heard any warning being shouted by the armed officers before they opened fire although the officers themselves either said they shouted a warning or heard one being shouted by their colleagues.

If, as they say, the officers genuinely believed that De Menezes was a suicide bomber about to detonate a bomb and kill everyone in the carriage, it would not have made any sense to shout a warning; he would surely have detonated his device if they had. If there was any doubt in their minds as to whether he was a suicide bomber, with a bomb, about to detonate, bearing in mind he was carrying nothing, was slim and in light clothing, being held in a bear-hug by a surveillance officer, they should have shouted a warning and then reacted to his response to the warning.

By Sunday, Brazilian foreign ministers were on their way to London and the IPCC were ready and waiting to take over the investigation into De Menezes's death.

The commissioner, meanwhile, was due to appear on Sky News with Adam Boulton at 10 a.m. This was when his earlier mistakes made on the morning of 7/7 came back to haunt him. That morning, the *New York Times* had done a large piece on Ian Blair's factual inaccuracies on 7/7. They criticised him for first getting the number of explosions wrong and then how he made a 'series of incomplete characterisations about the direction of the inquiry and, in some cases, public misstatements about the evidence. The missteps included statements about the timing of the bombs on July 7, whether the bombers in the initial attack had died with their bombs or were at large.'

When Boulton confronted Ian with this, the commissioner
replied, 'I would say that is an extraordinarily unfair criticism. I sat
in this studio an hour and a half after the first bombings, talked
about six, because there were tube bombs and people came up
through two tube stations. These things move incredibly fast. I am
not complacent and of course we are capable of making mistakes but
I actually believe that the investigation since 7/7 has been at an
astonishing speed.'

Boulton then said: 'Are you in a sense under pressure to say too
much which may be wrong and then they damage your credibility?'

'We are always under pressure from you and your colleagues to give
out information. But what you will notice is that in the press conferences we are very, very careful about what we say.'

Boulton also picked up Ian on the fact that the shot man was
'directly linked' to the investigation: 'From a police perspective do you
know what went wrong? Because you did initially say that this was
firmly linked to the investigation, now of course there isn't a firm
link.'

'Well I don't think that is quite true. I did say it was firmly linked
and it was firmly linked to the ongoing operation. The house from
which Mr de Menezes came out was a house that was subsequently
yesterday raided by armed officers and the pictures are all over these
newspapers. What we have got to recognise is that people are taking
incredibly difficult, fast-time decisions in life-threatening situations.
That is what has happened; this will obviously be a matter for inquiry
and investigation.'

Of course it was not a house but a block of flats that De Menezes
had come out of, through the communal doorway to the street, and
it was a different flat that was subsequently raided by armed officers,
not the one where De Menezes lived (a mistake made by the commissioner in the 3.39 p.m. press briefing on the day of the shooting
which went uncorrected in numerous press statements released
throughout Friday and Saturday). People watching might have been
forgiven for thinking the link was not as firm as the commissioner
appeared to be saying it was. There were in fact operations at two
addresses: numbers 17 and 21 Scotia Road, one of which was still

running on 23 July. According to Brown's evidence to the inquiry, the commissioner directed that no press release should be put out declaring the dead man's innocence until both operations had finished.

On the Sunday morning, a request came in from Kate Hoey, the Labour MP for Vauxhall, for the commissioner to attend a community meeting being held at Lambeth Police Headquarters. I spoke to him about the request and, realising I knew the Lambeth community well, he asked me to represent him.

This was the last time he told me that I had his full confidence.

I was doorstepped by the BBC as I left, and I told them that the IPCC would take over the investigation into De Menezes's death on Monday. Accompanied by the borough commander and a community officer whom I had known since I was a sergeant, we went to visit Brixton mosque, where we had a warm welcome and a constructive discussion.

On the way to the mosque my mobile phone rang; it was Roy Clark. Roy had been a deputy assistant commissioner in the Met but was now the director of investigations for the IPCC. I knew Clark well and I had the utmost respect for his ability and integrity. His boss, Nick Hardwick, had just seen my BBC interview and was not happy. Clark told me it was not true that the IPCC were going to take over the investigation from Monday; they had been involved from the word go.

This was news to me and I checked with the Press Bureau at New Scotland Yard. The lines that they had agreed with the IPCC were that they were going to take over the investigation from Monday. Sensitivities were clearly running high. The fact that I now had Roy Clark's mobile phone number in my 'received calls' list proved to be useful later.

I had about an hour or so before I was due to attend another community meeting which was this time open to anyone who wanted to attend. We went to a restaurant in Coldharbour Lane (which is just off Brixton Road) and had dinner.

Although I had felt perfectly safe in the restaurant the backlash from the community against the police was building. At a packed Stockwell

Community Hall full of concerned locals, a band of political activists tried to make things very difficult. For me, it was just like being at a Lambeth Police Consultative Group meeting.

At the first Metropolitan Police Authority meeting after the shooting, instead of an assortment of Management Board members who usually attended, there was just the commissioner, Sir Ian Blair, the deputy commissioner, Paul Stephenson, and me. I took this as a sign of the high regard in which I was held by both the commissioner and the Police Authority. The commissioner said we were engaged in our greatest operational challenge since the Second World War. John Roberts, the representative for Lambeth, voiced the concerns of many when he said that community trust had plummeted after Stockwell; I passed the commissioner a series of notes such as 'shoot to save life policy' to help him in what was his most difficult full authority meeting to date.

The commissioner did not help, however, when he appeared to suggest to Jon Snow on Channel 4 News on 26 July 2005 that since 7 July the Met had come close to shooting seven people because they were believed to be suicide bombers. Senior Metropolitan Police sources clarified Sir Ian's comments as meaning that officers came close to being ordered to shoot a suspect dead on seven separate occasions. Although he was trying to highlight the pressure that armed officers were under, this was not really the reassurance people were looking for.

CHAPTER THIRTY-THREE

Three weeks later, on Sunday 21 August 2005, I was in Brighton when *The World at One* called me on my mobile. They wanted me to comment on what the commissioner had said that day about the Stockwell shooting. I had no idea what they were talking about; they told me that Ian Blair had done an interview with the *News of the World*. It quoted him as saying: 'The key component was that at that time, and for the next twenty-four hours or so, I and everybody who advised me believed the person shot was a suicide bomber.'

I could not believe what I was hearing. The *News of the World* must have got it wrong. Surely the commissioner must have known within twenty-four hours that the dead man was not one of the suspected bombers; from what I had been told, *not* 'everyone who advised' him believed 'the person shot was a suicide bomber'. His two closest advisors had told me as much and Assistant Commissioner Alan Brown had provided us with Jean Charles's name at around 4 p.m. on the afternoon of the shooting, giving three senior officers the impression that we should prepare for the fact that we had mistakenly shot an innocent man.

I did not know it then but that same month, as well as the *News of the World*, Ian Blair had given an interview to the *Guardian* newspaper as part of a series about his first year as commissioner. It was not until 30 January 2006 that the *Guardian* published the following in response to their question to the commissioner about when he had known that the deceased was a Brazilian: 'I'm quite sure that by 7.30 p.m. at night we still had nothing that was identifying him . . . otherwise we wouldn't have been putting out the messages that we were putting out.'

Here was the commissioner, some days after the shooting, telling the *Guardian* that he was quite sure at 7.30 p.m. on 22 July the Met had nothing that was identifying the man we had shot even though the deceased's wallet containing a Brazilian photo ID driving permit in the name of Jean Charles de Menezes had been found at 3 p.m. Later, Stockwell 2 revealed that identity checks had continued running until at least 9 p.m. on 22 July, and the commissioner was not told until 10 a.m. on 23 July by AC Brown and Mr Fedorcio that Jean Charles de Menezes was apparently unconnected with terrorism. The commissioner would also tell the inquiry that his words had been taken out of context by the *Guardian*'s removal of the preceding sentence in which he had said it was possible that others in the Metropolitan Police Service might have correctly known or guessed De Menezes's nationality.

I thought to myself, if people come to believe that the commissioner was lying or was withholding vital information from the public, then this would be disastrous for the Met; it would leave our reputation in tatters at the most crucial time in our history when we needed the public's confidence more than ever. If, on the other hand, on the day of the shooting he had remained uninformed while his immediate staff believed that the person shot was not a suicide bomber, then he needed to know that, and action needed to be taken against them for not sharing this information with their boss.

I was not alone in my concerns. Alf Hitchcock found me the day after the *News of the World* article was published and asked me what we were going to do; what the commissioner had said in the newspaper was untrue. I asked Alf whether he would be happy to support my recollection of events if I decided to take the matter further and he was.

I was going to have to take this further but before I did I had to make sure that the *News of the World* had not got it wrong. I asked for the Met Press Bureau's own transcript of the interview. Somewhat surprisingly, the Press Bureau let me have the transcript and even more surprisingly (based on my own painful experiences with the press), the newspaper had the wording exactly right, although they had left out part of the sentence (although the commissioner emphasised to the Stockwell Inquiry that this change made a significant difference, as far as I was concerned it did not change the meaning of what he said). The full quote was: 'The key component was that at that time, and for the next twenty-four hours or so, I and everybody who advised me believed the person shot was a suicide bomber or a potential suicide bomber, and either one of the four for whom we were looking, or even worse than that, someone else.'

I realised even then that the information I had was potentially career-ending for me if not handled properly. There were three people in whom I had complete trust. I spoke briefly with John Grieve, the former head of the anti-terrorist branch and Sir Ronnie Flanagan from Her Majesty's Inspectorate of Constabulary and I then called Roy Clarke at the IPCC. They all agreed; I was in a very difficult position and that I should think very carefully about what I did next.

I went to see Catherine Crawford (clerk and chief executive of the MPA). She had always been supportive of me and was a supporter of Ian's, and she had been present in the Management Board meeting on the day of the shooting. I thought she might have useful, objective advice and she did: 'You must tell Ian.'

I told my boss, Tim Godwin, that I needed to speak to the commissioner and explained what it was about (it was not done for your boss to find out that you had seen the commissioner without him knowing). He reported back that Ian was willing to see me.

In no time at all, I was with the commissioner. Usually commissioners have their chief of staff with them on such occasions, but we were alone.

One of the first things that Ian Blair did when he became commissioner was to order the refurbishment of his office; an exercise carried out at great expense to the Met. For decades, the room had been lined with dark wood-panelling, except for one section which had a life-size full-length painting of Sir Robert Peel, the founder of the Met. An old chiming clock sat on a large antique desk. This cross between a gentleman's club and the library of a stately home had seemed timeless rather than old-fashioned, giving the occupier a sense of gravitas.

The decor was very different now. The green carpet had been replaced with a beige oatmeal affair, just like the one I had in my lounge at home. The imposing dark-wood formal writing desk in the centre of the room had gone and was replaced by a light-coloured modern desk set back at the far end, almost as if it had been pushed out of the way. Matching light-wood panels had replaced the dark-wood panels on either side. Sir Robert Peel had been usurped by a huge plasma television. A round coffee table with modern suede leather chairs set around it on a circular rug had replaced the traditional sofa and armchairs.

It looked and smelt like a DFS showroom.

This meeting was going to be very different from any other I had ever had with any commissioner. As far as I was concerned the future reputation of the Met (and my career) rested on its outcome. It all depended on what the commissioner's response would be when I asked him about what he had told the *News of the World*. For the moment at least, I was there as a friend.

I am a traditionalist at heart and when I first went to congratulate Ian on becoming commissioner I told him, 'I have always called you Ian in the past, but now I am going to call you Commissioner.' He appreciated the sentiment.

I reminded him of this and added as we shook hands and took our seats: 'Well, this is different. I'm going to call you Ian.' This was going to be a heart-to-heart, man-to-man conversation – not subordinate-to-boss.

From a note of the meeting that I made within an hour of it ending, I remember I started by talking about the 3.39 p.m. press conference on the day of the shooting and how Stewart and Murdoch had by then already confirmed to me that a Brazilian tourist had been shot, clearly implying that we had killed the wrong man.

The commissioner interrupted. He told me that I must have got the wrong time. He had gone through the timings with Caroline Murdoch, his chief of staff, and they had agreed between them that it was about 7 p.m. on the Friday that he was told that the person who had been shot was Brazilian. (This is how I remember it. The commissioner later denied making an admission on timing here.)

In any event, he said, an Argentinian had been arrested at Gatwick for carrying a grenade onto an aeroplane, so the Brazilian could still have been a suicide bomber.

I explained that up until this last Saturday I had not been too concerned. Up until then I had managed to convince myself that saying De Menezes was 'directly linked to the anti-terrorist operation' was arguably correct, in that he came out of a building that we had under observation.

The commissioner leapt on this: 'Exactly, that's exactly what I said.' I wondered whether he was trying to convince himself or to convince me.

I made it clear that I had not talked to him about who had been shot or what nationality he was or whether he was a terrorist or not, on the day of the shooting. We had not been in the same room on the day of the shooting when any discussion had taken place as to whether or not the dead man was a suicide bomber or not. I could not say what the commissioner knew or believed on that day.

The issue for me was, he had said '. . . *and everyone who advised me believed that the person who was shot was a suicide bomber . . .*' The impression I was given by his staff officer and his chief of staff, his two closest advisors, on the day of the shooting was that they did not believe the shot man was a suicide bomber. I told Ian Blair that if they had not told him of their concerns, then in my opinion they should have done.

I told the commissioner the other reason I could not have got the wrong time was that I had told Alf Hitchcock at about 3.45 p.m. that we had shot a Brazilian tourist.

The commissioner interrupted again; 'Well you must have got the wrong day.' He remembered Alan Brown sanctioning a press release on the Friday evening that would have contradicted that.

I told the commissioner, not only that I had told Alf Hitchcock at about 3.45 p.m. on the Friday but that, as a result of the smaller meeting following the Gold Group, those present were left in no doubt that what Alan Brown was asking Alf Hitchcock and Rob Beckley to do was to prepare a Community Impact Assessment on the basis that we had shot the wrong guy. The police computer system still showed the Community Impact Assessment as having been created minutes after five o'clock on that Friday afternoon of the shooting.

The commissioner reiterated that he distinctly remembered being in his office at 10.30 a.m. on the Saturday morning with Dick Fedorcio, the Met's Head of Public Affairs, when Alan Brown came into his office and told him we had shot the wrong man and he had thought 'what a disaster'.

The commissioner appeared to concede that I must be right. He said he did not know what I wanted him to do. I said that I did not want him to do anything but that I thought it was important that he knew, not only what I believed but what other senior colleagues believed, on that Friday afternoon. The commissioner said he could only say what he believed and that is what he had said all along.

The commissioner then said that he was telling the truth and added: 'You must do what you have to do but we both know the penalty for not telling the truth.'

This strange statement caused me some concern. What did he mean?

I reiterated that I was being completely open, honest and upfront with him and that I believed it was important for him to know. I still considered him to be a friend as well as a colleague and I was torn as to what I should do. I had not come to confront him; I wanted to help him.

He said, 'If I were you, I would tell as few people as possible for as long as possible.' (Although the commissioner had no note of the meeting, his recollection when he was interviewed by the IPCC was that he told me to take it through the proper channels and 'not to spread it about').

I asked the commissioner whether I could tell Alf Hitchcock about our conversation. He agreed. I shook the commissioner's hand and left his office.

I called Alf Hitchcock and he made notes as I spoke to him. I then spoke to Catherine Crawford before calling Roy Clarke on his mobile.

Most importantly, I sat down at my computer terminal in my office and wrote down everything I could remember of the encounter. As I look at the printout of the MPS computer screen now, it shows the document was last modified at 6.45 p.m. on 22 August 2005, less than an hour after I had left that fateful meeting with the commissioner.

CHAPTER THIRTY-FOUR

The Stockwell 2 inquiry was launched on 14 October 2005 but the IPCC took an inordinately long time to get round to interviewing me and I was not seen until February 2006. I met with Mike Grant (the IPCC's lead investigator for Stockwell 2, a former detective superintendent) and another investigator. We ran through my evidence with both detectives taking copious notes. Afterwards he said the IPCC could translate the interview into a statement for me if I wanted. Instead I elected to write it myself.

In July 2006 the commissioner was interviewed under caution and videotaped. Grant called me the same evening and I was not surprised but still shocked when I thought of the possible consequences after he told me that Ian Blair had denied almost everything I had said.

Grant told me that when Ian asked if I had any notes of our meeting, following the publication of the *News of the World* interview, and Grant told him I had, the commissioner turned his eyes skywards. During the interview, the commissioner reiterated that he believed the deceased was involved in terrorism until around 10.30 a.m. on 23 July, some twenty-four hours after the shooting. He understood that to be the position of all those, without exception, who were providing him with advice. During many discussions throughout the day he said no contrary view or information was expressed to him. He said that if anyone had thought that De Menezes was not connected to terrorism then it was their duty to say so.

He was certain that at the top of the organisation they did not know the identity of De Menezes by 7.30 p.m. on 22 July and he said this was entirely supported by a conversation he had at 7 p.m. with Maxine de Brunner, staff officer to Deputy Commissioner Stephenson. This conversation took place outside the deputy commissioner's office where the commissioner asked her whether she knew who the man was we had shot and she said 'No, sir.' When the commissioner was asked by Stockwell 2 investigators to confirm de Brunner's memory of their conversation, he said that he could not recall it.

Ian Blair was then questioned about the 5 p.m. sub-meeting of the Management Board on the day of the shooting, variously described by the attendees as a continuation of the initial meeting but with fewer people present. In attendance were the commissioner and his top team; in this case Assistant Commissioner Andy Hayman, Assistant Commissioner Alan Brown, Dick Fedorcio (in charge of media relations), Deputy Commissioner Paul Stephenson, Deputy Assistant Commissioner Richard Bryan (who briefed the international media), Commander Sue Wilkinson (from the Serious Crime Directorate), Len Duvall (chair of the Metropolitan Police Authority, MPA), Catherine Crawford (chief executive and clerk, MPA) and Caroline Murdoch.

There was one notable exception. Me.

On that day, I was an acting assistant commissioner, the head of Territorial Policing, a key member of the senior management team who outranked two of those who did attend, and I still do not know why I was excluded from this meeting; there was certainly no duty that would have prevented me.

Fortunately, the Stockwell 2 investigators were able to recover two sets of written notes taken by Caroline Murdoch at this meeting. In one section Murdoch wrote 'Commissioner (check): In terms of the link with the investigation how about "the man shot today at Stockwell was under police surveillance after he left the house under observation as a result of our inquiries following the incidents yesterday"'.

She appeared to be quoting the commissioner (apparently noting she should check with him that she had accurately recorded what he said) as asking whether this form of words would be okay for a press release. They were clearly being very careful about framing the wording.

Caroline Murdoch's notes go on:

'Len Duvall: People watching must understand that the intelligence led the police there and that you thought he could be dangerous.

'Dick Fedorcio: I will craft something for the public. [Fedorcio denied to the IPCC investigators that he used the word 'craft']

'Andy Hayman: There is press running that the person shot is not one of the four bombers. We need to present this that he is believed to be. This is different to confirming that he is. On the balance of probabilities, it isn't. To have this for offer would be low risk.

'Commissioner: Also his behaviour reported at the scene added to the circumstances. So, he came from the address, his behaviour, he was followed by officers, this led to shooting.

'The second point is that for the time being the CT [Counter Terrorism] investigation is pre-eminent. In due course we will discuss handing over to the IPCC. We must have this space.

'Action agreed that Dick Fedorcio is to produce the above and issue as an official statement. The IPCC will take over Monday.'

The commissioner appeared to have accepted, what was later shown to be mistaken eyewitness testimony (which can be notoriously unreliable), that there was something wrong with De Menezes's behaviour: that he had 'vaulted the barrier' and he was wearing bulky clothing. This was more likely to have been a description of the police officers who were in pursuit of De Menezes.

The commissioner was then asked what was meant by Murdoch's notes of the meeting which referred to the person shot not being one of the four and Andy Hayman's comment that 'We need to present this that he is believed to be'. He stated he did not understand it and had no memory of it and was genuinely puzzled.

He denied that anything untoward had taken place at the meeting stating that he would not have presided over a meeting where press statements were designed to deliberately mislead.

At about 9 p.m., the commissioner left New Scotland Yard.

Why, on one of the most crucial days in police history, did the commissioner of the Metropolitan Police leave his office still not knowing who it was his officers had shot in the first ever deployment of Operation Kratos?

At 9.45 p.m. on 22 July, a senior investigating officer of the Anti-Terrorist Branch told the detective superintendent from the Department for Professional Standards that the Anti-Terrorist Branch did not consider Jean Charles de Menezes to be linked to the events of 21 July and handed over the scene at Stockwell to the DPS. This was formal acknowledgement that an innocent man had been shot. If there had been any residual doubts about his involvement in terrorism, the Anti-Terrorist Branch would have retained control.

Would it have been unreasonable to have called the commissioner then, before ten o'clock in the evening, to tell him the terrible news? Apparently, nobody did. He told the investigation that he left no instructions that he should be contacted should anything happen, but that was anyway unnecessary as he is available twenty-four hours a day. When an IRA bomb had gone off outside the BBC, I called the commissioner at two in the morning and this was far more serious.

In connection with the meeting the commissioner and I had had about the *News of the World* article, the commissioner was asked whether there was any bad history between us. He said there was not. When asked whether I was lying he said I was 'very seriously mistaken' and asked to see a copy of my witness statement. Following a break in the interview when the commissioner was provided with a copy of my statement and that of another officer (an unprecedented step, for a suspect to be shown crucial witness statements in the middle of an interview under caution), he said he was disappointed with what I had said.

He thought our meeting had only lasted for about a minute when it had gone on for much longer but did add that 'there were resonances of the conversation that he was prepared to accept.' In particular, he referred to having mentioned an Argentinian. Having detailed why he disputed my statement, he was again asked if he knew of any reason why I was saying what I was. He responded by saying that he had a number of ideas but it would be unfair to me to make those points and he needed to stop at that. He stated he fundamentally disagreed with the statement and had concerns about why I should have said what I had, but without more knowledge, it would be unwise to go any further. He confirmed that this was his position and declined to say what his ideas were.

It is interesting that the commissioner remembered having mentioned the Argentinian. Why were we talking about the Argentinian, who had been arrested at Gatwick with a grenade, allegedly 'an Argentinian terrorist'? One possible explanation could have been that the commissioner *did* tell me that he had been informed on the day of the shooting that the dead man was Brazilian – but that this did not mean that he was not 'a Brazilian terrorist'.

This could have been a possible explanation but for Caroline Murdoch, the commissioner's chief of staff, having no recollection of coming to this conclusion about the nationality of the deceased with the commissioner on the Friday (although she had been told about the deceased's wallet and the Brazilian driving permit that afternoon). If the commissioner is right, that it does not make sense to say he had heard that the deceased was Brazilian on the Friday, why on earth were we talking about Argentinians in our meeting?

Prior to Grant's phone call I hoped that the differences between the commissioner and I might not be fatal to our relationship and to my career. These hopes had been dashed. I said to Grant, 'You won't be surprised to hear I stand by every word I've said.'

'I don't doubt it for a minute,' he said. 'I didn't phone you up to even suggest that might be the case. Since we first met you, we haven't had any doubts that you have told us the truth, and nothing we have learnt since has changed our minds.' Mike Grant recently confirmed

this conversation and went on to say that looking back on it, everything in my statements to the IPCC is accurate.

As the Stockwell 2 report later said, 'DAC Paddick made detailed
notes of his 22 August meeting with the Commissioner. Those
notes . . . appear wholly consistent with the evidence that he has now
given.'

People named in the IPCC Stockwell 2 report were given the
opportunity to make representations if they were criticised in the
report or if their evidence was contradicted by others, before the
report was published (commonly known as 'the Salmon process').

On 29 January 2007, my solicitor was contacted by the commissioner's solicitor. Was I prepared to approach the IPCC to ask them to
remove all references to the 23 August meeting from the report? The
commissioner had been led to believe that no further action would be
taken against him in relation to Stockwell. As a result, his solicitor
claimed that the meeting was no longer relevant. This was an extraordinary request; I believed the Salmon process was designed to allow
those criticised to make representations to the IPCC, not allow them
to change the focus of the inquiry.

Grant denied that the 'Salmon process' had resulted in any major
changes and said that all the report's conclusions had remained the
same. Having read parts of the draft report supplied to me under the
Salmon process and having compared this with the final version, I can
tell you that, in my opinion, substantial changes were made.

'It depends how you define "substantial" Brian,' Grant told me
later.

The Stockwell 2 report cleared Ian Blair:

> There is no evidence that the Commissioner or any other member
> of the MPS knowingly released the incorrect information to the
> media and public that Mr de Menezes had been challenged and
> that his clothing had added to their suspicions. Whilst they did
> release this information it was believed by them to have been cor-
> rect at the time . . . The complaint against the Commissioner is
> not substantiated and there is no evidence of misconduct.

However the MPA should consider why the Commissioner remained uninformed of key information emerging during July 22 2005.

The report concluded:

> The investigation team find it somewhat surprising that in the days following the shooting, let alone by November, nobody sought to inform the Commissioner that Brown's and Hayman's knowledge of the emerging post shooting events of July 22 was considerable, whilst his own was negligible. However, he maintains that at the time he gave the interviews to the *News of the World* and the *Guardian* it was his belief that all those who advised him also believed at that time that the dead man was involved in terrorism.

The IPCC accepts that the commissioner is telling the truth. The mystery remains; neither the Stockwell 2 report, nor the commissioner and his senior command, nor I can explain why Ian Blair was not told that De Menezes was not a suicide bomber for twenty-four hours.

As soon as Stockwell 2 was published, I spent some time going carefully through it and I was struck by just how many people had received crucial information about the shot man before the commissioner, the one person who needed this information more urgently than anyone else in the Met. Specifically, at least twenty-five police officers of senior rank and civilian staff based at Scotland Yard knew before Ian Blair that either Brazilian identity documents had been found on the deceased man and/or that he was not one of the four bombers we were hunting and/or suspected that he might be an innocent man. Most of them had learnt this while they were at Scotland Yard on the day of the shooting, and several of them had seen the commissioner after they found out.

Detective Superintendent Stephen Kavanagh, staff officer to Assistant Commissioner Alan Brown had briefed his boss by 3.10 p.m., almost thirty minutes before Ian Blair gave his first press conference about the shooting (this was also when Stewart and Murdoch also learnt the victim was Brazilian). Perhaps even more remarkably, some of these twenty-five had briefed civilians and civil servants before they briefed the commissioner.

For example, Helen Bayne, head of the Terrorism and Protection Unit at the Home Office was at the Home Office when she was informed about the shooting by Jeremy Page, head of the Government Liaison Team. He gave her an update following Alan Brown's 3 p.m. Gold Group meeting 'that there was a strong suspicion that the victim was not one of the four suspects for the failed bombings.'

Brown advised Page at 6.20 p.m. that property from a Brazilian male had been recovered from the scene in the identity of Jean Charles de Menezes, born São Paulo 7 January 1978 (described in a detective superintendent's decision log as 'the wallet of the deceased'). He told Page that he could confirm to the Foreign and Commonwealth Office (FCO) and the Home Office that property in the name Jean Charles de Menezes had been recovered from the scene.

Yet, four months after our meeting and two months after the Stockwell 2 investigation had began, on 22 December 2005, speaking to BBC Radio 4's *Today* programme, Ian Blair denied he had been 'kept in the dark' about the killing of De Menezes.

'Do you think,' the presenter asked him, 'looking back on it, that you were kept in the dark?'

'No, I was not kept in the dark,' the commissioner replied. 'I mean the answer is to all of this, that, you know, we will have to account for what happened. It was a dreadful set of events but there's no suggestion at all that, you know, that the commissioner or anybody else was kept in the dark.'

Nevertheless, the Stockwell 2 report concluded that 'No direct evidence has been found which suggests that following the shooting of Mr de Menezes on 22 July 2005, the commissioner was informed that day about an emerging identity for him, the recovery of any items from his body and the likelihood that he was not involved in terrorism.'

The report cleared everyone, everyone it seemed apart from Assistant Commissioner Andy Hayman. When Hayman was interviewed by the

Stockwell 2 team, he said that while he remembered the meeting it was difficult to recall the detail of what was said between him and the commissioner before the 3.39 p.m. press conference.

This is an extraordinary statement to have made. This is the man with overall responsibility for apprehending the terrorists but he has no record of what he has said to the commissioner or when he might have said it. One of the first things we are taught in major incident training is that in such situations you get a loggist, a trusted junior officer who records everything you do and say as it happens, in preparation for the inquiry that will inevitably follow. Five hours after the shooting, Andy Hayman still had no one taking notes although the senior investigating officers from his own Anti-Terrorist Branch and those from the DPS, and Alan Brown, the other assistant commissioner, all had their loggists in place.

I was present at a Management Board meeting in the weeks following the shooting where we discussed installing recording devices in the commissioner's conference room. There was already a microphone amplification system in the room which could have easily been connected to a voice recorder. It was even suggested that we could have a camera installed to create video records of meetings for use in such circumstances.

It was agreed by the majority of those present that the Management Board would sometimes have conversations that it would not want recorded.

Hayman could not recall when he was told that the deceased had documentation on him in the name Jean Charles de Menezes or whether he had ever been told at all. He could not be sure if he was told about the recovery of the wallet and mobile telephone. He said he did have a recollection of being told at some point during the day that there were papers on the body and a possible name which did not accord with the four they were hunting. He stated there were lots of possible scenarios which could not be resolved until the deceased was definitively identified.

Hayman stated that he did not know that the deceased was not one of the four wanted men until the Saturday morning. Yet he had briefed the Crime Reporter's Association (a select band of trusted journalists) at 4.30 p.m. Hayman could recall none of the detail of this briefing when he was interviewed by the Stockwell 2 investigators but at 5.10 p.m., 22 July, *BBC News 24* had reported: 'A line just in about the shooting in Stockwell earlier. The man shot dead at the tube station is not thought to be one of the four men shown in CCTV pictures released this afternoon.' Reporters later said that Hayman had told them that De Menezes was not one of the bombers but that he was a terrorist. It was this, along with the recovery of Murdoch's note which changed the status of Hayman from a witness to being under investigation.

On Saturday 23 July, Hayman got to work mid to late morning. He could not recall who briefed him but he was told the deceased was not one of the four bomb suspects. He stated that he could not recall when he was told that the deceased was innocent.

The report placed all of the blame on Andy Hayman. While the report does say that Hayman withheld vital information from the commissioner for reasons that have yet to be explained, I believe that it was not just the Met that shot the wrong man – the IPCC has too. While I would not describe Hayman as a friend or a supportive colleague (we have clashed many times in the past) I think it is grossly unfair for him to have been singled out when the report concludes that others could have passed information to the commissioner that day.

For example, the report said that '[Assistant Commissioner Alan] Brown agrees he was receiving [the] information during 22 July 2005 and whilst aspects of it were passed on directly or indirectly to numerous parties including ACC Beckley, the MSF, FCO and the Home Office Government Liaison Team, he did not tell the Commissioner.' Yet Brown, who has since retired from the Police Service, has escaped further criticism.

Why did neither Caroline Murdoch nor Chief Superintendent Moir Stewart, who held crucial knowledge about the Brazilian's identity, decide that the commissioner did not need to know? Both explained their position to the IPCC and were cleared. Stewart subsequently stated, in response to the Salmon process, that a huge amount of information had been passed to him and they made a conscious decision not to overburden Ian Blair with unconfirmed reports.

Surely it is for the commissioner to decide whether such potentially crucial information should be taken seriously or discarded?

Staff officers are invariably senior police officers themselves, and the commissioner's is a chief superintendent, the level of seniority that is usually in charge of policing a London borough. One of the staff officer's most important jobs is to look after the commissioner's back.

Earlier in my career I had been a staff officer to one of the most senior officers in the Met. I wondered what I would have done in this situation. My boss was about to go in front of the world's media and talk about what was arguably the most contentious incident in British policing history – the deliberate shooting of a suspected suicide bomber at close range.

If I had been given an unconfirmed report, that documentation relating to a Brazilian named Jean Charles de Menezes had been found in the wallet of the dead man, a man we thought was an Asian by the name of Osman, what would I have done? Not many people would have had the courage to tell the commissioner's staff officer such an important and potentially disastrous piece of information unless they expected it to be passed on to the commissioner. If they had been wrong, their career would have been finished; they would not have told the commissioner's staff unless they thought it was significant.

So what would I have done? I would have questioned the informant as much as I could. How do you know he was a Brazilian tourist? ('We found a Brazilian driving permit on him.') What evidence have we got that he is not a terrorist? ('There was nothing on him, no gun, no bomb, nothing to suggest a terrorist connection and he is not one of the four bombers we're looking for.') Who did we think he was, as opposed to who we now know he is? ('He came out of the block of flats where Osman was living so we thought it was him.') What makes you think he was Brazilian? ('His Brazilian photo ID driving permit looks genuine and the photo is a good likeness.')

At 7.30 p.m. on the Saturday, a family member was able to formally identify Jean Charles de Menezes. A close friend who also viewed the body told the *Sunday Times* how 'Every bit of colour had left his face but apart from that it was normal.' There was a photo ID driving permit and facial recognition was possible.

Two things are certain. If I thought the information was good enough to pass on to an acting assistant commissioner, and I was two levels above the staff officer and two levels below the commissioner at the time of the shooting, it would have been good enough to pass it on to the commissioner. If I thought it was unreliable or 'unconfirmed', I would have warned the commissioner 'be careful', there are 'unconfirmed reports' or 'someone has told me . . .' If you are doing your job properly, you are not going to let your boss go out there and make a fool of himself because he does not have the same potentially vital information that you do.

What if the commissioner had made an unequivocal statement that we had shot a suicide bomber and he subsequently found out that the staff officer had known we had shot an innocent man? Surely that would be the end of the staff officer's career?

The commissioner's staff officer and his chief of staff are his two closest advisors. If they believed the wrong man had been shot, and if they did not tell him of their concerns, then in my opinion they should have spoken up.

I do think people would have understood if the Met had confessed promptly to shooting an innocent man – the press and the public were talking about a war-time situation that summer and people were largely sympathetic towards the extremely difficult investigation the Met was running and the pressures our officers were under. There could have been a genuine fear that the media and public attention would have been distracted from the hot pursuit of the four bombers if news that the person shot was innocent had got out; vital information from the public could have been lost and the trail could have gone cold. If Jean Charles's identity had been released, the ongoing surveillance operation at Scotia Road could have been compromised with the media turning up while there were still terrorists inside.

What would I have done if I was commissioner and I thought it was operationally necessary to withhold information from the media in case we lost the bombers? I would have issued as brief a statement as possible along lines that we had shot somebody and that urgent enquiries were being made to establish the identity of the person. The Independent Police Complaints Commission were in charge of the scene and investigating what had happened (I would never have kept them out and I would have trusted them to keep quiet). I certainly would not have done a press conference; nothing looks worse than saying 'no comment' to a whole string of questions.

Then, as soon as we felt that we could not hold the line any longer, or that the period of operational necessity had passed, I would have explained, together with the IPCC in a joint press conference, that the shot person was innocent and we had not been able to make that fact public because of operational necessity. I would have made sure we did not say anything about the circumstances, about the way he died, as that was a matter for an independent investigation and a coroner's inquest to decide. The IPCC would have supported that stance. The Met and the IPCC would have been on the same side rather than being seen as enemies as happened in reality.

CHAPTER THIRTY-FIVE

Since my days at Merton, I had always tried to maintain good relations with as many journalists as possible but now this was proving to be a pain. Before the IPCC Stockwell 2 report was published, enormous pressure was put on me by numerous media contacts to reveal what I knew. Although they were relentless, I held the line; I would always speak to them or return their calls but I would not discuss anything that they did not already know. The breakdown in my relationship with Ian Blair and the worry over what this might mean for me only added to the stress and I struggled to conceal my concern.

One day, Tarique Ghaffur, picking up on my body language, appeared in my office and asked me whether I was okay. He was an assistant commissioner and a member of Ian Blair's 'cabinet'. We had had long discussions in the past about the various difficulties we faced as members of different minority groups in the Met and we had personally supported each other. In confidence, I said in general terms what was troubling me – that I had been told on the afternoon of 22 July by someone in the commissioner's private office that we had shot the wrong man, and that this had brought me into conflict with the commissioner.

Ghaffur suddenly cut our conversation short and left.

The following day at 5.15 p.m., the BBC's crime correspondent Margaret Gilmour phoned and asked if she could see me. I met her in an Italian restaurant on the corner of Marsham Street, just across from the new Home Office. Over a cappuccino Margaret told me she had heard from a reliable source that I had told the IPCC that people in the commissioner's office suspected by the afternoon of the 22nd that we had shot an innocent Brazilian.

Margaret told me that earlier on that day she had attended a press conference given by Ghaffur. Once it was over, he had ignored all the other journalists and said to her, 'Margaret, let's go out and have a coffee.'

'You're in uniform,' Margaret said, 'we can't.'

'Well, come up to my office.' Gilmour and a Met press officer went up to Ghaffur's eleventh-floor office at NSY.

At the door Ghaffur turned to the press officer and said, 'I don't need you any more.'

Moir Stewart, who had been the commissioner's staff officer at the time of the shooting but had since been promoted to acting commander, happened to be on the eleventh floor at the time and saw the press officer being dismissed before Ghaffur let Gilmour into his office and shut the door behind them.

Margaret told me she had spent an hour with Ghaffur but would not disclose what they had discussed. Clearly, journalists are bound by the principle that they never reveal their sources. She told me she was going to broadcast the facts as she understood them on the BBC *Ten O'Clock News*. I neither confirmed nor denied the story.

I nervously switched on the TV at 10 p.m. only to see that a live football match had gone into extra time so I was forced to wait for an extra nail-biting forty-five minutes. Huw Edwards dramatically introduced Margaret, who was sitting at the same desk with him in the studio. She said little more than what she had told me earlier, that she understood a senior officer at Scotland Yard had told the IPCC that a member of the commissioner's private office team believed that the wrong man had been targeted just six hours after the shooting. In fact it had been within five hours, and it was two people, not one person, who had told me.

Understandably, in the absence of any other information, the commissioner and his deputy assumed I was the source of the leak (a habit they never grew out of for the rest of my service). Nothing was said to me, but the following day my attention was drawn to a statement that had been issued by the Met police press bureau at 2 p.m. in response to Gilmour's broadcast.

The statement said: 'We are aware of the suggestion, who made it and which officer is alleged to have had the information. However the officer in the commissioner's private office has categorically denied this in his interview with, and statement to, the IPCC investigators. We are satisfied that whatever the reasons for this suggestion being made, it is simply not true.'

The statement did not name anyone, but on the back of Margaret Gilmour's piece on the *Ten O'Clock News*, it was obviously about me. I pointed out to the Met that it was quite obvious who they were referring to (a number of reporters had phoned me during the day asking me to confirm I was the source of the story). As far as I was concerned my own organisation was calling me a liar and there was no way I could let the matter rest. So began a public row between me and the Met.

I was summoned to see Deputy commissioner Paul Stephenson. Thinking I probably needed a witness for what was about to happen, I brought along my staff officer. Martin Tiplady, the head of Human Resources was waiting for me along with Stephenson. When Tiplady saw my staff officer he said, 'I don't think it's a good idea for your staff officer to be here, this might be embarrassing for him.'

I reluctantly sent him away. The deputy commissioner wanted me to issue a press release that I had misinterpreted what the Met had said and that I accepted that the Met was not calling me a liar.

I replied that it was the Met who had issued the statement and therefore it was the Met who should correct it. At this, Stephenson became very angry. 'You're not listening to what I am saying,' he said, '*you* have got to issue a press release.'

I started to say, 'Look there are two sides to this,' but as I tried to speak he talked over me, and each time I tried, he told me again and again not to interrupt. I was not going to be bullied. I said, 'If that's your attitude, I'm leaving.'

As I got up to go Martin Tiplady said, 'Let's see if we can resolve this.'

It very quickly became apparent that we were not going to sort this out between us; Stephenson was intransigent. I told them that I needed to seek legal advice. I telephoned my excellent libel lawyer, Tamsin Allen, who agreed that the press statement issued by the Met was clear, unambiguous and libellous.

She emailed Martin Tiplady to say that unless the Met published a correction and paid our costs, we would instigate libel proceedings.

When Tiplady tried to deal directly with me, I told him to talk Tamsin. After about a week of tense negotiation, the Met issued the following press release:

'It was reported recently that DAC Brian Paddick had taken legal advice about the content of a statement put out by the Metropolitan Police Service concerning his own comments and statement to the IPCC. Deputy Commissioner Paul Stephenson has clarified that the Metropolitan Police Service did not intend to imply that DAC Paddick or any officer had misled the IPCC. Any misunderstanding is regretted.'

That battle had been won but the war was not over. Highly placed sources told me that officials at the Home Office had decreed that Paddick should be dealt with.

As far as I was concerned, I had stuck to the commissioner's request and had told as few people as possible. I had no intention of taking my evidence into the public domain; that had been done by somebody else.

This had not been the first involvement of Margaret Gilmour in the Stockwell affair, as you might expect from the BBC's Home Affairs correspondent. About six weeks before, on 14 February 2006, I was at a conference at one of the Met's headquarters buildings, the Empress State Building on Lillie Road in West Brompton, a twenty-seven-floor building which used to belong to the MoD. The Met has taken over all but three floors of the building. Surprisingly, despite its height, it is a very difficult place to get decent mobile phone reception. I had received a voicemail from Margaret, and in trying to call her back I was wandering from room to room trying to get a signal.

On this particular floor, people were on courses; it was lunchtime and the rooms were fairly empty. It did not bother me in the slightest that police officers and others were around as I had nothing to hide and was not going to reveal any sensitive information. I was being called by journalists every day at this time and was well used to coming up with the appropriate phraseology without giving away my evidence to the IPCC.

Finally, I got hold of Margaret, who asked me, 'What's happening with Stockwell 2?'

'The investigation by the IPCC is under way.'

'Have you given evidence to the IPCC?'

'Off the record, yes I have.'

'Can I use that?'

'I'd rather you didn't. You're the only one who knows that. Things are already difficult between the commissioner and me. If he finds out I've given evidence it would make things even more difficult.'

'Do you know of any other senior officer who knew [that an innocent person had been shot] on the Friday?'

Trying to be helpful but not *too* helpful, I recalled a story that had been put to me by other journalists; that a senior officer had been told while he was off duty at a cricket match on the day of the shooting that the wrong man had been shot.

'This is third-hand, only a rumour,' I said. 'It may be worth pursuing a line of enquiry but it's not strong enough to use.'

I didn't realise it at the time, but a police officer had overheard part of this conversation: '. . . you're the only person who knows that . . . cricket match . . .' They decided to report me for leaking information to the press.

On the day I had the fateful meeting with the commissioner, Roy Clark told me not to worry about the *News of the World* story because there were other senior officers who believed what I did, that the wrong man had been shot, within twenty-four hours of the shooting. This is what I had been talking to Margaret Gilmour about.

In his evidence to the IPCC, Mr Clark said he believed that some senior MPS officers were attending a cricket test match at Lord's during the afternoon of 22 July 2005 and had become aware that the Stockwell shooting was a 'terrible mistake'. He could not remember the source of the information but believed he was told it in a telephone call.

DAC John Yates (now the assistant commissioner of 'cash for honours' fame) had attended a cricket match at Lord's on 22 July. He told the IPCC that at some point during that morning he was contacted on his mobile telephone and advised that the MPS had fatally shot a person at Stockwell. He could not recall who telephoned him. He said that he had received a number of calls throughout the day. When a national newspaper suggested Yates had been told that the shooting was a mistake while he was at the cricket match, he denied this was the case, threatened to sue the paper and the story was withdrawn. The IPCC report later concluded: 'The evidence of Mr Clark suggests that he [Yates] may have been told that the shooting was a mistake.'

Two months later, I received a call one evening from Tim Godwin. 'I know you need this like a hole in the head at the moment, but there have been allegations that you've been leaking stuff to the press. The police authority is referring the matter to the IPCC and you'll be getting a letter from them soon.'

This was on a Friday; on the following Wednesday, I received a letter from the MPA notifying me about the allegation and that they had decided to refer the matter to the IPCC.

A few days later, I got a phone call from a freelance journalist. 'Don't worry,' he told me, 'the IPCC don't want to know.'

'How do you know that?'

'I have my sources.'

Four days later, I was told exactly that. The IPCC had referred the matter back to the Metropolitan Police Authority.

I then learned that Sir Ronnie Flanagan, by this time Her Majesty's Chief Inspector of Constabulary, had been asked to investigate whether a disciplinary offence had been committed.

What Margaret Gilmour had actually called me about was this: 'I want to pre-record a piece for when the commissioner resigns. It won't be shown until he goes, but would you be willing to do a piece to camera in case he leaves?'

I refused, and as soon as the conversation was over, I had phoned the Met's press bureau, and told my boss, Tim Godwin, exactly what Margaret Gilmour had said. I thought it was important for the commissioner and the Met to know what the BBC was up to.

If I had divulged inappropriate information about the Met and the

IPCC investigation to Gilmour, I would not have told the Met's media machine and my boss that I had been speaking to her. I would not have done it in a police building in front of potential witnesses, either, or used a police mobile phone.

ACPO officers are covered by legal protection insurance for such investigations so I was put in touch with a solicitor and we prepared a statement giving a full and frank explanation of what exactly had taken place. I was then interviewed by Sir Ronnie. 'I think the Police Authority is looking for some contrition from you,' he said. 'Would you say in hindsight it would have been inappropriate to speak to Margaret Gilmour about something which you didn't know to be fact yourself?' I agreed that it may have been unwise to repeat what Roy Clark had told me, even if other journalists already knew.

When he submitted his report to the MPA, it said that I accepted it was ill-advised for me to speak to a journalist about Stockwell. When the committee of the MPA delivered their judgement, part of it said 'Brian Paddick shouldn't speak to any journalists.' I immediately called the deputy chief executive of the MPA and told him that this was not what I had either said, or agreed to.

He said it was too late and that was their judgement. Despite this erroneous conclusion, I continued to take calls from journalists but without telling them anything that was confidential. Some people will say – did say to me at the time – that the safest course would have been not to talk to journalists at all, but I was concerned that when the Stockwell 2 report was published, there might be attempts to under-mine my credibility because my evidence was contentious. I thought it was vital for my own survival to maintain good relationships with the media for this very reason. I recalled how, when I was the borough commander for Lambeth, the media had kept my name in the public eye and covered the extraordinary public support I was receiving, thus making it very hard for the Met to do anything underhand.

It was not long before another case took centre stage, a case in which the commissioner was accused of misleading the MPA. Brian Haw had set up a 'peace camp' on the green in front of the Houses of Parliament made up of an array of poorly drawn protest banners, flags and posters. It was widely agreed that his anti-war protest, however effective, was a general eyesore and the government was keen to get rid of him.

The Met used new legislation which had been introduced in 2005 to remove Haw. All his belongings, including his banners, posters and flags, were placed in a huge container which was put in storage, and he was arrested.

At a Police Authority meeting, the commissioner was asked by Jenny Jones, Green Party member of the London Assembly, how much the operation had cost. Jones was a champion of free speech and wanted to make the point that the operation was a waste of taxpayers' money. Ian replied that it had cost the Met £7,200 to arrest Mr Haw (£3,000 for overtime, £4,200 for transport).

When I heard media reports of how much the operation cost, it was obvious to me that this was a considerable underestimate, bearing in mind the number of officers involved and the logistics of the whole operation. I had always promised every member of the Police Authority that I would be completely open and honest and had told them, 'If you really want to know what is going on, talk to me.' At about 1 p.m. I called Jenny Jones and told her my concerns. Unknown to me, someone else had already told a journalist from the *Sunday Mirror* what had happened during a management board meeting where the real costs were discussed.

The *Sunday Mirror* had called the press bureau at 11 a.m. asking whether or not the commissioner had misled the Police Authority over the cost. As a result the commissioner sent an email to all the members of the Police Authority, clarifying that the total cost of the operation was in fact £27,754 rather than the figure of £7,200 he had given to Jenny Jones the day before.

I had gone off to another meeting when I received a telephone call from Commander Sue Akers, then head of the Directorate of Professional Standards. She had been asked by the deputy commissioner to establish whether anyone who had been in the management board meeting had spoken to journalists on that morning. I had been in the management board that morning when the costs of the operation were discussed and I had received two calls that morning from reporters who wanted to talk about Stockwell; I had made the usual excuse: 'Very sorry, I can't help but hopefully, in due course, I'll be able to talk about it.' Although the easiest option would have been to say, 'No, I have not spoken to any journalists', knowing Sue well and my own desire to be completely transparent I said, 'Yes I did, but I didn't speak to them about the meeting.'

'Oh dear,' said Sue.

'What do you mean?'

'You're the only one from the meeting who has admitted talking to journalists. This doesn't look very good for you.'

I have a real sensitivity, partly thanks to what happened at Lambeth, about being wrongly accused of things, and I was extremely worried about what information was going back to the commissioner (particularly in light of the Home Office's edict that I should be dealt with). I called Sue back and said, 'Look, I've already been under investigation recently. The last thing I'm going to do is put myself on offer by making calls to the press leaking damaging information about the Met. I might be a lot of things, but I'm not stupid.'

That Friday evening, I spoke to Catherine Crawford, the chief executive of the Police Authority and confessed that I had spoken to Jenny Jones.

'What time did you speak to her?'

I told Catherine I had called Jones at one o'clock. It was only then that she told me that the leak to the newspaper had happened at 11 a.m. We had a very long conversation, at end of which she said, 'I believe you and I will tell the chair of the Police Authority and Ian Blair that I believe you.'

I spoke to Sue Akers again. She said she had known me for a long time and she believed me as well. If I had been the source then I would have told her. Nothing more was said until the Tuesday morning after that Bank Holiday weekend when Derek Benson, the commissioner's new staff officer, came into my office and told me that only substantive members of the management board were required for the morning's meeting.

At that meeting, Ian had reassembled all the people from the Friday management board meeting except me. I can only assume he said something along the lines of, 'Somebody leaked this information to the press and I think it's Brian Paddick.' No doubt everyone in the room, including the person who really did leak the information, agreed with him.

I was summoned to see the commissioner at 1 p.m. Martin Tiplady, the head of Human Resources, was also present.

Ian told me he believed I was the source of the leak. I told him I was not.

'I don't believe you,' Ian replied. 'And in any event I've lost confidence in you. I can't have you attending management board meetings and I am therefore moving you from Territorial Policing to Management of Police Information with immediate effect.'

'Presented with the evidence you've got,' I replied, 'that I'm the only one who has admitted speaking to journalists, I can understand how you've come to this conclusion, but it's the wrong one. I did not leak that information to the press. You do realise our mutual enemies will be celebrating today.'

When you tell the truth and the Commissioner of Police of the Metropolis says 'I don't believe you' there is not much point in arguing.

I subsequently received an unsolicited letter from Catherine Crawford on Metropolitan Police Authority notepaper, introduced and signed in her own hand. She said that whilst the Department for Professional Standards had been asked to look into the matter of the leak, they had abandoned the investigation before establishing who was responsible. She went on to say that police misconduct is a matter for the Police Authority and as far as the Police Authority was concerned there were no misconduct issues relating to me that needed to be investigated.

She concluded by saying that any action taken as a result of the leak would be a misconduct issue, that this would be solely the preserve of the Police Authority, and whatever the reason the commissioner had for moving me, it could not have been because of the leak.

Not only did Catherine Crawford believe that I was not the source of the leak, she also believed that the commissioner had no right to move me over the issue. Catherine Crawford is a strong supporter of Ian's, so this was an unprecedented move on her part.

Later, when I did a newspaper interview after the publication of Stockwell 2, I said I believed the real reason for my being sidelined was because of my evidence in the Stockwell case (and perhaps because, when I was attacked by the Met and threatened to sue, the Home Office saw the public defence of my integrity as insubordination). The official response from the Met was that 'the reasons for his [Brian Paddick's] move from an operational to a non-operational post twelve months ago are well known to Mr Paddick, and were wholly unrelated to the events of Stockwell.' They did not, however, say what they were and I believe they were entirely related to Stockwell.

My boss Tim Godwin, who was very protective and supportive of me, was away on a long weekend when I was sidelined and told me what happened when he got back. He apparently asked Ian Blair where his evidence was and was furious to learn that there was none. He told me he was upset about what had happened while his 'back was turned'.

When I had become Tim Godwin's sole deputy we had not started off on the best foot, but after a few months we were working very well together and were beginning to deliver real results, so he was upset to lose me.

In the meantime, while Ian Blair had sidelined me, he had promoted Moir Stewart to temporary commander and put him in charge of reputation management. He was given a large team and was asked to gather and examine all the available evidence to ensure that the Met was not damaged by the Stockwell shooting.

Considering Stewart had apparently 'let down' the commissioner by not passing on the information he had that the person shot was Brazilian, it seems an extraordinary thing for Ian Blair to promote him. At the time of writing Caroline Murdoch remains Ian Blair's chief of staff.

CHAPTER THIRTY-SIX

I went from being in charge of twenty thousand officers and support staff to being responsible for five police officers, some assorted consultants and a couple of police staff. I was put in charge of running something with the rather uninspiring acronym MOPI. The Management of Police Information was part of the police's response to the Bishard Inquiry into the Soham murders. Ian Blair once told an MPA meeting that 'almost nobody' could understand why the murders of Holly Wells and Jessica Chapman had become such a big story. Unsurprisingly, he was forced to apologise. There was some irony then, in my being put in charge of this project.

MOPI was part of a wider programme called 'Impact', the aim of which was to produce a replacement for the outdated Police national computer so that any officer in the UK would be able to have immediate access to the latest information available on any individual. With the recent government record for failing to safeguard personal data held on national databases, people should be very concerned that it is planned to keep intelligence on individuals in this way.

While this was a very important project, it was very much 'back office' and not what I am good at or enjoy. I was not surprised to discover that my predecessor was a commander who had also made himself very unpopular; it was just that I was now even more unpopular than he was.

I was the senior responsible officer (SRO) for the project, a responsibility that was normally taken on in addition to a day job; I had no day job. I had little experience of managing a programme involving complex information technology as well as business change, so I employed a government consultant to advise me. He suggested that, though the work varied from project to project, someone in my position would be expected to commit about eight hours a week to being an SRO if they were taking their responsibilities seriously.

I was not overstretched.

Indeed, even though I was engaging with a project, on average, for only four hours a day, at the end of the year the head of the department, Ailsa Beaton, told me that I had delivered everything she had asked of me. I had turned the project around. By taking decisive action and through strong interventions I had given it a secure footing.

Following the 'You're fired!' interview with the commissioner, I got the distinct impression that I should not go to any meetings where Ian Blair was present. This included leaving senior officers' retirement functions early so I could disappear before the commissioner arrived to give his usual farewell speech.

The only exception was when I saw him and Martin Tiplady just before Christmas 2006, after it was decided that the commissioner should meet with each of his DACs for a 'Career Development Talk'. When my secretary was arranging my diary she asked me how long I thought the meeting would take. I suggested thirty seconds. Perhaps I should have said 'about a minute'.

At the meeting the commissioner said, 'I've noticed you've been avoiding coming to any meetings where I've been present; I think that's a very good idea.' We debated whether I should move (which I wanted to do) but the commissioner decided that I should stay where I was.

I had previously gone to see Denis O'Connor who was now Her Majesty's Inspector of Constabulary for London, to talk about the position I had found myself in over Stockwell. He told me there was 'no way back with Ian' and that I ought to move on. At that time the IPCC was still continuing their Stockwell 2 investigation and I certainly wasn't planning to leave until it had been completed, partly to make sure justice was done and also to make sure I was close to hand if I was needed.

It was clear by this time that my police career had reached the end of the line and I wasn't going anywhere as long as Blair was commissioner and still had 'friends' at the Home Office. It also became clear to me that the IPCC conclusions were not going to be fatal to the commissioner, so once they had concluded their investigations there was nothing more for me to do in the Met. I wanted to be free to speak about the Stockwell 2 report when it was published so I tried to time my departure as closely as possible to the date of the publication but, as it turned out, I left with a couple of months to spare.

One of the only two police staff I had at that time on MOPI was Laura Holford, who had also been my PA at Brixton. We didn't get on very well and she had not remained my PA for very long. Keen to put the past behind me, I went to see her and said I realised we had had our differences in the past and I explained how I had found myself in charge of the present project because of Stockwell. She replied, 'I was PA to [Deputy Commissioner] Paul Stephenson and I knew [we'd shot the wrong man] by 4 p.m.'

I was shocked. 'Have you spoken to the IPCC?'

'No.'

Stockwell 2 was about who knew what and when, and in particular what the commissioner and those closest to him knew. Laura was someone at the heart of the matter under inquiry. You would have thought, or at least hoped, that one of the first groups the IPCC would have interviewed would have been the staff who worked for those senior officers.

I phoned Mike Grant and asked him, 'Have you spoken to Laura Holford?'

'Who's she?'

'At time of the shooting, she was the deputy commissioner's PA.'

'Do you think she'd be worth talking to?'

'Yes, I do.'

And she was. She told the IPCC she was in the open-plan office with Ms Karen Scott, private secretary to the deputy commissioner, when Moir Stewart walked over to them from the direction of the door to the commissioner's office. She said that Stewart walked over to her and Ms Scott and told them, in a hushed tone, that the man who had been shot did not look like his Brazilian driving licence and said something like, 'they had got the wrong man'.

It was now eighteen months after the event and I had stumbled across a vital witness whom the IPCC had never heard of.

It was just after I had left the Met at the end of May 2007 that I found myself at Gay Pride. I met Mayor Ken Livingstone and we had a long chat before the parade about me running for his job. I had no intention of running for mayor at that time and I told Ken this was the case. The Liberal Democrats never gave up and it was a month or so later that I changed my mind and decided to run. In the afternoon I went back to the VIP area to get my umbrella at the same time as someone else was getting theirs.

'Hello, Brian. You were right to leave the Met when you did.'

This was someone I had never met before and it struck me as a rather unusual opening line.

'Why do you say that?'

This person said they worked in the mayor's private office. 'Caroline Murdoch phoned our office on the Friday afternoon to say that they'd shot the wrong person.'

I smiled politely and left.

I walked across Shaftesbury Avenue, went into a public call box and called Grant on his mobile. I repeated what I had just been told and he replied, 'Perhaps we should have seized the telephone records of all the calls made from the commissioner's office on the Friday. I wonder if they still have them?'

This was two years after the event. One of the first things the IPCC should have done was seize the telephone records, or at least establish whether such records existed.

Laura Holford had a grievance with the Met over the way she had been treated over a particular issue. As her ultimate line-manager, she came to see me, together with a police inspector who was acting as her 'friend', to lodge a formal grievance.

By coincidence, that afternoon she was going to give evidence to the IPCC with her formal 'friend' in tow. The 'friend' had recorded in his electronic diary, '11 a.m. meeting with BP and LH re grievance' and '2 p.m. meeting with LH and IPCC'.

The 'friend's' team had access to his diary. Someone from the team checked it, put two and two together, made five and called the commissioner's staff officer to tell him that Laura and I were conspiring over what evidence she was going to give to the IPCC.

We did not discuss Stockwell at that meeting. Luckily, the inspector found out about the call and he ended up making a statement to the IPCC that afternoon, telling them that there had not been any discussion about Stockwell in my presence. This is a typical example of how poisonous the atmosphere at the Yard had become.

The final straw for me came with the publication by Piers Morgan of his diaries in the *Daily Mail*. He said that he had been out for dinner at The Ivy and that I had approached him and had an emotional outburst, telling him that I was convinced that there was a cover-up over the Stockwell shooting. Piers is not well known for his photographic memory, and the fact that he clearly meant this to be an amusing anecdote rather than a serious comment was clear from the second part of his hazy recollection.

He made reference to the fact that the lead singer of Bananarama was also there and that I had approached her and said I was a great fan of hers. Piers had thought that this was an extraordinary comment coming from a gay man and wondered whether I had had too much wine.

If I *had* said I was convinced there was a cover-up over Stockwell, he would have been on to his editors immediately, and as soon as his book was published my comments would have been on the front page of every newspaper in the UK. The Met's media machine had no enquiries from any other media about his comments on his 'amazing revelations'.

The Metropolitan Police Authority did not take it in the same vein as the rest of the world. They wrote to me, claiming that this was an unauthorised disclosure of confidential information to the media, something I had undertaken not to do following the Gilmour incident. They required me to answer six questions so they could decide whether to start disciplinary proceedings.

The two most crucial questions were:

1. Did you have a conversation with Piers Morgan at the
   Ivy Restaurant on 20 September 2006 or around that
   time?
2. Whether you had any other conversations with Mr Morgan
   or any other journalist about Stockwell after May 2006?

I had by then already spoken to John Yates, by now an assistant commissioner with overall responsibility for investigating misconduct, and Sue Akers the head of DPS, where I had told them this was Piers Morgan hyperbole. They had told me that as far as the Met was concerned it was the end of matter, although they did say they did not know if the Police Authority was going to take any action.

In subsequent conversation with Catherine Crawford, she told me two very interesting things: first, that it was a senior officer at Scotland Yard who had alerted the Police Authority to the article in the *Mail*, suggesting that the MPA carry out an investigation. And second, that she regretted putting her name to the letter to me from the MPA and that it had not been her idea to conduct this investigation.

Once again, I had to instruct solicitors and I wrote back to the MPA, trying very hard to resist being facetious. It was at this point that I decided that I could not carry on in these circumstances and put in my papers. I could not go on being unable to speak to anyone about anything for fear of being investigated by the Metropolitan Police Authority, whether prompted into action by my bosses at the Yard or not.

It was only after they had my resignation in writing that the MPA finally told me that they would be taking no further action in relation to my after-dinner *tête-à-tête* with Piers Morgan.

CHAPTER THIRTY-SEVEN

After the investigation into the kiss-and-tell story was over, I had appeared on Radio 4's *The Choice*. The interviewer, Michael Buerk, asked me why had I said and done so many controversial things such as engaging with 'anarchists' on Urban 75, suggesting that police officers didn't arrest people for cannabis, and talking publicly about my sexuality. He wanted to know why I had not just kept my head down and become a chief constable – or even commissioner of the Met, where I could really have had an influence.

It was a good question.

I said I had seen too many colleagues who, after thirty years in the police service, had looked back on their careers only to realise that all they had achieved was becoming a chief constable. I told Michael: 'I joined the police because I wanted to make a difference – and I *have* made a difference.'

It was a good line but was it the whole truth?

Initially, when I joined the police I wanted to make a difference to the lives of the individuals with whom I came into contact. I wanted to protect those who could not stand up for themselves and, as I became a supervisor, I wanted to look after those under my command as well. This is not some form of Mother Theresa self-sacrifice; I get a kick out of helping people, whether they are the ones I love or complete strangers. This may stem from the lack of attention I received when I was a child; being able to alleviate that feeling in others now makes me feel good.

On the Strategic Command Course at the Police Staff College,

Bramshill, we were given a lecture by an academic on the difference between the superintending ranks to which we all then belonged, and the Association of Chief Police Officers (ACPO) ranks to which we aspired. He told us that, until then, we were expected to work within the existing paradigm; we were told how the world was and we were given the rules to operate within it, and we had to deliver within that framework. I had thrived within those professional constraints, although I had by then already broken out of the social constraints that I was born with.

He went on to explain that this was not the role of an ACPO officer. Police officers in the highest ranks were expected to challenge the existing paradigm, to look at the world differently and convince others that their view of the world was the right one – to literally think outside the perceptual box.

This was a potentially dangerous combination for me. When I was still a constable, I told my chief superintendent that I wanted to be a commander, the first rung on the ACPO ladder. Although I did not know at the time what that entailed, it became my benchmark for professional success. When I fulfilled that ambition, I was no longer concerned with promotion; I was instead committed to getting others to see the world the way I did.

In my first twenty-five years as a police officer hardly anyone had ever heard of me outside policing circles; I did exactly what I was asked to do and only operated within the rules. In my final five years, I was labelled as 'Britain's most controversial policeman' because I believe I did exactly what I was asked to do: change the existing paradigm and get the police service to look differently at the world and how it should deal with it.

Throughout my life, I have held on to the values my parents instilled in me from my earliest years – dignity, honesty and integrity. I left the police service because my own commissioner, supported by his Police Authority, had put me in a position where I could no longer make a difference, where he openly questioned my honesty and integrity, and where I believed the dignified thing to do was to leave.

At first, I found leaving the police because of doubts that had been falsely cast on my integrity very difficult to live with. I believed I had done nothing wrong, that I had done my duty by telling the whole truth and nothing but the truth to the IPCC about what had happened in the aftermath of the shooting of Jean Charles de Menezes. When the commissioner had told me, three weeks after the shooting 'We both know the penalty for not telling the truth' he didn't warn me that the penalty for telling the truth would be even greater. I was angry; why should I be the one sidelined, neutered, censured, while he continued in office?

This thought went through my mind, over and over again. When I confided in a much-trusted and respected friend, she accurately summed up my mood: 'It seems to me you only have two choices; shoot Ian Blair or throw yourself in the river.' At that moment I realised that this was not about the truth, it was about politics. Ian Blair was the commissioner, and whatever people thought about him personally he was the head of the Metropolitan Police and he would be supported. What I had said during our fateful meeting did not directly challenge Ian, but because of the way he responded to it, I had become a direct challenge to the Commissioner of Police of the Metropolis and I had to go. There was no point in reverting to childhood and shouting 'That's not fair!' 'I told you that when you were seven,' my Mother said, as I tried to explain what was happening.

I had never sat at the top table in my own right. I had never been one of the commissioner's top team, where my voice would have been heard and I could have had day-to-day influence over the greatest police force in the world. I am very disappointed that this never happened.

I am, though, very proud of having been a member of the Metropolitan Police for over thirty years, and I would go back as a constable and patrol the streets in uniform again if I had the chance. It is a great job, and the overwhelming majority of those who carry the badge deserve our respect, admiration and support, particularly those in uniform who face the public on our streets twenty-four/seven. They stand between us and anarchy, chaos and mayhem, and we forget this at our peril.

Although it was sad to leave in the circumstances that I did, being sidelined was a good way of weaning myself off the diet of status and adrenaline, off the long-hours culture and dedication to duty that takes over your life at the top of the Met.

It was shortly after I had been sidelined, in June 2006, that I went on holiday where I met Petter, a Norwegian from Oslo. I had written it off as a holiday romance, but when I heard he was coming to London to see a concert at Wembley, I took the risk and suggested he stay with me rather than booking a hotel. That weekend was one of the most wonderful weekends I had ever spent in my life and it has just got better ever since.

Strange how these things work out. I was devastated to have found my police career in ruins, but had I not fallen out so disastrously with Ian Blair, I doubt I would have become involved with Petter and entered into a relationship that we hope will last much longer than any police career.

What I could not give up though, was my addiction to making a difference.

I had spent over thirty years gradually learning and understanding more and more, not just about policing but about people, about London, about the issues and challenges Londoners face in so many ways – and about the unfairness of it all. I had also become more influential, not just because of my position but because of my experience. At the same time, it became ever more difficult to speak out as a serving police officer.

I needed a new platform from which I could continue to make a difference to people's lives, and the opportunity came when both the Liberal Democrats and the Conservatives approached me to stand as their candidate for Mayor of London. 'How can I stand for the Conservatives when I'm a card-carrying Liberal Democrat?' I asked my mother.

'Churchill did it. He crossed the floor.' She paused for a moment. 'But his mother never forgave him for it.' I would never have forgiven myself for it either.

Some people have said they support me, but ask, 'Why on earth are you standing for the Lib Dems?' Being openly gay does not make you very popular with some people but that is what I am. I can't help it. And I am a Liberal Democrat, and if people really took the time to understand what that means, most people would realise that they are Liberal Democrats too.

I do not think being openly gay or openly Liberal Democrat is what is really difficult. Being passionate about making a difference and being determined to be open and honest is what caused me most of the problems I faced during my police career. As I embark on my quest to become Mayor of London, it is those things – wanting positive change and telling it how it is – that are going to keep me in the line of fire.

INDEX

Abernethy, David, 38
accelerated promotion, 33, 117
Acceptable Behaviour Contract (ABC), 216
ACPO (Association of Chief Police Officers), 147, 192–3, 225, 243, 309, 324
  Terrorism and Allied Matters Committee of, 274
Adams, Bryan, 206
AIDS, *see* HIV and AIDS
Akers, Sue, 310–11, 320
Al Qaeda, 262
Allen, Tamsin, 196, 198, 306
All-England Club, 120
Allison, Chris, 254–5
Alowade, Alex, 152, 153
anarchism, 152, 165
Andrew, Prince, 207
Andria (Renolleau's landlady), 95–6, 110
anti-social behaviour, 215–16
anti-terrorism, 242, 244
  hotline, 260
  staff requested for, 262
  see also Anti-Terrorist Branch; Irish Republican Army; London bombings; Stockwell shooting
Anti-Terrorist Branch, 112, 147, 258, 259, 262, 283, 292
Any Questions, 168
ASBOs, *see* anti-social behaviour
Asian community, 105

Asian tsunami, 237–8
Associated Newspapers, 198, 199, 200
Associated Press, 257
Atkins, Vince, 133
Atlantic Bar and Grill, 205
Attitude, 205

Balcombe Street Siege, 245
Bamber, Andy, 212
Bananarama, 319
Barnet, 212
Barry (fellow officer), 31, 32
baton rounds, 82
Baxter, Doug, 10, 53
Bayne, Helen, 296
BBC, 173, 176, 255, 259, 278, 292, 304–5
  Any Questions on, 168
  BP traced by, 167–8
  Choice, The, on, 323
  drugs documentary of, 137
  London News, 192
  News, 24, 298
  Newsnight on, 232
  Radio London, 260
  Stockwell shooting and, 268
  Television Centre, 26, 147
  Today on, 141, 296
  undercover investigation by, 218–19
  World at One on, 281
  World Service, 102
Beaton, Ailsa, 316
Bec Grammar School, 6–7

Becker, Boris, 207
Beckham, Victoria, 207
Beckley, Rob, 272–3, 285–6, 298
Becks, Suzanna, 173, 240
Bennett, Derek, 149, 151, 152, 154,
    163
Benson, Derek, 311
Best, Mike, 133
Bethnal Green police station, 31
Big Issue, 166, 182
Bindman and Partners, 196
Bishard Inquiry, 314
Bishop, Ricky, 155–6
Black, Cilla, 205–6
black community, 23, 41, 45, 105,
    150–1, 152–3, 181–2
  police baton assault and, 150–1
  stop-and-search policy and, 113–14
  see also hate crimes; Lawrence,
    Stephen; MacPherson Report;
    race and racism
Blair, Sir Ian, 125, 144, 147, 157, 178,
    224, 226–7, 231, 232–3, 241–4,
    311–12, 313, 316–17, 324–5
  BP's criticism of, vii
  Commissioner appointment of,
    239–40
  detention issue and, 245, 246
  Gilmour's request concerning, 308
  Haw protest and, 309–10
  Investigating Rape book by, 249
  London bombings and, 255–6,
    276–7
  more counter-terrorism staff
    requested by, 262
  political nature of, 243–4
  refurbishment of office of, 283–4
  restorative-justice programme
    sponsored by, 213
  Soham murders and, 315
  staff officers of, 299–300
  Stockwell shooting and, 267–72
    passim, 274, 276–8, 279, 281–7,
    289–300 *passim*, 303, 304, 307
  Stockwell 2 report clears, 294–5
  support officers pioneered by, 209
  on *Today*, 296
  'trousers down' gaffe of, 246–7

  Urban 75 website and, 166
  Virdi and, 232
Blair, Tony, 243–4
Blake, Ivor, 18
Blake, Lord, 63
Blakelock, Keith, 42, 221
Blauel, Renate, 207
Blige, Mary J, 206
Blind Date, 205
'Blue Book', 53, 54, 115
Blunkett, David, 144, 145
Blunt, James, 207
Boulton, Adam, 276–7
Bowman, Ivelaw, 163, 184
Bragg, Susie, 92–2, 254
Brent, 212
Bridger, Martin, 212
British Celanese, 5
British Transport Police, 229–30, 256
Brixton, 35, 37, 41–2, 44–7, 85, 89,
    114, 123, 125, 132, 134, 139, 152,
    163, 182, 199
  Coldharbour Lane in, 159
  drug dealing in, 159–60
  National Domino Championship in,
    147
  prison in, 133
  racism in, 223
  riot in, 41–2, 44, 133
  see also Lambeth
Broadwater Farm Estate, 42
Bromley, 158
Brooks, Dwayne, 111
Brooks, Tony, 212
Brown, Alan, 269, 272–3, 274, 278, 281,
    282, 285–6, 290, 295–6, 297, 298
Browne, Desmond, 197
Bryan, Richard, 290
Buerk, Michael, 323
bullet- and stab-proof vests, 89
Burns, Jimmy, 162
Burt, Peter, 58

Cahill, Paul, 72
Camden, 161, 212, 230
Campbell, Naomi, 197
cannabis, 45, 46, 114, 137–43, 170–1,
    172, 176–7, 187, 198, 231

BP's no-arrest policy concerning, 139–45, 181
reclassification of, 144
smoked in BP's flat, 115, 172, 175, 176, 188, 191
sting operation concerning, 137–8
Canon Row, 187, 223
Carroll, Simon, 87–8
CCTV, 131, 149, 153, 155, 250, 262, 273, 298
Central London Crime Squad, 93, 95
Chambers (née Pilborough), see Pilborough, Fiona
Chaplin, Charlie, 184
Chapman, Jessica, 314
Cheam Baptist Church, 38, 58
Chelsea FC, 52
Chief Inspector of Constabulary, 130, 152
see also Inspectorate of Constabulary
Choice, The, 323
CIB (Complaints Investigation Bureau), 79, 106, 138
City of London Police, 123
Clapham, 125, 134, 152
see also Lambeth
Clark, Charles, 187, 188–9
Clark, Peter, 258, 262
Clark, Roy, 278, 283, 286, 307, 309
closed-circuit television, see CCTV
COBRA, 255
cocaine, 130, 139, 141, 142, 144, 154, 156, 159
Combat 18, 262
Community Impact Assessment, 273, 286
Condon, Sir Paul, 97, 98–9, 111, 229
counter-terrorism, see anti-terrorism
Cox, Patrick, 129
crack cocaine, see cocaine
Craggs, Noel, 163
Crawford, Catherine, 283, 286, 290, 311, 312, 320
Crime Academy, 195–6
Crime Reporters' Association, 263, 297–8

Crime Squad, 32, 34, 57
Crime Stoppers, 129
Crimewatch, 26
Crown Prosecution Service (CPS), 141, 191, 215, 226
Croydon, 66, 261

Daily Mail, 167, 180–1, 184, 196, 197, 200, 207, 319, 320
Daily Mirror, 125, 170, 179, 181
Daily Telegraph, 4, 11, 54
Daly, Mark, 218–19
Danes, Shirley, 19, 25
date rape, 250
Davis, David, 238
Day-Lewis, Daniel, 73
de Brunner, Maxine, 290
De Menezes, Jean Charles, 265–79, 281–7, 296–301, 303–9, 313, 318, 325
Dear, Geoffrey, 57
death in police custody, 154–6, 220
Department for Professional Standards, 223, 226, 292, 312
Deptford, 65–6, 212
Diana, Princess of Wales, 100–1
Dick, Cressida, 266, 275
Directorate of Professional Standards, 310
Dizaei, Ali, 212, 224–7
domestic violence, 19–20, 85, 109
Donovan, Tim, 192
Douglas, Brian, 108
Douglas, Jennifer, 150
drink driving, 22
Dunn, Paul, 216
Duvall, Len, 290–1

Ealing, 212
Earnest Bevin Comprehensive School, 7
Edwards, Huw, 305
Elms, Robert, 182
Elton John AIDS Foundation, 206
ethnic-minority recruitment, 217
European Convention on Human Rights, 196
Evening Standard, 140, 144, 170, 184–5, 245

Fedorcio, Dick, 179, 207, 282, 286, 290–1
Ferguson, Sarah ('Fergie'), 207
Financial Times, 162, 246
Finsbury Park mosque, 262
Fitzwilliam College, Cambridge, 120
fixed-penalty notices, 229, 230
Flanagan, Sir Ronnie, 185–6, 283, 308, 309
Flynn, Paul, 182
football matches, policing of, 51–3
Foreign and Commonwealth Office, 237, 296
Freemasons, 10, 53–4
  Knights of St James lodge in, 54
Fulham, 47, 51–3
Fulham FC, 52
Fuller, Mike, 105, 144, 192
Furnish, David, 129, 205–6
  stag night and civil partnership of, 206–7

Gately, Stephen, 206
Gausden, Keith, 150
Gay Police Association (formerly Lesbian and Gay Police Association), 72, 86
Gay Pride, 318
gay role models, 7–8
G8 summit, 254
General Election (2005), 243
Geoff (friend), 168–9
Gerard, Sergeant, 68, 69
Ghaffur, Tarique, 195, 231, 262, 303–4
Gilligan, Andrew, 245
Gilmour, Margaret, 303–5, 306–7, 308–9, 320
Godwin, Tim, 147, 148, 209, 213, 230, 242, 246–7, 270, 283, 308, 313
Gold Groups, 112, 223, 238, 256, 272
Goodbye Yellow Brick Road, 205
Graeff, Roger, 249
Grainger, Daniel, 81
Grant, Mike, 289, 293–4, 317–18
Grayson, Larry, 7
Greater Manchester Police, 218–19
Green, Michael, 59

Gresham Ballroom, 18
Grieve, John, 112–13, 187–8, 191, 192, 245, 283
Guardian, 182, 268, 281–2
'Gucci Michael', *see* Michael (partner)
Guinness Book of Records, 245
guns, 88, 133, 160
  cigarette-lighter-shaped, 149

Hardwick, Nick, 278
Haringey, 220–1
Harold Scott House, 29, 31
Harris, Lord, 165, 179
Harrow, 212
hate crimes, 85, 111, 112–13, 233
Haw, Brian, 309–10
Hayman, Andy, 124–5, 129, 138–9, 150, 226–7, 232–3, 244
  London bombings and, 258, 262
  Stockwell shooting and, 269, 270, 271, 273, 290–1, 295, 296–8
Helm, Dieter, 60
Henderson, Paul, 175
Hendon Training School, 12, 13, 195–6, 205, 218
heroin, 130, 139, 141, 142, 159
Hewlett, Andy, 126
Hill, Keith, 132
Hillingdon, 212
Hippodrome, Leicester Square, 72
Hitchcock, Alf, 272–3, 282, 285–6
Hitchens, Peter, 184, 200–1
HIV and AIDS, 87, 126–7, 206
Hoey, Kate, 133, 278
Holford, Laura, 317–18, 319
Holloway, 14–35
HOLMES2 computer system, 237
Home Affairs Select Committee, 143
homophobia, 31, 34, 71–2, 80, 85, 90, 91, 92–3, 182, 222, 233–4
  see also police service: homophobic culture of
homosexuality, 73–4, 162
  BP's, 6, 7–8, 29–31, 63, 71–3, 73–5, 85–7, 90, 91, 92–3, 117, 326–7
  female, 72
  force support and, 71
  school pupils and, 9

'sexual orientation' versus 'sexual
    preference', 85
  see also Gay Police Association;
    homophobia
Hornsey Road police station, 14
Hounslow Heath, 83
Human Rights Act, 196
Hyder, Ken, 139–40, 250

Iddon, Brian, 182
Independent Police Complaints
    Commission (IPCC), 267–9,
    273–4, 276, 278, 286, 289, 294,
    298, 301, 304–5, 307–8, 316–18,
    319
  see also Stockwell shooting
Independent, 144, 182
Inspectorate of Constabulary, 151–2,
    193
  see also Chief Inspector of
    Constabulary
institutional racism, 111
Instruction Book for Constables and
    Sergeants, 13–14
Investigating Rape: A New Approach for
    Police (Blair), 249
Irish Republican Army (IRA), 147,
    245, 258, 292
Islington, 212
Israeli Secret Service, 256

Jacquinandi, Stella ('Jacqui'), 5, 7
James, Graham, 79
Jarman, Rod, 269
Jasper, Lee, 193
Jenny (first fiancée), 31–2
John, Elton, 129, 205–6
  AIDS Foundation of, 206
  stag night and civil partnership of,
    206–7
Johnston, Ian, 229–30
Joint Terrorism Analysis Centre, 253
Jones, Jenny, 310, 311
Jones, Ken, 274
Jowell, Tessa, 132–3
July 2005 bombings, see London
    bombings
Junior Police 5, 26

'justice gap', 229, 230, 231

Karen (fellow officer), 67
Kavanagh, Stephen, 269–70, 295
Keating, Ronan, 207
Keith (driver), 187
Kennington, 125, 134, 152
  see also Lambeth
Kevin (fellow officer), 21, 24
King, Rodney, 150
Knight, India, 184
Knightly, John, 149
Knights of St James, 54
Koutsoyiannis, A, 60
Ku Klux Klan, 219

Lambeth, 108, 123, 130–45, 148–68,
    172–3, 179, 181–4, 192–3, 233,
    278, 309
  BP given command of, 125
  BP's loyalty to people of, 158
  cannabis no-arrest policy in, 139–45,
    181
  Community Police Consultative
    Group (CPCG) in, 133, 140,
    150, 152, 154, 155–6, 163, 182,
    183
  Community Relations Council, 41
  crime hotspot, 130
  Crime Prevention Trust in, 133
  crimes solved in, 193
  debt of, 158
  improvement in sight in, 157
  Inspectorate's review of, 151–2
  'lawbreaker culture' in, 131
  MORI polls concerning, 142, 181
  police baton attack on black man in,
    150–1
  public perception of safety in, 158
  raided wake in, 161–2
  rioting in, 149–50
  Sexual Offences Investigation Techniques
    (SOITs) officers in, 148
  strained police–community relations
    in, 130
  youth-crime project in, 214–15
  see also Brixton; Clapham;
    Kennington; Streatham

Lawrence, Stephen, 99, 111, 162, 219
   see also MacPherson Report
Len (friend), 168–9
Leon, Lloyd, 133
Lesbian and Gay Police Association, see
   Gay Police Association
Lewis, Jason, 175
Lewisham, 46, 66, 67–71, 188
Liberal Democrats, 133, 318, 326–7
Life on Mars, 223
Lifeline, 182
Little Britain, 207
Littlejohn, Richard, 155, 181, 184, 201
Live 8, 253
Livingstone, Ken, 182, 184, 209, 210, 318
London bombings, 68, 253–63, 276
   see also anti-terrorism; terrorism
   attempted repeat of, 265
London School of Economics, 221
London Underground, 131
   bombings on, 68, 253–63
Long, Nick, 163
Luke, Sue, see, Thomas (née Luke), Sue
Lulu, 205–6

McCullough, Ray, 90
McNee, Sir David, 27
MacPherson Report, 99, 111–12, 162,
   217
McWhirter Foundation, 244–5
McWhirter, Norris, 245
McWhirter, Ross, 245
Madame Prunier's, 6
Mail on Sunday, 162, 169, 170, 171,
   175–6, 180, 181, 182, 196–9, 206,
   207, 232
   Renolleau's story sold to, 169–71,
      175–9, 182, 187–92, 196–9Mail on
      Sunday, 162, 169, 170, 171,
      175–6, 180, 181, 182, 232
   BP sues, 196–9, 205, 206, 207
Major, Derek, 14
Management of Police Information
   (MOPI), 315–16, 317
Mandarin Oriental Hotel, 175, 199
Mark, Sir Robert, 27
Marshall, Geoffrey, 57–8
media – broadcasters:

BBC, see main entry
Channel 4, 148–9, 279
ITN, 255
Sky, 255, 256, 276
media – print and agencies:
   Associated Press, 257
   Attitude, 205
   Big Issue, 166, 182
   Daily Mail, 167, 180–1, 184, 196,
      197, 200, 207, 319, 320
   Daily Mirror, 125, 170, 179, 181
   Daily Telegraph, 4, 11, 54
   Evening Standard, 140, 144, 170,
      184–5, 245
   Financial Times, 162, 246
   Guardian, 182, 268, 281–2
   Independent, 144, 182
   Mail on Sunday, 162, 169, 170, 171,
      175–6, 180, 181, 182, 196–9,
      206, 207, 232
   Metro, 266
   New York Times, 256, 276
   News of the World, 170, 180, 268, 281,
      282, 284, 289, 292, 295, 307
   Observer, 245
   People, 176
   Pink Paper, 182
   Positive Nation, 126
   Renolleau's story sold to, 169–71,
      175–9, 182, 187–92, 196–9
   South London Press, 184
   Sun, 130, 166, 181
   Sunday Herald, 257
   Sunday Mirror, 179, 180, 310
   Sunday Times, 184, 299
   Time Out, 182
   Times, 167, 259
   Voice, 133, 181–2
Mental Health Act, 220
Merton, 100, 105–6, 144–5, 152
   Mitcham in, 105
Metro, 266
Metropolitan Police:
   Anti-Terrorist Branch of, 112, 147,
      258, 259, 262, 283, 290, 292
   BP's pride in serving, 325
   bullet- and stab-proof vests issued by,
      89

business-degree scheme of, 77–8
canteen culture in, 45
Central London Crime Squad in, 93, 35
change of culture in, 192
CIB in, 79, 106
CID's office-luncheon tradition in, 90
CID's reputation in, 33–4
Criminal Justice Unit of, 141
cuts in CID overtime in, 91
Department for Professional Standards in, 223, 226, 292, 312
Directorate of Professional Standards in, 310
Equal Opportunities Unit in, 92
ethnic-minority recruitment and, 217
Gold Coordinating Committee of, 254
Gold Groups in, 112, 223, 238, 256, 272
Home Office review of, 222
homophobia in, 34, 222
Impact programme in, 315
Internal Investigation department in, 124, 137, 138, 155, 239–40
Legal Services department in, 232–3
Livingstone promises more funding for, 209
Management Board of, 178, 279, 283, 290, 297
Management of Police Information (MOPI) in, 315–16, 317
Management Resource Centre in, 99
more recruitment needed in, 12
occupational-health department in, 81, 88
officer's rape allegation in, 223–4
pageant to mark 150th anniversary of, 26
Personnel and Training department in, 77
police community support officers (PCSOs) employed by, 210–11, 213
policing by objectives in, 55–6
Resource Allocation Formula (RAF) in, 157, 158
restorative-justice programme in, 213–14
restrictions placed on officers in, vii
riot training in, 12
Safer Neighbourhoods initiative of, 210–11, 241
seen as macho organisation, vii, 72
sexism in, 222–4
Special Constabulary in, 211–12
Specialist Crime Directorate in, 231
Specialist Operations department in, 240
Street Crime Investigation Unit in, 91
targets and, 55, 217, 230
tenure-of-post policy in, 97–9, 124, 189
Territorial Policing HQ of, 187, 209
see also police service
Metropolitan Police Authority, 123–4, 191–2, 308–9
Haw protest and, 309–10
Stockwell shooting and, 279, 320–1
Michael (partner), 128, 129, 163, 166, 167, 169, 176, 187, 198, 205–6
connections of, 205
toll taken on relationship of, 207
Michael, George, 206, 207
Minogue, Kylie, 206
Mirror Group Newspapers, 196
Misuse of Drugs Act, 188, 189
Modern Micro-Economics (Koutsoyiannis), 60
Montgomery, General, 4
Moore, Brian, 166
Morgan, Piers, 179, 181, 319–21
MORI polls, 142, 181
Morris Inquiry, 240
Movement for Justice, 152–3, 163
Murdoch, Caroline, 270, 284, 290–1, 293, 295–6, 298, 313, 318
Muslims, 245, 246
see also Finsbury Park mosque; London bombings
My Beautiful Laundrette, 73–4

National Criminal Intelligence Service, 129, 195

National Domino Championship, 147
National Front, 105, 262
National Intelligence Model, 195
Nationwide, 26–7
Neil (friend), 96
Neumann, Peter, 57
New Scotland Yard, *see* Metropolitan
    Police
New York Police Department
    (NYPD), 209
New York Times, 256, 276
Newman, Sir Kenneth, 53–4, 55–6,
    115
News International, 167
News of the World, 170, 180, 268, 281,
    282, 284, 289, 292, 295, 307
Newsnight, 232
Nicklin, Matthew, 197
Noel (staff officer), 187
Norman, Barry, 212, 226, 227
North Sutton, 63
Not One of Us (Dizaei), 225
Notting Hill, 89–91, 95, 113, 212
    Carnival, 10, 12, 80–1, 101

Observer, 245
occupational-health department, 81, 88
O'Connor, Denis, 100, 209, 316
Olive House, 14
Olympic Games, 253, 262
Operation Helios, 212, 224–7, 240
Operation Kratos, 267, 274–5, 291,
    292
Operation Sapphire, 223–4
Operation Swamp, 41, 44, 139
Operation Trident, 160–1, 173
Order 23/25, 20
Orr, Deborah, 184
Osbourne, Ozzy, 207
Osbourne, Sharon, 207
Osman, Hussain, 265–6, 273, 299
O'Toole, Tim, 259
Oxford, 57, 58–64
    youth club in, 62
Oxford Union, 29

Paddick (née Stone), Mary (wife), 5,
    58–9, 62, 63, 73–4, 162, 179–80

BP's long hours and, 71
BP meets, 38–9
BP's sexuality and, 74–5
marriage of, 58–9
separation from, 74, 86
trust of, 73
Paddick, Anthony (father), 3–4, 109
BP's sexuality and, 74–5
Freemason, 10, 53, 54
heart attack suffered by, 5
military service of, 4
technical job of, 5
Paddick, Brian:
academic prize won by, 63
accelerated-promotion scheme
    accepted by, 33
acting sergeant's role of, 34–5
AIDS scare concerning, 126–8, 134
Amsterdam trip of, 76–7
anti-surveillance training offered to,
    130
baptism of, 38
becomes acting chief inspector, 67,
    70
becomes acting sergeant, 34
becomes chief inspector, 85
becomes detective chief inspector, 89
becomes divisional commander, 101
becomes inspector, 47
becomes sergeant, 35
becomes superintendent, 96
becomes temporary superintendent,
    89
biology, chemistry and physics
    chosen by, 9
birth and early life of, 3–10
Blair's support of, 157, 178
'Brian the Commander' online ID
    of, 164
Bristol posting of, 43–4
Brixton postings of, 35, 37, 41–2,
    44–7, 85, 89, 132, 139
candidate's selection complaint
    against, 85–6
cannabis no-arrest policy of, 139–45,
    181
cannabis smoked in flat of, 115, 172,
    175, 176, 188, 191

Central London Crime Squad
    posting of, 93, 95
CID experience of, 33–4
co-director's interview taken by,
    117–18
'Commander Crackpot' label applied
    to, 166
commander post applied for by,
    123–4
commander post given to, 124
community group meeting demands
    reinstatement of, 183
Conservatives approach, 326
crime-squad transfer of, 32
criminal allegations laid before,
    188–90
Daily Mail sued by, 197
death encountered by, 65–7
Deptford posting of, 65–6, 212
Diana's funeral and, 101–2
Early Day Motion concerning, 182
end-of-training examination taken
    by, 13–14
fellow officer's sexual approach to,
    29–30
Financial Times 'outing' of, 162
Fiona engaged to, 33
first cadaver seen by, 15
first gay relationship of, 86–7
first sexual encounter of, 29–30
at Fitzwilliam College, Cambridge,
    120
Freemasons joined by, 53
Fulham posting of, 47, 51–3
Gilmour story and, 304–6, 320
'greatest South Londoner' poll won
    by, 184
Harris praises, 179
at Hendon Training School, 12, 13,
    205, 274
Hendon project of, 195–6
hire-car affair concerning, 118–19,
    125
Holloway posting of, 14–35
inaction complaint by, 232–3
injury to, 43–4
insufficient evidence in Renolleau's
    allegations against, 191

isolation felt by, 8
James assaults, 109
James meets, 95
James's separation from, 120–1
Jenny engaged to, 31
Lambeth posting of, 125, 130–45,
    148–68, 172–3, 179, 309
Lambeth resignation speech of, 179
Lewisham posting of, 67–71
Liberal Democrat candidature of,
    318, 326–7
Mail on Sunday interviews, 175–6,
    184
Mail on Sunday sued by, 196–8, 205,
    206, 207
malicious Crime Stoppers phone call
    concerning, 129–30
Management of Police Information
    (MOPI) post of, 315–16, 317
Mary engaged to, 39
Mary marries, 58–9
Mary meets, 38–9
Mary's separation from, 74, 86
mayoral election and, 318, 326–7
Merton posting of, 100–2, 105–8,
    144–5
Met's alleged libel against, 306
Nationwide appearance of, 26–7
New Scotland Yard post of, 77
Notting Hill posting of, 89–91, 95
'outings' of, 92, 162
at Oxford, 58–64
Paul's separation from, 92
personnel department posting of,
    96–100
petition demanding Lambeth
    reinstatement of, 182
Police Authority closes case against,
    191
police career chosen by, 9–10
at Police Staff College, Bramshill,
    37–8, 43–4, 324
post-traumatic stress suffered by, 81
press-leak allegations against, 307–9,
    312–13
probationers' examination taken by,
    29
pub-quiz 'outing' of, 92

Paddick, Brian – *continued*
  rape-investigation review undertaken by, 200, 249
  recruitment interview of, 11–12
  religion of, 38–9, 59–60, 63, 180
  Renolleau's allegations against, 169–71, 175–9, 182, 187–92, 196–9
  resignation from Met of, 317, 321, 324–5
  rumours concerning sexuality of, 85, 91
  school bullying of, 8–9
  sergeant's examination taken by, 33
  Serious Crime Directorate posting of, 195
  sexual-assault case affecting, 69–70, 73, 77
  sexuality of, 6, 7–8, 29–31, 63, 71–3, 73–5, 85–7, 90, 91, 92–3, 117, 326–7
  staff officer post of, 79–80, 82–3
  Standard commissions sympathetic article on, 185
  Stevens receives open letter concerning, 182
  stop-and-search paper and lectures of, 114
  Strategic Command Course and, 108, 117–20, 125, 324–5
  in Territorial Support Group, 83
  Territorial Policing HQ posting of, 187, 209
  training of, 12–13
  in university sport, 60–1
  Urban75 website and, 163–9, 172, 173, 184, 232
  variations in rape investigations in, 249
  at Warwick University, 77–8
Paddick, Evelyn (mother), 3–4, 7, 32, 180, 325
  BP's partner accepted by, 109
  BP's sexuality and, 74–5
  early views of, on homosexuality, 8
  Telegraph feature article on, 4
Paddick, Graham (brother), 3, 5, 6
  BP's sexuality and, 75

Paddick, John (brother), 3, 6, 7, 58
  BP's sexuality and, 74–5
  early views of, on homosexuality, 9
  head prefect post of, 8
Paddick, Sally (sister-in-law), 75
Paddington, 249
Padraic (fellow officer's partner), 73
Page, Jeremy, 296
Patmore, Chris, 12
Paul (partner), 86–7
  BP's separation from, 92
Peel, Sir Robert, 283
People, 176
Petter (partner), 326
Petty France, 92, 95, 96
Phil (fellow officer), 70–2, 74
Phillips, Melanie, 180–1, 200
Pilborough, Fiona, 32–3, 38, 180
Pimlico, 92
Pink Paper, 182
Police Academy, 195
police community support officers (PCSOs), 209–11, 213
Police Complaints Authority, 154, 156
Police Federation, 80, 106, 187, 210
Police Foundation, 142, 249
police service:
  ex-servicemen join up to, 11
  Freemasonry inconsistent with, 53
  homophobic culture of, 31, 80 (*see also* homophobia; Metropolitan Police: homophobia in)
  macho image of, 72
  moves to abolish senior ranks in, 89
  national computer of, 315
  pay of, 11
  race an emotive issue in, 112
  racism in, 218–19
  targets and, 55, 217, 230
  truncheon carried by, 13
  uniform of, 12–13
  see also Metropolitan Police
Police Staff College, Bramshill, 33, 37–8, 43, 324
policing by objectives, 55–6
Polkinghorne, Chief Superintendent, 29
Pollock, Jackson, 86

positional asphyxia, 221
positive discrimination, 117
Positive Nation, 126
Povey, Sir Keith, 152
Prince's Trust, 97
prostitution, 250
pub quizzes, 92
Public Order Training Centre, 82

Queen's College, Oxford, 57

racism, 44–5, 105, 111, 112, 231
  institutional, 111
  BBC undercover investigation and,
    218–19
Radio London, 260
Railton Road patrol, 45–6
rape, 108, 148–9, 215, 223–4, 249–51
  black women and, 250
  Blair's book about investigation of,
    249
  date, 250
  documentary about, 148–9, 249
  Met's review of, 200, 249
'reassurance policing', 209
Reed, Alan, 65
Release, 182
religion, 38–9, 59–60, 63
Renolleau, James (partner), 95–6, 98,
    108–10, 114–15, 119–21, 124,
    126, 168–71, 205
  allegations in story sold by, 169–71,
    175–9, 182, 187–92, 196–9
  BP's AIDS scare and, 127
restorative-justice programme, 213–14
Roberts, John, 279
Ross, Ruth, 96
Royal Tank Regiment, 4
Royal Ulster Constabulary, 185
rubber bullets, *see* baton rounds

Safer Neighbourhoods initiative,
    210–11, 241
St Aldate's Anglican Church, 59
St Paul's, Bristol, 43
Salmon Process, 294, 298
Scarman, Lord, 44, 45
Scarman Report, 133

Scissor Sisters, 205–6
Scotland Yard, *see* Metropolitan Police
Scott, Karen, 318
Scrouston, Mr, 7
Sean (fellow officer), 15, 18–19
Secret Policeman, The, 218–19
7/7, *see* London bombings
sexism, 222–4
Sexual Offences Investigation
    Techniques (SOITs) officers, 148
Seymour, Jim, 87–8
Shadow Lounge, 128–30, 232
Shawcross, Valerie, 182
Sheehy Report, 89
Sieff, Rt Hon. Michael, 59
Sir Arthur Conan Doyle Foundation,
    97
Smith, Harriet, 133
Smith, Jane, 65–6
Smith, Jim, 274
Snow, Jon, 279
Soham murders, 314
Soley, Clive, 46
South London Press, 184
Southwark, 181
Sparrow, Malcolm, 38
Special Constabulary, 211–12
Spencer, Lord, 102
Starr, Ringo, 207
Steph's Restaurant, 72
Stephenson, Paul, 263, 279, 290,
    305–6, 317
Steve (fellow officer), 66–7, 261
Stevens, Sir John, 99, 124, 141, 144,
    147–8, 151, 162, 173, 178, 192–3,
    212, 240–1
  BP's formal complaint to, 185
  Dizaei case and, 226
  Grieve's clashes with, 188
  NYPD visit of, 209
  open letter to, 182
  Urban 75 website and, 166, 169, 172
  Virdi and, 231–2
Stewart, Moir, 245, 255, 270, 284,
    295–6, 298, 304, 313, 318
Stewart, Rod, 206
Sting, 206, 207
Stockwell Community Hall, 278–9

Stockwell shooting, 256, 266–79, 281–7,
    296–301, 303–9, 313, 316–21, 325
  BBC and, 268
  Blair and, 267–72 passim, 274,
      276–8, 279, 281–7, 289–300
      passim, 303, 304, 307
  Gilmour and, 303–5, 306–7, 320
  Hayman and, 269, 270, 271, 273,
      290–1, 295, 296–8
  Metropolitan Police Authority and,
      279, 320–1
Stoke Newington Police Station, 96
Stone, Hilary, 38
Stone, Mary, see Paddick (née Stone),
    Mary
Stone, Norman, 38
Stone, Richard, 73
Stonewall, 196
stop-and-search, 44, 45, 113–14
  see also black community
Strategic Command Course, 108,
    117–20, 125, 225, 324–5
Stratford Shopping Centre, 210
Straw, Jack, 238
Streatham, 125, 134, 152, 222
  see also Lambeth
Street Crime Investigation Unit, 91
Street-Porter, Janet, 207
Sun, 130, 166, 181
Sunday Herald, 257
Sunday Mirror, 179, 180, 310
Sunday Times, 184, 299
Surrey, 5, 87, 166, 209, 242
'sus' law, 22–3
Sutton, 7, 63, 261
Sutton and Cheam Swimming Club, 7
Sutton Manor High School, 7
Swain, Steve, 274–5
Sweeney, The, 54
Sylvester, Roger, 219–22
Sylvia (secretary), 187

Tate Britain, 239
Taylor, Shaw, 26
Television Centre, 26, 147
Tendler, Stuart, 259
Terrence Higgins Trust, 126
Territorial Support Group, 83

terrorism:
  anti-, 242, 244, 259, 260, 271, 290,
      292
  detention issues concerning, 244,
      245–6
  Joint Analysis Centre for, 253
  perceived reduced threat of, 253
  see also Anti-Terrorist Branch; Irish
      Republican Army; London
      bombings; Stockwell shooting
terrorists, detention of, 244, 245–6
Thames Valley, 59, 249
Thomas, Mark, 182
Thomas (née Luke), Sue, 35
Thornton Heath, 83
Time Out, 182
Times, 167, 259
Tiplady, Martin, 305–6, 312, 316
Today, 141, 296
Todd, Mike, 140, 150, 151, 157, 173,
    177, 178, 185, 213, 219
  Flanagan investigates, 185–6
  Urban 75 website and, 166, 169, 172
  Virdi and, 232
Too2Much, 206
Tookey-Dickson, John, 14, 16
Toronto Airport, 258
Toxteth, 46
Transform, 182
Trotter, Andy, 256, 259
Truss, Richard, 182
Tuffy, Mark, 108
Twist, Peter, 86

Union Jack Club, 152
Urban75 website, 163–9, 172, 173,
    184, 232

Vagrancy Act, 23
Vaizey, Lord, 59
Vauxhall, 128
Veness, David, 238
'violent disorder', 229
Virdi, Gurpal, 231–2
Voice, 133, 181–2

Wacky Races, 19
Walsh, Dr, 9

Warhol, Andy, 86
Warwick University, 77
Webb, Alan, 83
Webb, Chris, 255
Wellings, Bob, 26–7
Wells, Holly, 314
Wembley Stadium, 80
Westminster (borough), 123, 128, 129,
    158, 193, 249
Westminster Technical College, 5
Whittaker, Rachel, 124
Widdecombe, Anne, 141
Wilding, Barbara, 232–3
Wilkinson, Sue, 290
Wilson, Bill, 83
    BP comes out to, 86

Wilson, Jacqueline, 86
Wimbledon, 105, 106, 108, 113, 120,
    253
Windsor Great Lodge, 59
Wingett, Fiona, 169–70, 176–7,
    199
World at One, 281
Wormwood Scrubs, 212
Wright, Steven, 196, 201
Wrout, Penny, 158, 177

Yates, John, 307–8, 320
York, Duchess of ('Fergie'), 207
York, Duke of (Prince Andrew),
    207
youth crime, 214–15